Opothleyaholo and the Loyal Muskogee

Dedicated to the memory of

Opothleyaholo and his followers; my daughter, Marilee Susan Brockway; my husbands, Gene Brockway and Tom Tindle; my son-in-law, Larry Dice; my brother, Bill McBride; my cousins, Stan Harper and Tom White, all of whom died too soon; my grandmother, Virginia Isaphine (Allen) McCray who pointed the way and George Lowther, Westport, Connecticut, who encouraged me to keep writing; my friends, Edith Greathouse and Austin "Double Ugly" Cook; and my parents, Weldon L. and Mary Edith McBride.

Opothleyaholo and the Loyal Muskogee

Their Flight to Kansas in the Civil War

by
LELA J. MCBRIDE

McFarland & Company, Inc., Publishers
Jefferson, North Carolina, and London

Acknowledgments: A work of this size could not be accomplished alone. I wish to thank the following institutions and people for their help:

Barbara Shoop and staff, W.A. Rankin Library, Neodesha, KS; Lucy Horton and staff, Fredonia Public Library, Fredonia, KS; Jo Anne Beezley and staff, Government Documents, Leonard H. Axe Library, Pittsburg State University, Pittsburg, KS; Public Library, Independence, KS; Kansas State Historical Society, Topeka, KS; Oklahoma Historical Society, Oklahoma City, OK; Library of Congress, Washington, D.C.; Indian Springs State Park, Flovilla, GA; Fort Leavenworth Museum, Fort Leavenworth, KS; Special Collections, U.S. Military Academy Library, West Point, N.Y.; Interlibrary Loan Dept. SEK Library, Iola, KS; Creek Nation, Okmulgee, OK; Delaware Indian Tribal Headquarters, Bartlesville, OK; Wilson County Historical Society, Fredonia, KS; Thomas Yahola, National Council member, Muskogee Nation, Wetumka, OK; Ed Sterling, Texas Press Association, Austin, TX; Terry Peck, Neodesha, KS.

Also, thanks to Dave Cheshier, Neodesha, KS, my mentor, in appreciation for all of his assistance; my family and friends for their encouragement; and to my Lord Who helped me every step of the way.

Library of Congress Cataloguing-in-Publication Data

McBride, Lela J.
    Opothleyaholo and the loyal Muskogee: their flight to Kansas
    in the Civil War / by Lela J. McBride.
       p.   cm.
    Includes bibliographical references and index.
    ISBN 0-7864-0638-0 (library binding : 50# alkaline paper) ∞
      1. Opothleyaholo, ca. 1798–1862.   2. Creek Indians—Kings
    and rulers—Biography.   3. Creek Indians—Wars.   4. Creek
    Indians—Relocation.   5. United States—History—Civil War,
    1861–1865—Participation, Indian.   I. Title.
    E99.C9O677   2000
    973'.04973—dc21   99-48305
                                         CIP

British Library Cataloguing-in-Publication data are available

Manufactured in the United States of America

McFarland & Company, Inc., Publishers
Box 611, Jefferson, North Carolina 28640
www.mcfarlandpub.com

Contents

Preface

On a bitterly cold Kansas day in January 1961, I visited the site where the crudely constructed Fort Row (Roe) had stood adjacent to the Verdigris River in my native Wilson County. The countryside was blanketed with a light snow, and the northwest wind buffeted me and my companions as we tried to envision that long ago scene. The years, the flooding Verdigris River, and the plowman had erased the little stockade and all evidence of the tragic affair that had occurred there in the winter of 1861–62.

This visit was to help me absorb, as nearly as possible, how the Loyal Indian Refugees must have felt on their journey and during their stay in Wilson County. They had fled northward from their homes in Indian Territory at the beginning of the Civil War. They were called loyal because, despite abandonment by the Federal Government in 1861, they had battled their own people and the Confederates to remain true to the Union.

I had been assigned to write several historical articles for the *Fredonia Daily Herald*'s Courthouse Edition slated to be published that spring. Wilson County's charming Victorian courthouse was being replaced by a more modern edifice. Fort Row and the Indians who had suffered and died there would be remembered in the issue.

Wally Olds, the editor and newcomer to Fredonia, wanted to visit the site, also, and offered the transportation. My good friends, Austin "Double Ugly" and Isabelle Cook of New Albany, accompanied us. Jake Spillman, a farmer whose land contained the site, was our guide.

Adequately dressed for the winter day, we endured the raw, cold wind as long as possible, listening while Spillman supplied historical facts. My toes became so cold I knew I could snap them loose from my feet without difficulty. In our haste to get back to the heated car, we stumbled over the once mellow loam clods of the plowed field, now rock-hard from the freezing temperatures. As for myself, I never considered how fortunate I was for the modern convenience. I accepted it as a part of my life.

1

But what about the refugees who had had no such warmth available? I knew the greater share of them were in rags or naked and starving. As I sat there shivering, wrapped in a winter coat, I wondered what adjectives could describe sufficiently the horrific event that had occurred there.

What of the abject misery they had faced when they lost family and friends in the three battles they had fought in Indian Territory before fleeing to Kansas? From what depths within them had come their incredible stamina and courage?

I was humbled that wintry day. It would take many years of research in seeking the truth before I would understand their desperation and the political machinations involved.

This book did not have its beginning with me in 1961. Rather, it had started when I was a small girl during the Great Depression.

I was privileged to share a bed with my grandmother, Virginia Isaphine (Allen) McCray. She was an Ohioan and the only grandparent I was fated to know. And she was a storehouse of information.

On those cold Kansas nights snuggled down in the feather bed next to grandmother, our feet warmed by the cloth-wrapped heated bricks, I heard that one of Gen. Custer's saddles was in the family. I knew that Gen. George Armstrong Custer (he was actually only a lieutenant colonel at the time) and five companies of his regiment had been wiped out by the Sioux at the Little Bighorn in Montana in 1876, but didn't know the circumstances which had caused the battle. Now, as the gusts rattled the windows and moaned in the chimney, grandmother's reminiscences would turn to the little Fort Row situated near where her parents, Henry C. and Sarah Allen, had settled.

Although grandmother was never fond of the "savage" Indians, as her generation knew them, still she was amazed by the unimaginable sufferings of the refugees at Fort Row, Delaware Springs and above New Albany on the Fall River. She had come to Wilson County in 1876 and even then the bones of the Indians and their ponies were still being found. Very heady facts for a young girl to comprehend. My education about the Indians was beginning.

At a tender age, I was to discover "the only good Indian is a dead Indian." If you wanted to retrieve something you had traded you were an "Indian giver." And you never wanted to be the "redskin" in the childhood game of cowboys and Indians. We were inhibited with the idea that the Indian was a filthy, barbarous thing, bent on destroying the white man. The history books, society and Hollywood had done their work very well with my generation. The name Geronimo conjured up within me a terrifying picture of the fierce, bloodthirsty Apache coming for my scalp.

Wilson County was a part of the Osage Diminished Reserve, their last domain in Kansas before being removed to Indian Territory. Lizzie Skaggs, my late first husband's grandmother, had been raised on the bottom land of the Fall River, a portion of it being the Osage Hunting Trail. Lizzie described the Osage as tall, blanket Indians who demanded some payment, preferably precious white bread, for allowing the family to live on their land.

I was intrigued by the fact that I was living in Osage country. West Mound where I have lived outside of Fredonia the past 50 years was a favorite location for Chief Little Bear of the Osage. At the top of the hill one can have an panoramic view of the countryside—an excellent position to watch for white interlopers on the Osage land.

Thus, gleaning bits of information from family and friends, I began my research about the Osage, who were more than tall, blanket Indians; Fort Row and the Indian refugees. Yet, even with the knowledge that Opothleyaholo, the Creek who had led them to Wilson County, had fought in the historic Battle of Horseshoe Bend I could not accept him other than just another Indian. I was terribly mistaken.

Opothleyaholo was a great leader of his people the Muskogees, called Creeks by the white man. He was a medicine man and speaker, a distinguished position in the Creek Nation. He had never been a chief. In his lifetime, he experienced two battles of Horseshoe Bend: one in Alabama in 1814, and one in Indian Territory in 1861. He had endured two "Trails of Tears," one in 1836 when he and his people were removed from Alabama to Indian Territory, the other at the beginning of the Civil War. Opothleyaholo met with two presidents, John Quincy Adams and Andrew Jackson, during treaty negotiations. He knew Sam Houston personally.

Some of these facts I did not know when I began my research. My enlightenment would emerge slowly through the years, temporarily shelved while I dealt with personal tragedies in my own life. But I always returned to Opothleyaholo and his people.

I have often wondered why we do not celebrate Indian History Month. What would we learn in those 30 days of profiling an Indian nation and personalities? Would we be amazed to find the Native People had the same basic instincts as we do to defend our homes? The invasion of the Europeans was welcomed peacefully by the Native People. And we repaid their hospitality by gaining their country insidiously and were contemptuous of the "heathens" when they chose to fight.

The United States is called "the home of the brave." Yet, the word "brave" was the appellation given by the French and North Americans in the 17th century to the Indian warrior. But did it mean fearless, or were they implying the archaic definition of "wild," "savage"?

This book tells a story that ranges from Oglethorpe and the Georgia colony through the Revolutionary War, the War of 1812, the Mexican War, Kansas-Nebraska Territory and Kansas statehood to the beginning of the Civil War and the retreat of Opothleyaholo and his followers to southern Kansas.

A retreat during the most inclement winter weather ever recorded in pioneer days up until that time.

One early historian's work led to another. I resisted the temptation to accept their opinions. I had to see the documents they had researched for myself. I ordered reports from the National Archives, Library of Congress, and researched the Government Documents Department of the Axe Library, Pittsburg State University, Pittsburg, Kansas. I studied myriad microfilms of old newspapers loaned by the Kansas Historical Society, Topeka. When I queried them about Opothleyaholo, I discovered they did not have much on file about him. I determined that if I had anything to do with it, they would have in the future.

I became completely absorbed in the research. And in my absorption, I came to realize how we as Americans had been deceived by history. But I was not alone in the realization. For quite some time we have been seeing and hearing on television and in the movies the truth about the Indians. Where once it was a stigma to have a drop of Indian blood in one's ancestry, now many Americans are proud to have had a native person in their family tree.

We were and still are horrified by the Holocaust. We find it difficult to accept how the German people were misled by the Nazi propagandists. Yet, we had our own propagandists who worked diligently to infect Americans' minds that the Indians were subhumans who must become extinct like the dinosaurs.

The truth is that the white men broke the treaties repeatedly in order to secure the Indians' land. The result always was bloodshed involving many innocent people, white and Indian. Barbaric acts by Americans toward the Indians, at first, were difficult for me to assimilate. However, the facts could not be disputed. This work shows the white men's cruelty, savagery and cunning.

The Creek Nation was powerful in their ancestral Alabama and Georgia. They were manipulated by our own esteemed political figures, pitting half-bloods against full-bloods with the ignoble plan of breaking their power. Their land was fertile, well-suited for the Southerner and his slaves.

The Creek Nation struggled constantly to keep their southeastern homeland. Finally, weakened by years of exploitation and civil wars within their nation they were removed to Indian Territory where they believed they would live peacefully "as long as the waters run and the grass grows." They were assured by the treaty that white men would leave them alone.

They readjusted to the wild country and became prosperous. Soon, the agents and superintendents of the Southern Superintendency governing the area for the Indian Bureau began reporting the Indian Territory was no longer considered a worthless part of the United States. Indeed, the Americans could live there and do quite well. As most of the agents and superintendents were Southerners, it behooved the South to turn their attention toward Indian Territory. It had to become a part of their slave power.

The reader will accompany Lt. William Averell on his mission from

Washington, D.C., to Indian Territory with secret orders to close the Federal forts in 1861—forts that had been built as a result of treaties, bound to provide protection for the Creeks, Seminoles, Chickasaws, Choctaws and Cherokees. The closing of the forts gave the South an invitation to woo the nations to the Confederacy without opposition.

The South perceived that John Ross, Cherokee chief, would be hard to convince. The Creeks and the others would give them no trouble. They had forgotten about the annulled Indian Springs Treaty of 1825 and the man called Opothleyaholo.

This narrative not only concerns Opothleyaholo and the Creeks, it also reveals little known facts about states' rights, the fraudulent funding of the Pony Express, the Civil War, and Kansas and Indian Territory's prominent roles in the rebellion. And through it all, Opothleyaholo was there, a highly important man who has been neglected in this country's history. He deserves the recognition long denied him, and should rank alongside such historical Indian figures as Chief Joseph, Tecumseh, Crazy Horse, Sitting Bull and Geronimo.

I asked Thomas Yahola of Wetumka, Oklahoma, a lineal descendant of the leader, what his people wanted to be called. "Muskogees," he answered. "What about Native Americans?" I asked. "No," he replied. "We were here before this was America. We want to be known as the Native People."

History has been plagued by errors. As an example, it was Fort Row, not Roe as misspelled in the official reports. Although Fort Row cannot be found in the old forts listing in the military archives, it played its part in the Civil War.

The plight of the loyal Indian refugees is considered by many historians to be a minor incident of the Civil War. How does something so disastrous stay minor? Is it because it happened to Indians and thus, is really not important? Or has it been treated in the same way as Kansas, the Indian Territory and the West? If this part of the United States was so insignificant in the rebellion, then why did the South involve themselves so prominently in the area?

Another error publicized recently is that the followers of Opothleyaholo called him "Hope." When I asked Thomas Yahola if this was true, he answered, "No. They called him by his name." Opothleyaholo (O-Be-thle-ya-ho-la) was an extraordinary native person who personally tried to remain inflexible against the politicians, the army and the Southerners who intended to make him and his people a part of the Confederacy. Instead, they became inculpable victims of the Civil War and their ancient history and culture, which had instilled in them stamina, courage and faith, inevitably bringing them to a place called Roe's Fork.

Chapter 1

The Wolf Has Come

"We read history through our prejudices"
—Wendell Phillips

It was Sac and Fox Indian buffalo hunters returning from the Arkansas River to their reservation in Osage County, Kansas, who spotted the bloody footprints in the sleet-encrusted snow in southern Kansas, January, 1862.[1] The gory trail was coming from the southwest and heading off in a northeasterly direction. Bowing to the bitter northwest wind which was driving a sleet and snow mixture before them, the hunters slowly followed the ragged course. Soon the bloody tracks were intermingling with the prints of moccasins and unshod hooves across the snow-drifted tall grass prairie.

The hunters learned that the ones staggering through the snow were followers of Opothleyaholo, the elderly Creek leader and all of them were escaping Confederate-held Indian Territory. Miles to the rear, just inside Indian Territory, Billy Bowlegs and Haleck Tustenuggee, Seminole chiefs, with other warriors, were battling an overwhelming force belonging to the half-blood Cherokee Confederate Colonel Stand Watie and his Cherokees.

Opothleyaholo and his followers had been on the move since early November when the Secessionist Indians, many of whom were their own tribal members, and white Confederate forces had harassed them into this impromptu flight north to Kansas for Federal help. They had journeyed more than 250 miles from North Fork Town in the Creek Nation. The group of several hundred men, women and children were a small part of the survivors of three battles against the Confederate forces of Colonels Douglas Cooper, Stand Watie and James McIntosh in Indian Territory. In each battle they had lost personal possessions, food, cattle and ponies until they were destitute, bereft of any sustenance.

The Indians' trail to freedom had been marked with bloody footprints

7

and strewn with unburied bodies. Many had frozen to death and were left to be devoured by the wolves that paralleled their path. Babies were born and died in the snow.

Although desperate, the miserable beings were determined to follow Opothleyaholo to the Osage Trail which lay to the northeast along the Fall River in Wilson County, Kansas. The Creeks and Osages had been at peace with each other for many years, and Opothleyaholo knew he and his people would encamp in safety on this hunting branch of the Great Osage Trail. There, they would wait for the assistance of the Great Father Lincoln.

Among the refugees were the feeble, the sick, those with threadbare clothing, or none at all. Many were barefooted, their feet gashed, shredded, bruised and frostbitten. They had no tents and only a few tattered blankets and, on the virtually treeless prairie, they were without shelter from the inclement weather. When ponies had died, they had eaten them, but mostly, they were reduced to scraping through the hard-packed snow into the frozen earth for edible roots. And many had picked and eaten corn from the ponies' droppings.

The Sac and Fox hunters moved among the people, knowing they must do something to relieve their sufferings, if only in a small way. The men rationed the kill destined for their own families. When the supply ran out, they had to turn away from the anguished faces of the refugees, their purple, swollen hands raised in silent supplication for food.

As the Sac and Fox hunters made their way northward, they alerted any whites they met of the influx of refugees, which in time would stretch upward of 200 miles from the Arkansas River in southern Kansas to the Verdigris River in Wilson County, Kansas.

In the days and weeks ahead, W.G. Coffin, superintendent of the Southern Superintendency, would be appalled by the number of Creeks, Seminoles, Cherokees, Delawares, Euchees, Choctaws, Chickasaws, Caddoes and others of the Indian Territory that daily staggered into the Fall River Valley, their ranks soon swelling to nearly 8,000 souls. In his reports to William P. Dole, Commissioner of Indian Affairs in Washington, Coffin would be unable to describe the "destitution, misery and sufferings amongst them" in the Fall River Valley.[2]

George A. Cutler, Creek agent, held a council with delegates of the Creek, Seminole and Chickasaw tribes on November 4, 1861 at his home in LeRoy, Coffey County, Kansas. After the council, Cutler escorted the delegates to Washington, D.C. to confer with Dole personally.[3]

After listening to the delegates, Cutler was well informed about the war that was erupting between the Secessionist and Union Indians in the territory, as part of the larger war that was racking the nation. He was aware of the Confederacy's desire to gain that area for itself due to its strategic location and its wealth in Indian beeves, horses and crops. He was aware, also, of

Albert Pike, commissioned by the Confederacy to seek an alliance with the Five Civilized Tribes, an alliance that was promoting hostilities between the tribes. Yet, discounting the seriousness of the Indians' pleas for help, he believed he was well prepared with food and clothing for the few Indians, that might possibly escape to Kansas. He had not anticipated the arrival of Opothleya-holo, his remaining army, and the others who would follow the Creek Moses to Kansas, looking for the Great Father's army to drive the rebels from their country.

The Federal Government in the spring of 1861 would be the catalyst of one of the worst, if not the worst, events to occur in the Civil War, that of the plight of the Loyal Indian Refugees. And Opothleyaholo, far removed from his native lands in Alabama and Georgia, would do everything possible to save the lives of the refugees.

Chapter 2

Opothleyaholo and the Muskogees

A representative of Georgia, while debating the appropriations for the Indian Springs Treaty of 1826, called his name too long and barbarous to pronounce.[1] This man with the long and barbarous name would rise to power within the Creek Nation. His love of home land and fealty toward his people would cause him to fight for their survival, even to the giving of his own life. He would become esteemed by his people and in matters of treaties they would often say, "Opothleyaholo knows and that is all that matters."[2]

Properly his name was Hupuehelth Yaholo. The literal translation of Hupuehelth is "fog" and yaholo means "whooper, halloer." Yaholo comes from the time he was a lad, "halloing" as he helped serve the sacred black drink from a gourd to the chiefs and head men of the Creeks.[3]

The black drink ceremony is unique to the Creek Nation. The drink was made from the leaves of the Assi or Ilex Cassine which were boiled to make a tea. The ancient Etowans, whose ruins were discovered near Carterville in northern Georgia, indulged in the black drink.[4] It was drunk before each council meeting and other ceremonials and acted as an emetic. The decoction was repulsive to the white man who often witnessed the excessive vomiting that littered the public square. The Creeks believed the black drink had been given to them by the Great Spirit to cleanse them of sins. When preparing for the removal to the West in 1836, Opothleyaholo said, "We shall at that time take our last black drink in this nation."[5]

One variant spelling of Opothleyaholo's name was Poethleyoholo, recorded by historians as a result of the Indian Springs Treaty.[6] There are many spellings which begin with an "H," but Opothleyaholo or Opothleyahola are the ones which have endured.

His sobriquet, earned undoubtedly by his astute trading ability with fellow tribes and whites, was "Old Gouge." Old Gouge would be cited in official reports of the Civil War, newspapers of that era, and even reminiscences by the Texans who pursued him and his followers.[7]

In February 1862, Kansas newspapers reported the literal translation of his name as "Crazy Fog." This, like so many other details concerning the Native People, is in error. "Crazy" in the Muskogeean language is Harjo. There were many brave men who bore that name, but it is a misnomer when applied to Opothleyaholo.[8]

Opothleyaholo's age in historical reports has ranged from 60 to 102 years. If, as some believe, he was born in 1798, he would have been 62 to 63 years of age at the beginning of the Civil War. A person who was in his sixties during the 19th century would have been considered aged, which could account for such a variance in his years. Ethan Hitchcock, dispatched to Indian Territory in 1842, met Opothleyaholo and believed he was 40–50 years old at the time.[9] Thomas Yahola, a member of the great leader's line, believes he was nearer 75 years of age. Opothleyaholo's position of speaker for the nation in 1825 would have required him to be more mature at that time. Despite his reputed age, the three battles in Indian Territory which he led, and then the desperate retreat to southern Kansas during inclement weather, and on to Leavenworth for interviews with Lane, Hunter and Dole exhibited unbelievable stamina. In his youth, Opothleyaholo had developed stamina when he had endured the young man's rites to become a warrior of the Creeks.

When Opothleyaholo left his home on the North Fork of the Canadian River in Indian Territory because of the white man's war, he had done so with great courage and a strong heart. He had kept his eyes and ears open, had not feared the cold nor the enemy's arrows and always, even in flight, he and his men had shown they were true warriors.

As a man, Opothleyaholo was tall, well-built and known for his sagacity, calmness in time of adversity, and eloquence in speech. He was a Tuckabatchee (Tukvpvtce) of the Muskogee Nation, which was an amalgamation of at least seven tribes living in Georgia and Alabama. It is uncertain when the confederacy was formed, but DeSoto, in his explorations of 1540, found several of their towns each having a chief.

Perhaps these Indians united because of attacks from the northern tribes. By the 18th century the Muskogee Nation was powerful and well-equipped to defend themselves against the Iroquois Confederacy, the Catawbas, Cherokees, and Shawnees.

Tribes with different languages and customs which were taken into the confederacy soon abandoned their cultures, being absorbed by the Muskogeeans. There were exceptions, however. The Yuchis or Euchees always retained their language and customs and would side with the loyal Creeks during the Civil War. And the Naktache and Alabamas continued to observe their customs and speak their own language. More than 50 percent of the nation was of the Muskogean linguistic stock and it was the language that prevailed.

The Muskogee Nation like most of the southern tribes had African slaves. Their slavery practices created much difficulty with the slave-holding whites, who usually accused them of stealing or protecting runaway slaves.

The dominant power in the nation were the Indians living in towns along the Coosa and Tallapoosa rivers in northern Alabama, and along the Flint and lower Chattahoochee rivers on the Alabama–Georgia border. Because they lived near these streams, the white men had dubbed them Creeks.

Their towns would grow until they numbered 77. Each was governed by a chief, with a principal chief for the entire nation. There were also villages, but only the settlements called towns had public squares where the annual busk, dances and important meetings of chiefs and head men were held.[10]

Some of the Creeks living in the Lower Creek area abandoned their nation, whether as fugitives or in disagreements with fellow tribe members. They settled with the Indians in northern Florida and were called Seminoles from a Creek word meaning "wild" or "far off people." As they were in Spanish territory, they inevitably became separated from the Creek Nation. From this small tribe would come the celebrated Osceola; Mikanopy; Emathla (King Philip), Hal-pat-ter Tus-te-nuggee, Alligator, Ho-lota Mathla, Jumper, Haleck Tustenuggee and Halpatter–Micco (Billy Bowlegs) said to be the brother of Alligator, and the last Seminole chief to remove to the west.

Eventually, a distinction between the two Creek factions was made by the white man. The ones living in the northern section would be called Upper Creeks and those in the south, Lower Creeks. With the coming of the white man, and the intermarriages of the Creeks, particularly with the Scots, more and more half-bloods became chiefs among the Lower Creeks. The Upper Creeks, traditionally, were known as the full-bloods. This division, geographically, of the nation would be the tool that the white man used to bring about its diminishment.

Opothleyaholo was born near Tuckabatchee, the ancient and principal town of the Upper Creeks. Tuckabatchee was located about two and one-half miles below the falls of the Tallapoosa River in Alabama. When the Tuckabatchee people were weakened by wars, they aligned themselves with the Muskogees and though a singular people, they would become an authoritative voice in the nation.

It was the Tuckabatchees who brought to the nation the five copper and two brass plates that were used in their greatest religious ceremony, the annual puskita (busk) celebration of the green corn. It was this celebration that witnessed the lighting of the new fire. Opothleyaholo, when removal became imminent, had said he would put out his old fire and never make or kindle it again until he reached west of the Mississippi, there never to quench it again.

The ashes of the old fire were carried to Indian Territory where, carefully, a new fire was started over them.[11]

One ancient name of the Tuckabatchees was Isopokogi, legendary beings, who had instructed them in their ceremonies and had bestowed upon them the ceremonial plates. It is significant that a Tuckabatchee named Isopokogi Yaholo would gain prominence during the Civil War because of Opothleyaholo.[12]

With the signing of the Treaty of Paris in 1783, which ended the Revolutionary War, the United States came into possession of all the lands west to the Mississippi River. Basically, the young United States was bankrupt due to the war. Payments to the soldiers would have to be in land bounties. Although the government was feeling the pressure from their white constituents to settle in the area, they were not inclined to use force against the Indians. The veterans believed they had battled England for the rights to the Indian country. They saw the Indians only as tenants who should be replaced by another race that was destined to inherit "God's wilderness."

Alexander McGillivray was the son of Lachlan McGillivray, a Scotsman, and a half-blood Creek princess named Sehoy. After being educated at Charleston, South Carolina, he came home to live in the Creek Nation. He became a chief and was a British agent during the war. Perhaps McGillivray would not have remained so vengeful toward the Americans had the Georgia authorities not taken his property as punishment for his alliance with the British. He and his warriors began a campaign of retribution against all whites in the Cumberland Valley and east Tennessee.

The government feared McGillivray's power over the southern tribes and, most of all, his affiliation with the Spanish. He had declared he would not renounce Spain unless "obtaining a full equivalent for the sacrifice." His connections were "honorable and lucrative to himself and advantageous to the Creek Nation."[13]

In October 1785, five U.S. commissioners met with the Creeks at Galphinton, Georgia. The meeting was adjourned for lack of adequate representation by the nation. Absent were the Tuckabatchees, Hickory Ground and Hilebee delegates. However, Georgia representatives, taking advantage of the situation, treated with the Lower Creeks who ceded their lands between the Okmulgee and Oconee down to the St. Mary's River. This treaty with Georgia was not accepted by the Upper Creeks, and these lands would be disputed during negotiations for the 1790 Treaty.

Yet, in the 1785 treaty, the Georgians incorporated the Creeks into the colony. By this action, Georgia "took away from the Confederated Government," as it was then called, "all pretensions as to jurisdiction over them."[14] This particular article would be cited in future dealings with the Creeks. Joseph V. Bevan was appointed by the Georgia Legislature, in September 1825, to research the state's archives for documentary evidence that Georgia's rights were being ignored. Bevan's research was very thorough, citing agreements between the Lower Creeks and James Oglethorpe as far back as 1733. Summing up his findings, Bevan, because of the 1785 treaty, believed "at this early period in the history of the General Government, did the State of Georgia become a martyr to State Rights!"[15] The fact that Georgia was a colony and not a state in 1785 was never considered by Bevan or the Georgia Legislature.

The turmoil in Georgia escalated and in 1789 commissioners, selected by the president, advised the governor that in order to effect a treaty with the Creeks, the Georgians had to cease "all animosities"; a refusal by the nation to sign a treaty meant "arms of the Union" should be used to protect the Georgians as United State citizens; continued hostilities by the Creeks would brand them as "enemies of the United States" to be "punished accordingly."[16]

President George Washington in January 1790, fearing troubles on the "Southern frontier," communicated with both houses of Congress to effect a treaty with the Creek Nation. The Creeks were trading with the British using the Spanish ports to the south of the nation. Washington feared repercussions because of this foreign trade and wanted the United States to trade solely with the Creeks. A personal invitation from the president finally moved McGillivray and a delegation to travel to the capital, New York City, to treat with the United States. By that summer, Washington was able to present the first treaty with the Creeks to the Senate for ratification. The president was pleased by the treaty's terms and felt it would be "productive of present peace and prosperity to our Southern frontier." He, also, saw the treaty as cementing "the Creeks and the neighboring tribes to the interest of the United States."[17]

However, while the treaty contained the relinquishment by the Creeks of the Oconee lands to the State of Georgia, which claimed the area, they would not yield on another claim by that state. Georgia insisted that in their treaty of 1785 at Galphinton the land "to the eastward of a new temporary line from the forks of the Oconee and Okmulgee in a southwestern direction to the St. Mary's River" had been ceded by the Creeks. Washington thought the "generally barren" land along the rivers might be cultivated for rice and the timber used for shipbuilding. The Creeks found the area to be highly important to them as "valuable winter hunting grounds"; the delegation in New York City at the time refused to yield.[18]

The treaty was signed August 7, 1790, by Alexander McGillivray and other representatives of the Creek Nation. This treaty with the Federal Government was the fruition of seven years work on the part of the U.S. commissioners.

Georgia protested against the New York Treaty. The Georgia Legislature's fifth resolution censured the government's assertion that the Indian hunting lands within Georgia's limits belonged to the United States and not to the state.

Georgia had never granted this area to the Federal Government and, therefore, they insisted that they had retained their "sovereignty and right of preemption exclusively over the same."[19] The sixth resolution deplored the seventh article, which prohibited the whites from hunting on the Creek lands while the Indians were not banned from the white people's land.[20]

It was Washington who suggested in his fourth annual address to the Congress the placing of trustworthy men to live among the Indians. He believed the agents "would also contribute to the preservation of peace and good neighborhood." Washington was confident he had settled any disputes the Georgians might have with the Creek Nation. In 1794 he stated "the Creeks in particular are covered from encroachment by the interposition of the General Government and that of Georgia."[21]

Georgia was not through with the Creeks, though, and by 1795 they were charging them with depredations along the Cumberland River. Washington believed the Creeks still claimed that land and he deemed it important to trace the causes for this outburst of hostilities. He nominated Benjamin Hawkins of North Carolina, George Clymer of Pennsylvania, and Andrew Pickens of South Carolina as commissioners to hold another treaty session with the Creeks. That December, in his seventh annual message to Congress, Washington lamented the fact that Georgia citizens had committed "wanton murders" on Creek hunting parties. The Southern frontier was, once again, plunged into "disquietude and danger which will be productive of further expense and may occasion more effusion of blood."[22]

The Federal Government, however, refused to reimburse the Georgia militia that had been called out to check the Creek aggressions against the state.[23]

The new treaty was signed at Colerain, Georgia, June 29, 1796, and allowed the United States to establish trading houses and military posts within the boundary of the Creek Nation. Georgians believed their rights had been, once again, ignored by the government.

With each signing the Creeks had ceded more and more of their ancestral lands located in the area formed in 1798 and called the Mississippi Territory. As a result the nation had been assigned agents, the one in that position during Opothleyaholo's youth being Benjamin Hawkins. Supposedly, agents were there as a buffer between the two races. But their true work for the government was to bring about cessions of land. Also, the Creeks had been provided with blacksmiths and tools and implements for cultivation of the soil. Hawkins penned reports of their progress to the administration in Washington. The agent was pleased to see them adopting the white man's civilized life; they were plowing, raising cotton and livestock and the women were weaving.[24]

The Creeks were a proud people, loyal, industrious. Any visitor in their nation was received hospitably, and fed well by a generous host. Menus often consisted of beef, turkey, venison, pork, corn, potatoes, beans, rice and coffee.

They loved music and ball play was their favorite game. They had laws governing all aspects of community life. The custom of burial was different than most Native People. Generally, the deceased was buried in a square pit under the bed where he had died.[25]

Just as the Osages became known as "walkers," the Creeks were noted as great "talkers." When Opothleyaholo was appointed Speaker of the Creek Nation, he had attained one of the highest official positions possible in that nation. Whenever the principal chief had an important message to be given to the people, his speaker delivered it.

Opothleyaholo, in early historical accounts, has been called the son of Alexander Cornell. Cornell was a half-blood who served as an assistant and interpreter for the agent Hawkins. Other historians believed the speaker's father was David Cornell. Neither are correct. Although there is no documentation to support the Cornell link, still Opothleyaholo's parentage has been lost to history. What is known is his mother was a full-blood Tuckabatchee. Opothleyaholo was a full-blood and could not speak English. Had he been the son of either Cornell, he would have learned the English language from his father.[26]

However, Opothleyaholo had no need to be conversant in the white man's tongue. Through his interpreters it would become clear to presidents, their cabinet members, other government officials, and army men that Opothleyaholo was a formidable man, one who would never succumb easily to the government's ultimate goal in taking the Muskogees land for the Americans.

Chapter 3

The Europeans Invade

In 1733, James Oglethorpe and more than 100 persons landed on the southeast coast and formed the settlement of Savannah. Oglethorpe, former member of Parliament, who had created this new colony for the British, was appointed its governor. The new colony had been chartered by King George II to serve as an intervening power between the Spanish in Florida and the French in Louisiana. The area chartered was an east-west strip between the Savannah and Altamaha rivers and extended from the Atlantic to the Pacific oceans. Oglethorpe named the colony Georgia in honor of the English sovereign. Conflicts would ensue with the Spanish who claimed the territory, however. No regard was taken for the Native People who called the area "home." Indeed, the Native People had been used as slaves by the whites from the beginning. Columbus had shipped 500 of them to Spain to be used as slaves. Even the sanctimonious colonists in New England had Native People for slaves.[1]

Initially, Oglethorpe's plan was to offer the area as an asylum for those who had become debtors, some even prisoners of the crown. The plan extended to the oppressed German Protestants and others on the continent.

Rum and slavery were forbidden in this last, the 13th, English colony. However, when the colonists learned and eventually saw other people across the Savannah River in South Carolina profiting from slavery, they became discontented and hostile. Adding to this unrest, war between Spain and England erupted in 1739, putting Georgia in a precarious position. With the failed attempt by Oglethorpe and the Georgia militia to capture St. Augustine, and the taking of Fort St. Simon on the Altamaha River by the Spanish, the future looked very grim. Finally, the Battle of Bloody Marsh in 1742 saw the defeat of the Spanish. That same year the importation of rum was permitted and in 1749 slaves were brought into Georgia.

The colony, hard-pressed for money, petitioned Parliament for aid. When that was rejected, Oglethorpe returned to England and relinquished his charter

17

in 1752. King George II reorganized the colony and Georgia became a Royal province in 1754. After the French and Indian War, which lasted from 1755 to 1763, Georgia's southern boundary was the St. Mary's River and its western border the Mississippi River.

Georgia was subjugated by the British during the Revolutionary War. Savannah was captured in 1778 and occupied by the Red Coats until 1782.

Representatives from Georgia were sent to the Second Continental Congress. When the war ended the other colonies declared their independence from the crown. Georgia knew, with its vast landholdings, that it would become a power in the newly formed Union. On January 2, 1788, the colony became the fourth state, ratifying the Constitution. Georgia's power was felt when the Federal Government entered into a compact with the state in 1802. At that time, the state formally ceded to the United States the area to the west called Mississippi Territory with the condition that slavery would be legal there. The United States wanted to organize the territory and appoint a governor.

That same year the United States and the Creeks signed a treaty. This cession gave to Georgia, by a re-purchase of lands from the Creeks, the Talassee country, including the disputed area within the forks of the Oconee and Oakmulgee rivers. As part of the compact, the United States vowed to "extinguish the Indian title to all other lands within the state of Georgia."[2] This promise to remove the Native People from their home land would take many years to accomplish. President Thomas Jefferson knew the people would have to be moved farther to the west in the Mississippi Territory. Then in 1803 the French offered to sell Louisiana to the United States. With that purchase came the possession of the mighty Mississippi River and the Rocky Mountains, an 828,000 square mile area.

No longer would Jefferson have to wonder where to relocate the Indians. This President was the author of the Indian Removal Plan. His message to Congress on January 18, 1803, was, in part, devoted to the Indians and the extension of the U.S. territories. He believed the Creeks, whom he considered to be an important nation, should be applying their energies to raising stock, farming, and to "domestic manufacture." Jefferson foresaw the time when they would give up their "former mode of living." All of their "extensive forests necessary in the hunting life will then become useless." Of course, should their civilization occur, "they will see advantage in exchanging them for the means of improving their farms and of increasing their domestic comforts." Jefferson wanted to add more "trading houses among them." Such places would prove to the Indians that for domestic comfort this would be better than "the possession of extensive but uncultivated lands." Jefferson, it would seem, desired to prove to the Creeks that becoming civilized like the white man would encourage them to part with their land and, of course, the Americans were waiting to acquire them when they did.[3]

In 1804, the Louisiana Territorial Act was passed. It gave the President the power to remove the Indians from their lands east of the Mississippi River and relocate them to the west. There was much resistance by the settlers who would have preferred annihilation of the Native People.[4]

Jefferson was not concerned only with the Southern tribes. He became interested in the Missouri River and the aborigines in that area. He suggested that "an intelligent officer with ten or twelve chosen men" might be persuaded to explore that country "even to the Western Ocean."[5] The expedition of Meriwether Lewis and William Clark entered the Missouri River in May 1804, and in December 1806, Jefferson reported to the Congress that the endeavor had been successful.[6]

The exploration of the Red River in 1804 had failed, however, and that fall, efforts were concentrated "on an interesting branch of the river called the Washita."[7] The Spanish to the west of the Mississippi had been showing a force along the Red River. The Spanish territory included Texas to the Californias. Oregon Territory was claimed by Spain, England, Russia and the United States. As explained by Jefferson in his sixth annual message to Congress in 1806, Spain had "advanced in considerable force" taking post at Bayou Pierre on the Red River. Originally, it was French and eventually "was delivered to Spain only as a part of Louisiana." When Louisiana was returned to France and then sold to the United States, no one had noticed that Spain "continued a guard there" at the remote post.[8] The Sabine River became a "temporary line of separation" between the two countries. However, Spain crossed the Sabine intending "to occupy new posts and make new settlements" and advanced to the Adais. A U.S. army detachment was sent from Natchitoches. After negotiations, the "Spanish commandant withdrew his force to the west side of the Sabine."[9]

The removal of the Creeks from Georgia would not be so easily accomplished. It would be a slow, painful process. The powerful Creeks (and the Cherokees, to the north) posed a threat to the encroachment of the white man. Although they had seen most of their land ceded to create the great state of Georgia, the tribe still retained considerable acreage within the state. More forts had been erected in the Creek country, additional trading posts established, and roads had been built.

The Georgians, constantly referring to the 1802 compact, demanded that the Indians be removed from their state. The Indian-held lands were considered very fertile, and for the state to expand its cotton crop and slavery, it needed the room.

In 1811, William McIntosh, half-blood chief of the Lower Creeks, advised the tribe to enact a law whereby any ceding of lands must be done and approved in full council. Any one Creek chief who would treat with the Federal Government on the sale of lands would be tried and killed. This verbal transaction in full council would be refuted in 1825 by the Lower Creeks.[10]

Yet, McIntosh, son of a Scotsman and Creek mother, began leaning more and more toward the white man's way of living. McIntosh was no exception. Many were adopting the white man's dress, and to those trying to hold onto their own individual culture, it was as if the others were traitors. Discord was growing in the nation, and it would be Tecumseh, the Shawnee, who would be the spark to light their fears.

Opothleyaholo was a young man when, in 1811, Tecumseh visited the southern tribes. The Shawnee was a dynamic, persuasive Indian who was attempting to arouse the anger of all the Indian tribes. He was desirous of creating a confederated Indian nation which, with the help of the British, would drive the white man from the continent.

Tecumseh was not a stranger to the Creeks, having lived with them as a young man. His deeds of valor in the north were legend, and soon were being repeated in the southern tribes. Although he had not been successful with the Lower Creeks, he was able to stir the blood of the Upper Creeks when he visited Tuckabatchee.

Opothleyaholo was impressed with Tecumseh who exuded a magnetism as he spoke. The Indian was wrong to go the way of the whites. They must give up the white man's garments; their customary tillage of the land. It was degrading to the Indian who found honor in fighting and hunting. Tecumseh painted pictures in words of the desolation to come to their lands; more and more forests would be destroyed; white man's towns would be built; the Indian would become a slave on the lands the Great Spirit had given to them. They could not let this happen.[11]

It was impossible not to be moved by the Shawnee's words. Yet, Big Warrior, the chief of Tuckabatchee, did not appear to be swayed by the oratory. He knew the Americans could be a redoubtable foe. He was not particularly fond of them, but he feared any acts of war against them would inevitably destroy the nation. Tales of that era state that Tecumseh, realizing this man would never believe him, warned the chief that when he returned to Detroit, he would stomp his foot and they in Tuckabatchee would feel the earth tremble beneath them. Then they would believe in his power as given to him by the Master of Breath. Coincidentally, when the New Madrid earthquake occurred, sending the mighty Mississippi River to flow northward for a time, the earth moved at Tuckabatchee as elsewhere in the area. What more proof did the Creeks have to have, the young bloods wanted to know. Tecumseh was right. They would destroy the white man; reclaim their lands, and once again live as their ancestors had, free to roam and hunt as they pleased.

When Tecumseh left the Creek country, Little Warrior, a Creek chief, and 30 Creeks accompanied him on his journey north. Once there, they received full attention by the British officers. The Creeks always had been sympathetic toward the British, and on the surface, it appeared the feeling was returned. British spies had been active in the nation for some time, soliciting the help of the Creeks against the United States.[12]

When Little Warrior and the others were returning home they killed seven American families in the Chickasaw country, taking one woman as a prisoner to their nation. Hawkins, the agent, learned of the atrocities and called for the perpetrators to be punished. Chiefs, who desired to keep the treaty promises with the government, in council, ordered the arrest of the men. William McIntosh and Capt. Isaacs led two parties of warriors and soon they had apprehended all, except Little Warrior. The men were killed, and eventually, Little Warrior suffered the same fate.[13]

The killing of the Americans and the punishment of the Creeks precipitated a civil war in the Creek Nation in the spring of 1812, the same year the United States and Great Britain declared war.

Outrage after outrage continued in the Creek country with some Americans being killed. The friendly Creeks and those dedicated to the killing of the whites began battling each other. In retaliation for the death of Little Warrior and his party, the hostiles killed the chief, Capt. Isaacs, in 1813. Big Warrior and Tuckabatchee tried to remain neutral, but it was impossible. Death threats were made against the chief, and he was taken to a place of safety. Tuckabatchee suffered from raids with much destruction.[14]

All of this activity was watched closely by one man in particular, a man who as far back as Jefferson's administration had wanted to march his Tennessee militia into the Creek country for an all out war. Andrew Jackson, was, history has shown, "a war hawk," who knew Americans on the frontier would sanction any campaign against the Indians, and it would not hurt his political image.

Menawa, half-blood chief of the Oakfuskee towns in the Upper Creek district, believed in Tecumseh, and soon his youthful warriors and others in the nation were gathering strength in numbers. Francis, the Creek prophet, had been instructed in the Shawnee mysticism by Tecumseh's prophet who had stayed in the nation.

The Red Sticks learned the war dance of the Indians of the English lakes, which jerking and convulsive motions whipped them into a psychedelic state. All of the Creek warriors who fought against the United States became known as the Red Sticks due to the red war clubs they carried. The Red Sticks met secretly, waiting for a sign and threatened all who would not join them in their cause with death. They killed cattle and hogs, destroyed crops, anything that might be associated with the white man's life. Their fellow Indians were alarmed at the devastation, and believed a general outbreak in their country was imminent.[15]

Whites, Blacks, Indians and mixed bloods sought safety within the fortress built by Samuel Mims on his land, situated above the confluence of the

Alabama and Tombigbee rivers. The command of Maj. Daniel Beasley, half-blood Creek of the Mississippi volunteers, had been ordered to the fort, and in all, the total of people within the stockade has been estimated to number from 247 to 550.

Although warned of a possible attack by the Indians, Beasley ordered the fort gate open at all times, and to insure that, sand had been piled against it. It was a beautiful day that August 30, 1813, and the people were reveling in it. Only the day before, Sunday, more whiskey had been delivered and obviously from the sounds coming from within the fort, it had been drunk liberally.

Jim Cornell, a half-blood Creek, scouting the area for the Red Sticks, rode to the fort and warned Beasley, who was drunk, that the Indians were coming. Beasley disregarded him and all other warnings about an attack. Then, at the noon hour, swiftly and on foot, the Red Sticks led by William Weatherford, a half-blood Creek, moved through the open gate.

The fighting was bloody and disastrous to all within the fort. Weatherford, who was reluctant to join the Red Sticks, and had done so only when they had threatened to kill his family, had hoped to calm the frenzied warriors. He was unable to stop the carnage. Blacks were taken as slaves by the Indians, and they along with a half-blood family and about 20 whites, who escaped, were all that survived the massacre. It had taken five hours.[16]

Later that fall, the great Tecumseh lay dying in Canada. The British had made him a brigadier-general in charge of the Indian troops. Tecumseh's death would not bring an end to the hostilities in the Creek Nation. The Red Sticks, even if it were possible they knew of Tecumseh's death, would not be swayed from their crusade. Obviously, Tecumseh's medicine had been bad, indeed, they had witnessed bad medicine among their own comrades. Had it been good medicine, bullets and swords would never penetrate their bodies.

The Red Sticks believed the Master of Breath had ordered them to kill only whites and half-bloods.[17] This, possibly, was one of the reasons McIntosh had offered his services to the United States in putting down the Red Stick rebellion.

Boasting of their success at Fort Mims, the Red Sticks fervor to eliminate the white man from their country did not wane until 1814 and the Battle of Horseshoe Bend on the Tallapoosa River in Alabama.

Chapter 4

Annihilation at Horseshoe Bend

The peninsula called Tohopeka by the Creeks was in a bend of the Tallapoosa River and consisted of about 100 acres of land. Across its mouth the Red Sticks had erected heavily timbered walls with port holes, comparable to the civilized man's fortresses. Credit for these preparations was given to William Weatherford, who had many opportunities to visit Pensacola and Mobile to study how the Spanish engineered their fortifications.[1]

The Creeks believed they could escape across the Tallapoosa, if need be, but Gen. Andrew Jackson, realizing they would use it as an escape route, effectually dispatched John Coffee and his western Tennessee militia, together with a Cherokee contingent to seal it off. McIntosh and his Lower Creeks were present at Horseshoe Bend with the Americans. Jackson and his western Tennesseeans, among whom was Sam Houston, along with Cherokees and Creeks, numbering at least 2,000, twice as many as the total of Red Sticks, attacked the fortifications on foot and with cannons. Those escaping by the river were mowed down, and in just a short while, Red Sticks littered the battleground. Estimates have varied in the total number of Red Sticks killed, from 800 to 950, but one thing was certain: Jackson had vowed to annihilate them and it was a promise he had battled to keep.[2]

Dignitaries of the southern states and politicians alike all praised the war hawk, believing he had saved the country singlehandedly. Jackson was feted at a public dinner held in Nashville in May in appreciation for his victory against the Creeks. This victory would bring into the southern states most of the Indian lands they had coveted. Friendly Creeks and Cherokees who had fought against the Red Sticks would be penalized along with the hostiles, and all would be deprived of their heritage.

The treaty of 1814 was negotiated August 9 at Fort Jackson, formerly Fort

Toulouse, renamed by Jackson himself. His determination to have the very best of the Creek nation was debated by the Creeks but in the end, Jackson's mercilessness toward them would win out. More military posts, trading houses and roads to be established within the territory. The United States would have navigation on the rivers; all discourse with the British and Spanish would cease. Permanent peace was to ensue between the Creeks and the United States. Supplies of corn would be furnished to the Creeks due to the devastation of their crops, but only until they could raise a new supply.[3]

The biggest reward for Jackson in overpowering this proud nation was the material wealth gained in land for the South. In 1814 the Creeks had ceded almost 50 percent of the present state of Alabama to the United States. The expansion of slavery was a capital item, and as seen in Senate documents, and Sen. Thomas Hart Benton's "Thirty Year View," this expansion could never have occurred without the support of the northern politicians. The South had the North to thank as in the years following the Battle of Horseshoe Bend, removal of the Indians from their ancestral lands was completed for the sake of cotton and slavery. Then, within a few short years, the politicians would turn on themselves when slavery became an issue in the west.

Menawa, "The Great Warrior," had led his Red Sticks in the Battle of Horseshoe Bend. He was wounded. The callous attitudes of the soldiers toward his fallen comrades, those once youthful warriors with their painted faces, crowns of turkey feathers adorning their heads, and the cow tails that had been tied to their shoulders, to hang free to the wrist, moved Menawa to shoot one of the soldiers. Another soldier returned fire, wounding Menawa in the face. Sinking back into the carnage, he waited patiently for nightfall then crawled to the river and finding a canoe that Gen. Floyd's men had missed made his way to where the women and children had been hidden among the bushes along the bank. Menawa's penalty as participant against the whites was the burning of his village, destruction of his houses, cattle and merchandise. Menawa, once a wealthy man, was reduced to impoverishment.[4]

The federal government, in its desire for an accurate accounting of the dead Red Sticks, ordered the soldiers to snip off the nose of each dead Creek. As if this act was not barbarous enough, they were skinned, the strips becoming bridle reins for the soldiers' mounts.[5] These acts were committed by a self-proclaimed civilized race who had succumbed to the propaganda spread about the Creeks' hideous acts against the Americans. And the desire to eradicate the Red Sticks from humanity failed. Some survived the battle and became worthy citizens of their nation. Their memory lives on in the name of the capital of Louisiana: Baton Rouge, French for red war club.

Annuities for 1812 through 1814 had been withheld because of the war. By October 1814, many of the innocent and guilty were naked and hungry and without means to clothe themselves for the approaching winter. Jackson touted that he hoped justice would be done. Strange that it was long delayed, Secretary of War James Monroe advised in December that he had sent supplies, and they never arrived. A famine is a subtle way to decrease a population.[6]

Many historians believed Opothleyaholo was a Red Stick at the Horseshoe Bend battle. Certainly, he was a young man and had experienced many hardships as a result of the war. He would never forget the federal government's dedication to acquiring that which it pleased, and most of all, Andrew Jackson's unforgiving attitude toward the Creek Nation.

President James Madison, in his sixth annual message on September 20, 1814, praised "the bold and skillful operations of Maj. Gen. Jackson." The "principal tribes of hostile savages" had been subdued. "The recent and exemplary chastisement" had put an end to "their cooperation with the British enterprises which may be planned against that quarter of our country."[7]

In 1817, Mississippi became a state, followed by Alabama, 1819, the twentieth and twenty-second states in the Union, respectively. Both states were shaped out of Indian lands belonging to the Creeks, Choctaws, and Chickasaws. Still the Americans were not satisfied. They wanted all of the Indian country remaining in their respective areas.

William McIntosh would gain power in the Creek Nation and was given the rank of major for his devotion and aid to the United States during the Creek War. Some Red Sticks had escaped to Florida for safety among their fellow Seminoles. When Jackson continued on to the Spanish held area, McIntosh and his Creeks helped Jackson to round up the hostiles. McIntosh was then breveted brigadier general for his service to the United States. He received for his term of service, February 24 to May 9, 1818, $645.72, which included pay for forage and servants.[8]

The state of Georgia continued to press the government for a swift conclusion to the 1802 compact. Gov. Clark appealed to Washington and, finally in August 1820, commissions were sent to Col. Andrew Pickens and Gen. Thomas Flournoy to treat with the Creek Indians. However, Pickens resigned in September and Daniel M. Forney of Lincolnton, North Carolina, was appointed to replace him.[9]

John C. Calhoun, secretary of war, advised Flournoy that, despite Clark's insistence, that the Georgia commissioners had the right "to conclude and sign the treaty," only the United States had that power.[10] Flournoy encountered difficulty with the state commissioners and resigned in November. Earlier, Flournoy had given orders to Gen. D.B. Mitchell, Creek agent, to contract for rations and to request the Creek Nation to meet with the commissioners on December 20, 1820, at Indian Springs.[11]

Gen. David Meriwether of Athens, Georgia, was appointed to succeed Flournoy. There was a conflict of interest in that Meriwether was a Georgia commissioner and James Monroe, then president, deemed it "incompatible" and advised him to resign the state appointment.[12]

John Quincy Adams, secretary of state, had notified the Georgia governor that as the treaty negotiations had been requested by the state, it was the president's intention that the "freest and fullest cooperation" should exist between the U.S. and Georgia commissioners.[13] Thus, when the negotiations began in December, J. McIntosh, David Adams and Daniel Newman were there to represent Georgia.[14]

Forney and Meriwether delivered a talk to the Creeks. Property allegedly taken by the Indians had not been returned to the Georgians in accordance with previous treaties beginning in 1790.[15]

In their speech the Georgia commissioners pointed out that long before the 1790 treaty with the United States "the headmen of Georgia and your nation talked together and agreed to bury all differences and to have perpetual friendship." The Georgians reminded them of the treaties at Augusta, Galphinton and Shoulderbone with both the state and the United States at New York and Coleraine that promised that the Creeks would restore all property taken and pay for damages done to the state.[16]

The next day the state commissioners talked to the chiefs and presented "a statement of the claims of the people of Georgia against your nation." The chiefs were informed that the president "and the Governor of Georgia expect the red people to do justice to the white people. They ask no more."[17] With the justice Georgia asked for would not only be a payment of the claims, but a cession of more land, hopefully all of the Creek country within the state.

The Creeks had been appalled to learn of Georgia's claims against them. Tustunnuggee Hopoy or Little Prince, the principal chief of the nation, answered the Georgia commissioners through his speaker, William McIntosh. Little Prince had been unaware that in the course of the present negotiations he would have to make an accounting about the Georgia claims. He stressed the nation had cooperated in restoring Negroes and white prisoners to the state. Little Prince cited his venture when he had joined the American army under Col. Clinch "and proceeded to the Negro fort on the Appalachicola River and aided in its destruction." He had, also, joined Gen. Jackson's army and journeyed to Florida, and had recaptured some of the Negroes who were with the Seminoles. He had notified the U.S. agent and had delivered them to the authorities.[18]

Little Prince, in studying the claims, could not find any credit given to the Creeks for property returned. He was willing to refer all claims, including those of the nation against the white people, "to his father and Protector the President of the United States."[19]

Although the Georgia commissioners conceded the Creeks had displayed a "friendly disposition" in their answer, still the state pressed the issue. They could not believe the Creeks considered themselves not "bound to restore to us the property taken or destroyed by your nation before the treaty of New York." They charged that although the British had carried away or destroyed Negroes in the late war, the Creek Nation, in transporting the slaves to the scene of battle, was held responsible for those who had "belonged to the people of Georgia." The commissioners agreed to lay the matter before the President.[20]

With the agreement by both parties in regard to the claims, the land cession dominated the rest of the negotiations. On January 8, 1821, the Creeks ceded to the United States nearly 5 million acres for the sum of $450,000. In the opinion of Forney and Meriwether "no tract of country, of equal extent, within the Indian boundary, is as fertile or a desirable as the one now ceded."[21]

It is highly interesting to learn that a proviso of Article I states that "1,000 acres would be laid off in a square so as to include the mineral springs in the center thereof, as, also, 640 acres on the western bank of the Okmulgee River, so as to include the improvements at present in the possession of Indian General McIntosh." There were 26 signatures or marks to the treaty, including McIntosh, Little Prince and Etomme (Etome) Tustunnuggee.[22]

The U.S. commissioners believed they had accomplished "the views of the Government." However, they had "been considerably embarrassed in negotiating this treaty." The Georgians insistence about their claims against the Creeks had been "unpleasant." Two-hundred fifty thousand dollars was set aside out of the treaty money to pay any and all claims prior to the 1802 compact with the state of Georgia. Claims on both sides would be subject to the will of the president, but no dollar amount was ever set for Creek claims against the Georgians.[23]

The 1821 treaty did not settle Georgia's claims against the Creeks. Soon, there were rumors that Georgia intended to gain the remaining Creek land within the state.

A select committee in the U.S. House of Representatives reported on January 7, 1822, their findings on the extinguishment of the Indian title to land in Georgia. Having studied the treaty of 1814 they found that the Creeks, by ceding lands within the Territory of Alabama, had been driven to withdraw "within the limits of Georgia."[24]

In March 1817, acting secretary of war George Graham had written to William McIntosh and others of a Creek delegation. "Friends and Brothers: The land which was guaranteed to you by the treaty signed by Gen. Jackson, and your chiefs and headmen on the ninth of August, 1814 is your lands, and your father the President, who holds you and your nation fast by the hand, will take care that no part of it is taken from you, except by the free consent of your chiefs and headmen, given in council and for a valuable consideration."[25]

The select committee had determined that this guarantee by the War

Department and the 1802 Georgia Compact had created "very opposite and conflicting obligations." The committee recommended to the U.S. Congress that their resolve "to grant to the Indians fee-simple titles to land within the limits of Georgia is a violation of the sovereign rights of that State."[26]

However, the Creek Nation, particularly the full-bloods, would remember Graham's words of assurance.

Chapter 5

Georgia's 1802 Compact

The United States, with treaties through 1821, managed to provide Georgia with 15 million acres. In April 1802 the state was paid $1.25 million for lands west of the Chattahoochee River. Following the 1821 treaty, the Georgians wanted the 1802 compact completed. They did not like the schools for Indians, the constant introduction of improvements among them on the part of the federal government. Educating the Indian meant he would be more aware of the value of his possessions. He would never part with his property peacefully if he realized how valuable it was to the white man.

In 1824 a different man was the governor of Georgia. George McIntosh Troup, a plantation owner and an ardent state rights man, immediately upon taking office, began pressuring Washington to finalize the 1802 compact. Troup was also a cousin of William McIntosh.

In February, Troup, in a letter to Secretary of War John C. Calhoun, had defined Georgia's position in regard to the Indians in that state. "Of all the old States, Georgia is the only one whose political organization is not complete ... Georgia is not in the possession of her vacant territories—a territory waste and profitless to the Indians, profitless to the United States; but, in possession of the rightful owner, a resource of strength, of revenue, and of union."[1]

Yet, President Monroe was insistent "that the Indian title was not affected in the slightest circumstance by the compact with Georgia and there is no obligation on the United States to remove the Indians by force." The extinguishment of Indian titles within Georgia was, as agreed upon by the state and federal government, to have been "done peacably," reasonably. And as agreed to in that compact, "the Indians had a right to the territory in the disposal of which they were to be regarded as free agents." The president found forcible removal of the Native People as "unjust." Still, Monroe was ambivalent in his appraisal of the question. He felt strongly that "if they could be prevailed upon" to retire west and north of states and territories "the Indians security and happiness would be assured."[2]

29

George A. Cutler, M.D. and Creek Indian
Agent of the Southern Superintendency
during the Civil War. Reproduced from History of Kansas, 1883. *Kansas State Historical
Society.*

Troup argued that to extinguish the Indian claims "peacably
and on reasonable terms" would
leave them to do so whenever they
pleased. The governor cited the
1814 treaty to have been the
appropriate time to have procured
for Georgia "the Creek lands
within our limits." Should the
president and the federal government continue to ignore Georgia's
claims, Troup prophesied that the
1802 compact would become null
and void, "and leave no alternative to Georgia but acquiescence
or resistance." He even suggested
that if nullification should occur,
that Georgia should have her
lands back and the state would
repay the government. "And without making war upon the states of
Alabama and Mississippi, we will
run the risk of concluding with
them the best bargain we can."[3]

Georgia was determined to
have the Creek's land and that of
the Cherokees. Both nations were aware of Troup's crusade and they counselled
with each other. The Creeks emulated the Cherokees and agreed "not to sell."[4]

In June 1824 the Bureau of Indian Affairs was organized within the War
Department.

Finally bowing to Georgia's demands, money was appropriated enabling
Monroe to begin negotiations with the Creeks. Col. Duncan G. Campbell and
Maj. James Merriwether, both Georgians, were commissioned to begin the pre-
liminary work in the summer of 1824. Calhoun apprised them of their duties,
and that expenses incurred could not exceed the sum of $50,000.[5]

Calhoun, also, discussed the 1821 Creek Treaty. The federal government,
although averse to treaty failure, felt the price for the remaining lands should
not exceed that paid in 1821. It will be remembered that the Creeks were to
receive $200,000 in installments and $250,000 had been set aside for the Georgia claims. However, by 1824 $100,589 had been paid to Georgia in the set-
tlement of its claims. In the 1821 treaty, the Creeks were to receive in cash and
claims monies amounting to $450,000 for their lands. With the alleged claims

falling short of the $250,000, what became of the near $150,000 left in claim money? Undoubtedly, the Creeks never received it and the Georgia government complained to Washington. They wanted the balance of the money. But the War Department records and papers had been destroyed by fire in 1800. If there had been records they were no longer extant. Georgia remonstrated against this decision repeatedly, but Washington asserted "that the decision was made and could not be reconsidered."[6]

"The terms on which the land was then purchased under the treaty of the 8th of January, 1821 within the Creek nation, were considered very high," Calhoun advised Campbell and Merriwether.[7]

John Crowell, Creek agent, had informed the head chiefs that November 25, 1824, would be the commencement of negotiations at Broken Arrow near Fort Mitchell, Georgia.[8] The Creeks did not agree to the date, and set December 6 as the earliest time they could attend. The commissioners were unhappy with the prolongment and informed Crowell they would begin December 1 and no later.

When Campbell and Merriwether arrived at Princeton, near Broken Arrow on the Chattahoochee River on November 30, they found "the Indians convening in considerable numbers."[9] It would not be until December 4, however, that the commissioners would meet with the Indians in their council. Any business to be transacted would begin December 6, but heavy rains cancelled that meeting as it was to be held in the public square. At last, on December 7 the commissioners delivered their address in full council.

They explained to their "Friends and Brothers of the Creek Nation" about the 1802 compact with Georgia and its boundaries. "The President finds you entirely surrounded by white people" and there were encroachments on both sides. "He has extensive tracts of country under his dominion beyond the Mississippi which he is willing to give you in exchange for the country you now occupy. We make you an offer, not only for your territory within the limits of Georgia, but for your whole country."[10]

After considering the commissioners' address, the next day, Little Prince, O. Porthle Yoholo (Opothelayholo), speaker of the Upper Creeks, William McIntosh, speaker of the nation, and Hopoy Hadjo replied. They were unacquainted with the agreement between the United States and Georgia. They were convinced that such an agreement would promote an alienation of affections "of a just parent from a part of his children or aggrandizing the one by the downfall and ruin of the other." Removal beyond the Mississippi would ensue in that ruin. "It is true, very true, that we are 'surrounded by white people'" and that there were encroachments made. "What assurances," they wanted to know, "have we that similar ones will not be made on us, should we deem it proper to accept your offer and remove beyond the Mississippi?" The Creeks, also, were concerned they might be "encroaching on the people of other nations."[11]

The commissioners followed with another address that attempted to explain the connection of the Creeks to the government.

"We ask you, how did the Muscogee nation come to this country? You came from the west, and took the country from another people who were in possession." The commissioners then described the history of Georgia and the Revolutionary War. "The war lasted seven years and the British were conquered; you took part in that war, and were conquered, also." The country conquered they declared now "belonged to the conquerors." Only the "humanity and goodness of the new Government which was established after the war" had saved the Creeks from being "driven off" like the British. All of the Indian tribes since that war "have had no power in the United States."[12]

They assured the Creeks that the president "will always stand by you and protect you against want and against your enemies." The president wanted their race "preserved"; he wanted them to "live and prosper"; to be civilized. And the only way to accomplish the president's desires was to leave the South and go beyond the Mississippi. Out there those lands would be theirs forever. Should the Creeks object to removal, then "you must come under the laws of the whites."[13]

Concluding their lengthy address, the commissioners wasted no more time in eloquent speech. "We want the country you now occupy. It is within the limits of Georgia and Alabama. These States insist upon having their lines cleared."[14]

Little Prince, Opothleyaholo and McIntosh were dismayed to learn "that the Muscogees are not the original proprietors of this soil, that they came from the west, and obtained it by conquest." Their traditions had "impressed" them "with the belief that we are the original and sole proprietors of the soil. Brothers, the first white people that ever landed here found us here. The first red people that were known to visit the whites were from the Coweta town." The meeting of the two cultures they referred to was when the Muscogees visited Oglethorpe in 1735. This historic meeting and the fact that the Indians were from Coweta in the Lower Creek region would have a great bearing on the 1825 Indian Springs Treaty.[15]

The Muskogees believed the Great Spirit had given them this their "promised" land. They had come from the west guided by a divine hand. The Great Spirit had commanded them in the way they should worship Him. Obeying these commandments, their traditions and customs had been established.[16]

The Creeks recited their many treaties with the U.S. Government beginning in 1790, and iterated Graham's letter of 1817 that "the land" guaranteed in the 1814 treaty "is your land."[17]

Removal beyond the Mississippi was out of the question. "Again, we feel an affection for the land in which we were born, we wish our bones to rest by the side of our fathers."[18]

The commissioners continued their efforts to make the Creeks understand that the government had to comply with Georgia, the United States had to "lie together in a compact form." The Indians living within the states were a deterrent to "the protection and improvement of the nation" and "it was necessary they should go out of the limits of the States." They also warned the Creeks not to be "misled by the Cherokees and others."[19]

Little Prince avowed there was "no land for sale ... Gen. Washington" had given them "the balance and told them it was theirs, and that they never intended to spare another foot."[20]

Big Warrior, through his speaker Opothleyaholo, insisted "that he would not take a housefull of money for his interest in the land." The commissioners "might take this for a final answer."[21]

Campbell and Merriwether prevailed upon the chiefs, that due to the bad weather the negotiations should be conducted in a room, the expense to be paid by the government. They suggested "that the mass who were standing around," and occasioning great expense in rations, should be discharged. The Creeks answered that none of their people would be discharged and "they would meet nowhere but in the square."[22]

The commissioners became satisfied that "the chiefs within the limits of Georgia" would treat with the government. Rather than expose those chiefs to the council, Campbell and Merriwether decided a temporary adjournment was essential to allow Campbell to travel to Washington to obtain instructions as to "the validity of a treaty signed by a dividual council."[23]

Chapter 6

The Indian Springs Treaty

Campbell, in his lengthy communication to Calhoun and the War Department in January 1825, expounded about the intrigues used by the Creek Nation before the treaty negotiations at Broken Arrow. There had been two meetings, one at Tuckabatchee in May and another at Pole Cat Springs in November.[1]

John Ross, Cherokee chief, figured prominently in the Tuckabatchee council. Although Campbell and Merriwether had not seen the papers Ross had sent to Big Warrior, they allegedly "proposed a concert of action" and "advised a resistance" of the government's policy. Another purpose was to "depreciate McIntosh" and ultimately to "destroy his standing and influence." Campbell charged that the meeting consisted solely of the Alabama chiefs and they had worked "industriously" to promote their decision and to ignite fear into McIntosh and his minions. The sub-agent, William Walker, had recorded the meeting.[2]

Later, at Pole Cat Springs, the Creeks met at Walker's home. Alabama papers published the results of both meetings and Campbell and Merriwether had been unaware of them until shortly before the Broken Arrow negotiations. They believed Capt. Walker had "prostituted" his official duties and had intermeddled in the treaty proceedings.[3]

It was at the Tuckabatchee meeting that the Creeks asserted "we have a great many chiefs and head men, but, be they ever so great, they must all abide by the laws. We have guns and ropes and if any of our people should break these laws, those guns and ropes are to be their end." Their land was to be held in common, "as it always has been." All laws had been made for all, not "for any person in particular."

At Polecat Springs, Georgia, the Creeks judged it unwise to sell any more land. Any authority given "to any individual" had been revoked. As proof of their advancement in civilization, they cited how the Upper Creeks in the

Coosa and Tallapoosa rivers had manufactured in one year "upwards of thirty thousand yards" of homespun. Their agriculture was improving. They acknowledged that they were weak relative to the strength of their "white brothers." From "our white and Christian brethren" they expected justice. Both notices had been signed by Little Prince, Poeth-la-Halo (Opothelyaholo), Big Warrior, Etomme Tustenugge, Charles Cornell and others. They were published in *The Montgomery* (Alabama) *Republican*.[4]

While the Commissioners were aspersing Walker and the Alabama chiefs, at the same time they had been involved in intrigues of their own. They had had many conversations with McIntosh at Broken Arrow. They believed the half-blood to be astute in many topics, particularly the connections between the government and the Indian tribes. He realized the policy of removing the Indians west of the Mississippi was "very humane and advantageous." McIntosh was the opposite of Big Warrior and both exemplified the "very striking difference" between the Upper and Lower Creeks; the former "stubborn and unyielding," the latter "reasonable," ready to accept a treaty.[5]

Etome Tustunuggee was the head chief of Coweta and this town claimed to be the original one of the nation. Coweta was on both sides of the Chattahoochee and extended north from Broken Arrow to the Cherokee boundary. Here resided McIntosh and Little Prince who was an admirer and friend of the speaker. McIntosh maintained only Coweta town had the exclusive right "to dispose of the whole country."[6]

Campbell wanted to reopen negotiations and sought President Monroe's consent. He deplored the fact that the treaty could have been signed by the chiefs within the limits of Georgia, but Big Warrior had been too stubborn to let that happen.[7] The president and cabinet granted the commissioners the authority to reconvene the Creek Nation at Indian Springs, Georgia. In a separate letter, Campbell then asked for the power "to accept a treaty signed by the chiefs within the limits of Georgia," provided the nation's chiefs would accept abandonment of the land "by the emigrating party."[8] The date set for the convention was February 7 and the commissioners notified Crowell and the Creek chiefs.

In the meantime, Secretary of War John C. Calhoun apprised Walker that he had been discharged as sub-agent. Operating completely upon the commissioners' report, the president determined Walker had helped to defeat "the termination of the treaty." As to Agent Crowell, although he maintained neutrality in regard to the proceedings, his career depended upon more evidence of his dereliction of duty.[9]

President Monroe instructed the commissioners that they could not treat "with General McIntosh alone." The government would not object to an arrangement with McIntosh to quit the country and settle west of the Mississippi. Monroe believed the Lower Creeks did not have the power "to cede any portion of the land belonging to the Creek Nation." Only the nation had that right. If any agreement was made with McIntosh alone, without its consent, then individuals within the nation might believe they had the right to cede the land they occupied. This would lead to the destruction of the nation's independence which had been maintained "under the laws, treaties and usages of the Government." The President again cautioned that should McIntosh be agreeable, it could only be done with "the assent of the nation." And the arrangement had to be in treaty form.[10]

On January 25, 1825, at Coweta, a memorial was drafted by the chiefs of Coweta, Taladega, Cussetta, Broken Arrow and Hitchita towns to the president. They asked for protection from "the red sticks (or hostile party)" of the nation. They had received word that Big Warrior and his chiefs were in council and they believed decrees were being passed that were derogatory to McIntoshes safety. Earlier the Big Warrior party in council had "passed an order for the execution of McIntosh" and other chiefs who would be in favor of selling the Georgia lands. The Lower Creeks maintained that McIntosh and his chiefs held a "superiority" in the nation's council, based upon their support and defense of the U.S. in the Creek War. Furthermore, Big Warrior's chiefs had "forfeited their rights to the country" because of their hostility toward "the United States during the last war." There was "much trouble" in the nation, the agent was partial to the Upper Creeks, "the United States are failing to comply with what they once promised us—that is, protection."[11]

The chiefs, in a separate article, authorized McIntosh, Etome Tustunuggee, Samuel Hawkins, interpreter, and six others to meet with the President, or his commissioners, to make arrangements for exchange of lands west of the Mississippi. They stressed that their delegates' actions would meet the approval of the National Council as there were "six of our principal council" with McIntosh. All were "authorized to sign any treaty of that kind."[12]

The trouble in the Creek country filtered through the Senate and House of Representatives. Campbell, while in Washington, had met with politicians and suggested that Agent Crowell and his relatives, who were traders in the nation, had no wish to see the Creeks cede more land. Particularly as "the affairs of the State of Georgia were in the present hands"; the hands being Gov. George Troup. Senators notified the Committee on Indian Affairs of their dialogue with Campbell who believed McIntosh would be deprived of his power and his life should he not be sustained by the government.[13]

Despite all of the incriminations and recriminations dealing with the proposed treaty, the commissioners arrived at Indian Springs on February 7. The site chosen had become important when white traders traveled the area and discovered the mineral spring which was well known to the Indians. McIntosh had built his house there among his 1,000 acres of land. In 1823, the Indian Springs Hotel was opened and the area became an early day resort.[14]

Crowell told the commissioners there would be no interference on his part.

Almost 400 chiefs and head men were assembled and the commissioners advised them that they had prepared a large council room for the meetings. The Tuckabatchees said they were not ready and, moreover, would not meet in the room, rather they would meet with the commissioners in their own camp. Irrespective of the Tuckabatchee defiance, a meeting was held immediately and the propositions made at Broken Arrow were repeated. The Creeks were offered an exchange for the whole country with a cash settlement of $500,000 in payment for loss of improvements and the expense of removal.[15]

Opothleyaholo delivered Big Warrior's reply and his own opinions the following day:

> We met you at Broken Arrow, and then told you we had no land to sell; I then heard of no claims against the nation, nor have I since. We have met you here at a very short notice, and do not think that the chiefs who are here have any authority to treat. General McIntosh knows that we are bound by our laws, and that what is not done in the public square, in general council, is not binding on the nation. I am, therefore, under the necessity of repeating the same answer as given at Broken Arrow, that we have no land to sell. I know that there are but few from the upper towns here, and many are absent from the lower towns.
>
> General McIntosh knows that no part of the land can be sold without a full council, and without the consent of all the nation, and, if a part of the nation choose to leave the country, they cannot sell the land they have, but it belongs to the nation. From what you told us yesterday, I am induced to believe that it may be best for us to remove, but we must have time to think of it; and, should the chiefs who are here sell the land now, it might create dissensions and ill blood among the Indians. I have received a message from my chief, the Big Warrior, directing me to listen to what the commissioners have to say; to meet them friendly, and part in the same way, but not to sell the land. I am also instructed to invite you to meet us at Broken Arrow three months hence, when a treaty may possibly be made, and to return home. This is the only talk I have for you, and I shall return home immediately. I gave you but one talk at Broken Arrow and I shall give you but one here; such is the message I have received from the head chief, and I am bound to obey; tomorrow I shall leave here. I have now said all I have to say; I will listen to any thing further you have to say, but shall give no further answer.[16]

That night it was discovered that some of the Cussettas and Soowagaloos had departed for home. The commissioners were appalled and initiated an inquiry as to the cause of the precipitate departure. Opothleyaholo was implicated as the one who had come to the camps, telling them "to go and break up the treaty for the present and they would meet again, a few months hence, at Broken Arrow."[17]

Campbell told Opothleyaholo that if his party left the council, he, Campbell, would complete the treaty without the Tuckabatchees. Surely Opothleyaholo must have considered the commissioners daft, as he had explained in his address to the council that "what is not done in the public square, in general council, is not binding on the nation."[18] Broken Arrow was the national council square, not Indian springs.

Campbell and Merriwether concluded the treaty without the absent Lower Creeks, but McIntosh was reminded by Opothleyaholo that he was breaking a Creek law. "I have told you your fate if you sign that paper. I once more say, beware."[19]

Crowell advised the commissioners that the signatures to the treaty, "with the exception of McIntosh and perhaps two others," were either by low grade chiefs or not chiefs at all. "These signers are from eight towns only, when there are fifty-six in the nation."[20]

The preamble of this 1825 treaty states: "And whereas the chief of the Creek Towns have assented to the reasonableness of said proposition and expressed a willingness to emigrate beyond the Mississippi, those of Tokaubatchee excepted."[21] There was no doubt that the Tuckabatchees were in disagreement on this treaty.

As to why McIntosh was persuaded to sign a treaty that ceded southwestern Georgia and several million acres in Alabama for the same amount of acreage west of the Mississippi, cushioned by $400,000, was the belief he had been bribed by the federal government. He was to receive $25,000 for his acreage and improvements and the 640-acre McIntosh Reserve now located in Carroll County, Georgia. Another $15,000 was to be paid for his signature alone. Agent Crowell, in his defense filed with the Indian Office Manuscript Records, affirmed that McIntosh, angered at being removed as speaker of the nation, had sold his country out of revenge. Too late, McIntosh realized the offense he had committed against his people.[22]

Fraud had been committed by the U.S. commissioners and the Georgians. James Merriwether took the stage at Wilkes bearing the treaty to Washington. Campbell informed Troup they were in time for its "ratification by the present Senate."[23]

Soon, the differences of opinions in the Creek Nation and the troubles the Lower Creeks had mentioned in their memorial would emerge into bitter hatred in the nation.

The Big Warrior was dead. Campbell and Merriwether, learning the news at the conclusion of the treaty, knew that with his passing, "all opposition will now cease." They were satisfied that the "dissenting party" would treat and "re-unite with the emigrating party."[24]

As Americans, the commissioners were not educated in the Native People's culture, traditions and most of all, their laws. When Big Warrior had invited them to Broken Arrow, the national council square, they did not consider postponing treaty negotiations once again to even confer with the Upper Creek chief. Surely, this apathy toward the Big Warrior must have been received as an affront to his power in the nation. Campbell and Merriwether had not heeded Crowell's advice that fraud had been committed, and what that portended for the future of the nation. The commissioners were legally guilty of promoting dissension in the Creek Nation.

The treaty, concluded during President Monroe's administration, became a thorny gift to President John Quincy Adams. He had had no alternative but to ratify it after the Senate sanctioned its validity. William F. Hay, secretary for the commissioners, believed the treaty should never have been made. "But nothing could have arrested the progress of this iniquity after the selection of two Georgians as commissioners for negotiating the treaty." And he believed they had negotiated it "in face of their instructions."[25]

President Monroe had to have been cognizant that Campbell and Merriwether had erred in the completion of the treaty. Yet on February 28, he sent the treaty to the Senate. That august body did not examine it for any violation of the Creek Nation's rights; all they considered was the fact Georgia had gained the last of the Creek lands within its boundaries and removal of the Indians was sealed. Now everyone could breathe easier as Gov. Troup would no longer be pressuring the government to fulfill its obligations to Georgia. Troup would cease all talk about states rights.

Yet, McIntosh and his party were not so confident that all would be peaceful in their country. Why else would he, his son, Chilly McIntosh, Etome Tustunuggee and others travel to Milledgeville to meet with Troup?

These Lower Creeks dined with the governor on February 16 and the next day at Troup's office delivered a written message. Its theme was protection from the hostile party. They believed that as they had been warriors under McIntosh and had fought for the United States that they would be protected by "our father the President." Should the hostiles try to create "a disturbance with the friendly Indians" they would inform the president they needed protection.[26] A postscript read: "We wish to know from you in writing, whether you could protect us, should protection be necessary."[27]

Troup recorded the meeting held with the Creeks in the Executive Journal of Georgia. They had informed the governor that Agent Crowell was one of "their worst enemies." No protection from Crowell would be forthcoming. Could they "be certain" of the U.S. government's protection and that of Georgia's?[28]

True politician that he was, Troup replied in a positive way, congratulating them on their compliance with their great father's wishes. In exchange for signing the treaty they would receive better lands across the Mississippi and those lands "would belong to themselves and their children forever." There would be difficulties in removing them, the president knew. However, the treaty provided them with "ample provision" which in turn would enable them "to remove their women and children in comfort" and to cover any removal losses that might be occurred.[29]

As to protection prior to removal, Troup "had no doubt" their father, the president, would see that they had it. As to Georgia, the friendly Creeks should, "so far as depended on him, find protection at all times." As they "had fought and bled for Georgia in the last war," the Georgians would not forget them.[30]

McIntosh spoke of the Big Warrior "as having been inimical in his heart to the United States" during the Creek War. Fear had caused him to join the friendly party. McIntosh felt that he and his people had been right to dispose of the land without the consent of the hostile party.[31]

Troup cautioned his cousin, however, that the president and the Senate would "decide who had the right." They, and the Georgians, would remember that it was McIntosh and his warriors who had fought on their side during the late war.[32]

Etome Tustunuggee gave Troup a paper for him to keep. The chief admitted that at first he had been disinclined to sell the land. He had been deceived by white men, but afterwards "he had listened to the voice of his great father." Then, hearing Troup's words, "now he approved."[33]

Before leaving Milledgeville, the Creeks sent a message to Troup. They were satisfied that Georgia would protect them from their enemies. They were satisfied that Troup, at the first indication of trouble, would dispatch runners to the hostile party, and that he, as commander-in-chief of Georgia, would protect the friendly Indians.[34]

This delegation referred to the meeting in 1824 at Polecat Springs. They did not accept the law passed that if land was sold, "guns and ropes should be their end." They did not recognize it as a national law because it was not read before the national chiefs. The delegation assured Troup that their disposition was friendly and they would "treat all mankind as friends, brothers and relations. They would never impose on any man."[35]

Troup decided to issue a statement to the Tuckabatchee and Cussettas chiefs. He wrote to Col. Henry G. Lamar, his aide-de-camp on February 26, 1825, and enclosed the message. He instructed Lamar as to his duty, which was to impress the chiefs that other tribes were being moved beyond the Mississippi as evidenced in the enclosed president's documents and newspapers. Lamar was to tell them "that soon, very soon, they will all go; so that a red man will not be seen between the Mississippi and the lakes."[36]

Troup's message to the chiefs was a chastisement and warning. "I hear bad things of you," he began. After citing McIntosh and his signing of the treaty, Troup warned: "Now I tell you, take care and walk straight. McIntosh and his people are under my protection, as well as under the protection of the United States." The governor might very well speak for his state, but where did he obtain the authority to speak for the United States? "Do not let bad men persuade you that because you live in and near to Alabama you will be safe. If you commit one act of hostility on this side of the line, I will follow and punish you."[37]

Lamar reported that he had reached Tuckabatchee on March 4, 1825, and appeared immediately before the council. Lamar thought that Ho-po-eithlea Yoholough (Opothleyaholo) had succeeded Big Warrior and was acting as interim leader until a new chief could be appointed.

Lamar proceeded with the same rhetoric about McIntosh, the treaty and the president's wishes. The Tuckabatchees were attentive, politely waiting for him to finish his speech. At the conclusion, Opothleyaholo then spoke through an interpreter.[38]

The Speaker was glad of the opportunity to "contradict the reports which had reached Georgia." He loved "his white brother," their peace, and also McIntosh. On hearing that he (Opothleyaholo) wished to spill blood, "he was sick at heart and his blood was chilled." It was during this reply that Opothleyaholo stated how in the late war he had "fought with McIntosh and his white brothers to subdue the hostiles, and succeeded." In Opothleyaholo's words, he refuted all of the later historians' beliefs that he was a Red Stick. Clearly, he had not been.

Opothleyaholo disputed all rumors that he intended to kill McIntosh. "No one murmur had by him been placed on the winds, to be carried to Georgia, against his white or red brothers." When Hawkins was their agent, he had been instructed "to throw away his gun, quit the chase, and cultivate the land." It had been good advice. "His gun was now rusty, he could not see to shoot; instead of his gun, he used the plough and the hoe."

Lamar continued on to Cussetta, accompanied by Charles Cornell. Here he met with Little Prince and the Council on February 7, 1825. Lamar's speech reiterated the one given at Tuckabatchee, with additional warnings should McIntosh and his chiefs be harmed. Such an attempt would divide the nation. "Take a number of reeds, bind them close, you cannot break them." But should the bundle be divided, "the weakest of you can break them in pieces." The white men who surrounded them would become "your common enemies. They outnumber the trees in your forest." Lamar hoped they would listen to the governor and the president and go to the country west of the Mississippi. There the land would belong to them. "No nation, not even your father, could take it from you."

Little Prince denied there were "contemplated hostilities" against the treaty party. Furthermore, stories that had circulated about trouble had been judged by "the headmen" as not "worthy of notice."[39] Still, on March 4, the diminutive, principal chief wrote to the McIntoshes that he was "sorry" about "the fuss amongst my people." Little Prince assured them that "I love you as a son, and wish you home to your family." This message would be used against the aged chief as an instrument in stripping him of his authority over the Lower Creeks.[40]

Lamar's consensus was to leave the Creeks to themselves. They believed the president's power to be absolute, and if they understood his wishes, they would conform. Yet, the Creeks were fearful that "should they move beyond the Mississippi," their consequence would be "a perpetual warfare with the tribes" who lived there.[41]

Had the Creeks, with years and years of dealing with the white man, adopted his habit of using a forked tongue? Did Opothleyaholo and Little Prince decide to tell Troup what they knew he wanted to hear? And was it a ploy to reduce apprehension on the McIntoshes' part, and lull the Lower Creeks into a false sense of security? Or did the chief and speaker truly believe the treaty would never be ratified?

Chapter 7

Execution of
Chief McIntosh

On his way home from Milledgeville, Chilly McIntosh had met his friends, William Miller and A. Tustunuggee, at the Flint River. They told Chilly that hostiles had threatened to "cut their throats and set up their heads by the road for a show." The hostiles were determined to die, if necessary, and men had been appointed to kill McIntosh, Chilly, Joseph Marshall, Samuel Hawkins, James Island, Etome Tustunuggee and Col. Miller. Chilly, conveying this news by letter to Troup, was at Newnan and intended to remain there. As he had parted with his father at Indian Springs, he sent a runner to warn him and asked his father to come to Newnan.[1]

Troup, in response, was sorry to hear "the hostiles continue to be such fools and madmen." He believed Lamar should be in council with the hostiles by this time, March 5. Troup assured Chilly that if those Indians did not listen to Lamar, he intended to send the military "to the line, to keep them in order and punish offenders."[2]

When Troup received Lamar's report of Opothleyaholo and Little Prince's affability in regard to the state of their nation, the man apparently believed he had settled the dissension. And after the ratification of the treaty, he lost no time in contacting McIntosh for his consent to survey and run boundary lines in the ceded country.[3]

McIntosh assented, but stipulated only if it met with the approval of the United States and the hostile party.[4] Troup did not understand why McIntosh would bring the others into the picture. "We have nothing to do with the United States, or the agent, or the hostiles in this matter." He wanted only the treaty signer's consent. "If we wanted the consent of the United States, we could ask it." McIntosh informed his cousin he did not wish "to act contrary to stipulations" between the Creek Nation and the United States. McIntosh had to

43

have had great faith in Troup as he freely gave to the state of Georgia the right to survey.[5]

Troup was aware that surveying could not be done until all of the emigrating party had been removed. Article eight set the final date as September 1826. He was acting in defiance of the federal government, and, more importantly, he was capitalizing on McIntosh's feelings of self-worth. The megalomaniac Troup focused on Georgia and its right, the Creek Nation had lost theirs in the treaty. After all the years of failed attempts by his predecessors to finalize the 1802 compact, he, Troup, had been the one who was successful. Such feelings of his power against the United States and the Upper Creeks had blurred his reasoning. Troup disregarded any abiding danger to McIntosh.

Little Prince had notified McIntosh that a council of the nation would be held, April 19 at Broken Arrow. All Lower Creek chiefs were invited to attend. McIntosh would not be present due to ill health, but the other chiefs would. He did, however, expect to accompany the delegation to the west to explore the land as soon as treaty money was received for that expense.[6]

Troup wasted no time in asking for an advance from Merriwether and Campbell to be used to send a small party of Lower Creeks to explore the country west of the Mississippi. Two thousand dollars would be needed and Troup assured the commissioners that "I can advance the amount" should they not be "in funds," provided that it would be reimbursed by the government. Campbell advised the governor to advance Georgia money to McIntosh and they would be reimbursed. April 9, Troup notified McIntosh that the money was ready for his authorized agent to receive it. In all of the correspondence between the cousins, it is evident that Troup was the instigator. First, the survey and then the rush to send McIntosh on the exploration.[7]

It appeared that for the present there was an uneasy truce in the Creek Nation. Then, without warning, what had been feared for many months happened. It was in the morning hours of May 1, 1825, that McIntosh's home was surrounded by, in some estimates, 400 hostile Indians. Neighbors on the Chattahoochee heard the war whoop at daybreak and saw the flames. The chief's home had been set afire.[8]

Little Prince and Opothleyaholo had ordered the execution of McIntosh and the treaty signers. Menawa, the aged Red Stick, was appointed executioner.[9] Etome Tustunuggee, Chilly and Motey Kennard had stayed the night at the chief's home as they expected to depart with McIntosh for the west the next morning.[10]

Before torching the house, Menawa allowed the women and children and all whites to leave. Chilly and Motey Kennard escaped through a window during the bedlam. McIntosh and Etome Tustunuggee were shot as they came out. McIntosh's wife reported that nearly 100 balls had entered their bodies.[11]

Francis Flournoy, the U.S. Commissioner who resigned in 1821, had stayed the night at the chief's home. In his deposition dated May 16, Flournoy stated he pulled Etome Tustunuggee's body from the burning house. Other witnesses state that McIntosh and Etome had been shot as they escaped. Crowell and Walker were implicated in advising Little Prince and Opothleyaholo that in order "to get their land back, and keep it, was to kill all that had any hand in selling it." Flournoy deposed that even "the property of the white men," his included, was destroyed. This assertion does not correspond with an earlier message to Troup on May 6, in which Brig. Gen. Charles J. McDonald stated that both parties, friendly and hostile, were determined to execute Crowell. If McDonald is to be believed, relying on a Mr. Freeman's information, Crowell had communicated to the Indians the treaty's ratification and proposed they sell "that portion of the territory which had been reserved" and go beyond the Mississippi. The Indians never replied to his suggestion, but did ask "if he had signed the treaty." He answered that his signature was as a "witness."

McDonald believed Crowell needed help and "a small additional force could do no injury." Troup advised McDonald not to hesitate in securing the frontier and protecting the agent. "I hope that no harm has befallen him." The solicitous Troup would soon change his mind about Crowell when he learned the purported facts about McIntosh's death.[12]

Simultaneously, when the assault was made on McIntosh, other hostiles surrounded Samuel Hawkins's home, capturing him. He was bound with ropes and lay on the ground until Menawa arrived. At 3 P.M. the same day, Hawkins was shot like his father-in-law McIntosh. All of the bodies were left uncovered by the enemy, "exposed to the fowls of the air and beasts of the forest."[13]

The Chattahoochee was flooding and the hostiles were unable to reach Col. Miller, Hogey McIntosh, William's brother, and the Derrisaws.

Plundering occurred. Cattle and hogs were eaten; Negroes were captured along with other property.

Peggy McIntosh, William's Cherokee wife, and small children, Jane (McIntosh) Hawkins, Samuel's widow, and children escaped to Line Creek in Fayette County. Peggy sent a letter to Campbell and Merriwether revealing her husband's assassination. She blamed Crowell for encouraging Little Prince and Opothleyaholo to commit the heinous acts. She informed that at the recent Broken Arrow council the hostiles "had decreed that they would murder all the chiefs who had any hand in selling the land, and burn and destroy and take away all they had, and then send on to the president that he should not have the land."[14]

Jane McIntosh also wrote to the commissioners, describing the murders. Both women reminded the men that the assassins were the same ones who had opposed the United States in the Creek War.[15]

On May 2, Chilly and other chiefs had reached Milledgeville where they met with Troup. The governor lost no time in notifying President Adams. Troup blamed the federal government for not heeding the warning of possible trouble in the nation. He saw the Indian Springs Treaty as a measure that had "reconciled the State to the Federal Government." This tragedy "might have been averted" had the United States acted. Troup declared he had maintained peace in the country "despite ... every thing attempted to the contrary." He had dispatched messages "to the surviving chiefs to forbear hostility."[16] He told them, "My revenge I will have." A revenge he avowed "the Great Spirit would require, such as our Christ would not think too much."[17]

On May 5, Troup ordered Maj. Generals Wimberly, Shorter and Miller of the 5th, 6th, and 7th divisions to hold "in readiness their respective divisions to march at a moment's warning, either by detachments or otherwise," subject to Georgia's, or the commander-in-chief's authority. He notified Brig. Gen. Alexander Ware, at Fayetteville, that should "these infuriated monsters" invade the settled limits of Georgia, Ware might "have the opportunity to give them the bayonet freely." The bayonet was an "instrument they most dread ... most appropriate for the occasion." Ware was to provision the Lower Creek refugees using state funds that would be reimbursed from their annuities payable by the United States.[18]

Chilly and Roley, half-brother of William, traveled to Washington City, carrying Troup's letter and to alert the government of the murders. On May 15, they met with President Adams, who was appalled to hear the news. Adams advised the Creeks to visit with Secretary of War James Barbour the next day.[19]

The Lower Creeks charged Crowell with refusing to give rations to the McIntosh party at Broken Arrow and insisted that the agent had instigated the murders.[20]

Barbour, who thought Troup was a madman, sent a messenger to him, informing the governor that the United States had never interfered in any internal feuds among an Indian tribe. The courier would convey to the Upper Creeks a message to desist from violence, to return home, and they would be allowed to send a deputation to Washington in the winter.[21]

Adams approved of the messages, but thought they would be "insufficient." He viewed the recent massacre as a "signal for a ferocious Indian war, bursting upon us like a thunderbolt." He wanted Barbour to find out what military force could immediately be moved to Georgia's "menaced border."[22]

Little Prince had insisted that the execution of McIntosh conformed to a Creek law and they did not intend any hostility toward the white man. Chilly presented written charges against Crowell and claims for protection and indemnity. He cited Article Eight of the Indian Springs Treaty in which the McIntosh party, should they not remove immediately from their nation, were promised protection. In his mind the killing of his father was a violation of that treaty. Adams found the protection as "very insidiously introduced." Obviously, the Senate had not considered the import of the promise.[23]

The military believed that an Indian war with Georgia would be profitable for that state and Troup was seen as an extremely violent man. Gen. Edmund P. Gaines, of the Eastern Department of the U.S. Army, had been ordered to the Georgia frontier to ensure its safety. Should the outrages continue, Gaines would act accordingly.[24]

Adams, studying the charges against Crowell, named Maj. Timothy P. Andrews as U.S. special agent in the Creek Nation, but was hesitant to suspend Crowell, relying on Chilly's information alone. Andrews had the power to suspend him, but the evidence would have to be irrefutable; Adams was concerned any suspension of the agent might cause further unrest in the nation.[25]

The Investigation of General Gaines

The unrest in Georgia and the Creek Nation was not confined exclusively to that area. The press reported the assassination of McIntosh, and newspapers in the South wanted the government to withhold the Creek monies and force them beyond the Mississippi. The clamoring of the editors reached the North and eventually Europe. The European newspapers saw the affairs in Georgia to be the best evidence that the United States form of government could not last.[1] Ultimately, in the fall, there were rumblings in the North for President Adams's impeachment.[2]

Undoubtedly, the Press had turned McIntosh's death into a national issue, and finally, it would result in the first states rights confrontation in this country. History, either by design, or ineptitude, has failed to educate the student of how close this country came to a civil war in the summer of 1825, a civil war not started because of tariffs or slavery, but because of the Creek Nation and its need for justice.

President Adams was one of the more just executives in dealing with the Indians. He had wanted the Creeks to accept the Indian Springs Treaty, yet, he desisted from forcing them to do so.

General Gaines was a veteran of many Indian wars. He was experienced in dealing with the Indians, and felt strongly that they were being exploited by the white men. Although he, more than most of the military, understood the Native People, still, he had a duty to his country. He intended that the Creeks must understand the government's rights. He went to the Georgia frontier to sort out the problems and bring the calamitous affair to an end. However, before too much time had elapsed, he and Maj. Andrews became embroiled in an inflammatory clash of dispositions with Gov. Troup.

From the beginning, Troup was determined that he and Georgia would be successful in their demands. He notified Gaines that Georgia laws "extended over the ceded country." As governor he was bound "to execute them there." He had sent Capt. James Harrison, commander of the Twiggs County Cavalry, to the frontier to assess any depredations on the Georgia citizens by the hostile Indians.[3]

Gaines had requested that one cavalry and one infantry regiment of Georgia militia or volunteers should be held ready to assemble "at a moment's warning."[4]

Troup advised Gaines that he was apprising Alabama's governor with regard to running the boundary line between the two states. Should Alabama demur, Troup intended to survey the lands within Georgia's limits.[5]

Gaines saw the survey as a collision between "the views of your excellency" and the instructions given him by the Department of War. The general would have no alternative but to tell the Indians that the president had advised Troup to abstain from surveying the ceded land until their removal.[6] Troup vowed "the line shall be run and the survey executed."[7]

C. Vandeventer, chief clerk of the War Department, warned Troup that if Georgia persisted in the surveying, "the United States will not in any manner be responsible for any consequences which may result from that measure."[8] The governor arrogantly informed the clerk "to state to the President that the survey will be made, and in due time."[9] President Adams had not wanted to debate the issue with Troup and delayed an answer until after Gaines had counseled with the Creeks.

Troup had demanded of Andrews the suspension of Crowell. The special agent, averse to such an action, but, ostensibly wanting to pacify the hot-tempered Troup, suspended the agent as a courteous gesture to the Georgia authorities.[10] This letter was published in *The Patriot*. Andrews's obvious doubts about Crowell's guilt prompted Troup to warn Andrews to "consider all intercourse" between him and the Georgia government to be "suspended."[11]

The council was to be held on June 25 at Broken Arrow.[12] Troup sent Colonels Seaborn Jones, Warren Jourdan, William W. Williamson and William H. Torrance as Georgia commissioners. They were accompanied by Captains J.S. Thomas and William Bowens, marshals, and M.J. Kenan, clerk. They were charged to gather all evidence against Agent Crowell, and to participate freely in the council.[13] That was Troup's intention, but Gaines and Andrews felt differently and so did the Creeks. To prevent further upsets, Gaines allowed the state commissioners to attend as observers only.

The commissioners complained to Troup that all of their endeavors had been forestalled. They had tried to work with Gaines and Andrews, but their applications to Gaines had been deemed in conflict "with our instructions, it is therefore inadmissible." They were pleased to report that in regard to the treaty's abrogation, Gaines, in council, had stated that "such an occurrence was unknown in the history of diplomacy." He had urged reconciliation to the treaty and the federal government's policy.[14]

The Georgians persisted in their mission, however, and notified Gaines that they would take testimony from Little Prince, Opoithle Yoholo (*sic*) and others. They objected to William Hambly as interpreter; Crowell must select another. They would use Benjamin Hawkins. And the public square would not be used for the examination, rather they intended to avail themselves of Gaines's quarters, with his permission, of course.[15]

Andrews, replying for Gaines, stated that Williamson had been present when the Creeks refused conversations or examinations with the commissioners unless held in public, in the open square or in council. "All questions put to the Indians must be in writing." Gaines and Andrews wanted nothing to be "misapprehended." They had been bound to pursue this course, thought to be fair to the Indians.[16]

During council, Gaines conveyed the commissioners request. Opothleyaholo, as speaker of the Creek Nation, answered that "he would transact no business in private with the Georgia commissioners." Also, the Georgians plans "of taking them out of their square, had caused all their troubles," necessitating their coming here. "Private meetings, where persons do not adhere to the truth, make difficulties, and have brought General Gaines here." Opothleyaholo thought "their business was with General Gaines"; their present difficulties was due to the Georgians. "Georgia intrigues had brought them from their crops, which were necessary to feed their little children." The Speaker saw "the Muscogee nation and Georgia … like two children that quarrel, and if one is stronger than the other, he tells lies on him, puts him in the wrong, and then gets whipped for it." In conclusion Opothleyaholo remarked, "he supposed the Master of breath had decreed the Muscogee nation should be reduced and imposed upon, that the time has now arrived, and he presumed it must happen."[17]

The commissioners, smarting from Opothleyaholo's rejection of their proposal, rebutted that they had come to the conclusion that Opothleyaholo's remarks were "not the language of an untutored savage." Rather they viewed it as the work of the "wily and perfidious" Hambly. Furthermore, the man "whose vices and whose crimes are proverbial" was "the trustworthy and confidential interpreter" of the federal government. Hambly had been licensed "to abuse indiscriminantly the Government of Georgia, its public functionaries, and it's citizens." Hambly was so corrupt and unprincipled that he "disgraces and dishonors even Indian society."[18]

Finally, after all the asperity, Gaines and Andrews concluded the negotiations with the Creeks. In a letter to Troup, July 10, Gaines detailed his findings in regard to the Indian Springs Treaty.[19]

Prior to the Broken Arrow council, he had met with the McIntosh party who "demanded retaliation" for the recent deaths of their chiefs. The hostiles were to restore all property taken and destroyed. They based this claim on Article Eight of the treaty.

The alleged hostile party consisted "of nearly forty-nine fiftieths of the whole of the chiefs, headmen and warriors of the nation." Gaines had recognized many of them as having served in the late war; he knew they had been friendly to the United States "as any of our Indian neighbors could have been known to be." He found "the supposed hostile party" represented the Creek Nation. These Creeks assured Gaines they would be peaceable and friendly to the McIntosh party and the United States. They objected to the late treaty. It was a fraud that countered a Creek law and the nation's will. They refused all treaty money.

Gaines met with the McIntosh party again at Joseph Marshall's ferry. The chiefs agreed to the proposition put forth by the hostile party. The chiefs of both parties assured Gaines they would "remain at peace with each other" and the United States citizens. Thus, the general was happy to report that Troup would not have to use the state's militia or volunteers.

While at the ferry, Gaines obtained a certificate signed by Marshall, a Creek half-blood, and William Edwards in which they attested that McIntosh had not granted Troup's request about the survey. The two men had accompanied the governor's express to McIntosh who had said he would confer with the chiefs before giving his answer. Gaines enclosed a copy of the certificate in his report to Troup, commenting that "your excellency" would now unhesitatingly abandon the survey. Such action would be a relief to Gaines as it would be painful to oppose "the venerated authorities of an enlightened and patriotic member of the United States" for whom he had pledged "under solemnity of oath, to serve them honestly and faithfully."[20]

Angered, Troup called the procurement of the certificate a "malignant villainy." He had in his possession three assents given by McIntosh in his own writing. Marshall had lied; he had verified to Troup that all the friendly chiefs had agreed to the survey. The same chiefs declared their assents to Troup. The Georgia commissioners asserted that in the council, the governor's oath passed "for nothing." "Any vagabond of the Indian country" could now "discredit him." The people of Georgia, however, would uphold his oath. They had "never refused credence to the word of their Chief Magistrate." Troup did not believe they would now, "unworthy as he may be." Frankly, he did not "like the complexion of things" as told to him by the commissioners and he hoped Gaines would never regret his part in them.[21]

Gaines answered at length, denying there was any skulduggery in obtaining the certificate; it had been voluntary. The one thing he had regretted was "to differ with you in opinion" which had brought the general "acrimonious censure" by the governor.[22]

Troup, after a long delay, received an answer from the president about the survey. Adams had been disappointed that the Creeks had not accepted the late treaty. However, disregarding the impeachment of the treaty, Adams cited the eighth article whereby the United States "had solemnly pledged to protect the Creek Indians from any encroachment till their removal in September, 1826." Therefore, surveying "would be an infraction of the treaty" and it would not be permitted.[23]

Barbour notified Gaines of the president's regret that a reconciliation to the treaty had not been obtained. As the majority of the Creeks had opposed it, Adams had determined the allegations should be investigated "and their effect decided by the proper authority." As to Troup's plan to survey, in defiance of the federal government, "a collision by overt acts between the Executive of the Union and that of a State, is so against the theory of the constitution." It would be repugnant to the president and "only under a solemn sense of duty" would he determine "to do an act by which so serious a result would be produced." Should Troup persevere, Gaines was authorized to use the military to prevent surveyors entering the land and should they be found in the country, he was to arrest them, "turn them over to the judicial authority" to be dealt with by the law.[24]

Troup backed down, reasoning that with the president referring the treaty to Congress, it put a stop to the survey for the present. "The Executive of Georgia has no authority in the civil war with which the State is menaced to strike the first blow, nor has it the inclination to provoke it."[25]

In several letters to the president, Troup maligned Hambly, Opothleyaholo and Gaines. Hambly was "a base and unworthy fellow ... a confidential friend of the agent." Yoholo (*sic*) had lied when he had detailed "the circumstances connected with the late negotiations at Indian Springs." Williamson, the commissioner, who had attended at Indian Springs told Gaines that "he knew of his own knowledge, the statements of Yoholo [*sic*] to be false." Gaines had answered "that he would not believe the congregated world if it were to say so."[26]

Letters, purported to be from Gaines to Troup, had been printed in local papers. They were insolent and deserved the president's "reprobation of his conduct." "I demand, therefore, as Chief Magistrate of Georgia, his immediate recall, and his arrest, trial and punishment, under the rules and articles of war."[27] The President dissented from Troup's demand for Gaines arrest. Gaines received Adams's regrets that the letters had been published, and asked that he abstain in the future.[28]

Andrews had found Crowell innocent of the "charges preferred" against him by Troup and believed the Creek agent to have been "a much injured man."[29]

On September 19 Andrews publicly answered the Georgia commissioners who had had three reports published in the *National Intelligencer*. One by one, the special agent attacked the veracity of the commissioners. Jones was known as a "certificate man," one "who in the absence of other testimony" obligingly would give "his certificate, or make a report, whenever the interests of the political party to which he is attached are in jeopardy."

Williamson, brother-in-law of Commissioner Campbell, "stands convicted ... in attempting to bribe various persons to betray their duty and honor." Andrews had sent all evidence against him to the War Department. The evidence showed Williamson had "offered a bribe" of $8,000 to the U.S. interpreter. As he would be in charge of the disbursement of the Creek removal funds, he would see that Hambly received some of the profits if he would support Campbell and Merriwether in getting the treaty signed. Hambly had refused, and Williamson campaigned to destroy his character. This commissioner had been paid $1,000 for his services and had received $25,000 to $30,000 of United States funds which had been placed in the hands of Campbell and Merriwether for use in the Indian Springs Treaty. Since February, Williamson had used the money to speculate "in negroes, as a common negro trader."

Torrance had been convicted "of a disgraceful slander" and fined considerably as a punishment.

Jourdan had been publicly accused "of having screened a notorious smuggler." During the late war, Sancho Panza "had smuggled a large quantity of blankets into Georgia from Amelia Island."

Bowen and Thomas, the two marshals, had been deputies of the former Creek agent, Gen. D.B. Mitchell. Mitchell had been dismissed from office when it was learned that he had smuggled between one and two hundred African Negroes into the Indian nation from Amelia Island. Bowen and Thomas had obtained and carried the negroes into the nation. They were compelled to leave the Creek country. Thomas had done everything possible to "counteract the measures of General Gaines in the Creek Nation." Andrews, acting upon the evidence, charged it was Bowen who had written "the correspondence signed in the name of General McIntosh to the Governor of Georgia," agreeing to the survey and leading to McIntosh's death.

Kenan, the commissioners' secretary, was "a young gentleman of capacity and merit."

Alluding to private acts by the Georgia commissioners, Andrews described the introduction of whiskey ("through the woods, and at night") into a back building in Princeton. Liquor was "always prohibited in the neighborhood of an Indian council in session." Bowen had jeered the Indians about Gaines refusing them liquor. "If they would go to the lodgings of the commissioners, they should have as much as they wanted." The nation presumed, according to Andrews, "that the whiskey was introduced to produce confusion among the Indians through the agency of Captain Bowen."

The commissioners had brought close to $6,000 to Indian Springs. Andrews explained that their personal expenses could not have amounted to more than $20 to $30 apiece in the nation. Possibly they had intended for Williamson to use the money for bribes. Andrews left the explanation of "so much money" up to the commissioners.

"The charges and insinuations against General Gaines ... and those against the missionaries will be known to be untrue," Andrews wrote. "And, from that cause, if from no other, I found a strong hope that those against myself will be generally discredited." The four commissioners, Andrews declared, had tried to circumvent him "at every step" in his faithful discharge of duty.

Andrews concluded by quoting Troup, who in his message to the Legislature in November, had said: "The Government of Georgia, in the employment of agents to superintend its various interests, has been peculiarly unfortunate."[30]

Chapter 9

Opothleyaholo Meets President Adams

Jefferson, and the lawmakers of his era, had heard of the many dangers encountered by settlers who had chosen to go west and take up residence in isolated locations. Away from the government's protection, and being far from each other, they were fair game for the French–Canadian coureour du bois and the Mexican plunderers. The Indians, the politicians conceived, should they be removed west of the Mississippi and established on their own lands, might effectually protect the white men from the vicious foreigners. The venerated lawmakers' audacity in considering such a plan exemplifies their willingness to sacrifice the Native People to save the Americans. What they had not considered was the fact that the Indians never feared the French–Canadians as many of the trappers married Indian women. As to being a defense for the white man in any conflict with the foreigners, the scheme was totally inane. It was the Indian who needed to be protected from the white man. In addition to this scheme, the politicians knew they would have to treat with the many Indians who lived in the area of the Louisiana Purchase before moving any tribes to the north and west of the Mississippi.[1]

The government considered most of these tribes "hostiles"; the Cheyenne, Kiowa, Comanche, Arapaho, Pawnee, Sioux, Osage and Kansa. Fortunately, they would, at this time, only have the Osage and Kansa to treat with in land cessions related to the southern tribes.

The Osage, Great and Little bands, and the Kansa were of Siouan stock which had dominated later Missouri, Arkansas and Oklahoma since the 17th Century. The Kansa, or Kanza, later Kaw, had at one time been Osage, but legend states they became embroiled in an argument over buffalo meat which brought about the split in the tribe.[2]

The first treaty with the Osage was in 1808, but it was not ratified until

1810. In each treaty leading up to the one in June 1825, the Osage had lost more and more of their land. The Treaty of 1818 definitely was a fine and punishment, culminating when U.S. citizens and Cherokees in the Missouri Territory claimed the Osage had stolen property and never returned it. William Clark, of Lewis and Clark fame, was governor of the Missouri Territory and Superintendent of Indian affairs. He acted as commissioner on behalf of the United States in conducting this treaty.

In Article I, the Osages, who were never paid but a paltry sum for their cessions, in comparison to the annuities of the southern tribes, were unable to pay for the stolen property out of their funds as that would leave them destitute. Instead, the government chose to show its magnanimity. They would not charge the Osage annuities, rather they would take more land as payment.[3]

Missouri was admitted to the Union in 1821. Depredations by the Osages had been claimed by the Missourians who were not content to have any Osages living in the state. Finally in June 1825, the same month as the Creek agreement of pardon toward the McIntosh faction, the Osage, once again, were penalized and ceded all their lands within the state of Missouri and in the Arkansas Territory, which included what would later be termed Indian Territory. Now the U.S. had somewhere to send the southern tribes. But they were not through with the Osage.[4]

For many years, traders from Missouri had been using the Great Osage Trail which crossed from east to west in the northern part of future Indian Territory, to travel to Santa Fe in Spanish territory. Then, in 1822, William Becknell decided to strike out across Indian country (later Kansas) from Fort Osage, Missouri to Santa Fe. As a result of his suggestion that a road might be made from Fort Osage to Santa Fe, commissioners met with the Great and Little Osage at a large grove on the Neosho River, 160 miles west of Fort Osage in August 1825. U.S. Commissioner, George C. Sibley, named the place Council Grove which would become known as "the last stopping off place" on the Santa Fe Trail. Here, people would purchase supplies and mail letters to anxious friends and families.

A great oak tree was marked at the edge of the timber for the council meeting. William Sherley "Old Bill" Williams, mountain man, whose half-blood Osage children had been allotted tracts in the June treaty, was the Osage interpreter.

For the sum of $800 in cash and merchandise, the Osage granted all privileges to the United States for "a road to be marked out from the western frontier of Missouri to the confines of New Mexico." The Kansa, likewise, would grant the same privileges and the Santa Fe Trail thus became an important thoroughfare for trade and travel.[5]

In November 1825, Opothleyaholo along with Menawa and others traveled to Washington to have the Indian Springs Treaty annulled, and to make a new one. Two young Cherokees, Joseph Vann and John Ridge, accompanied them. They had been named secretaries for the delegation, chosen by Opothleyaholo. Paddy Carr, a half-blood Creek, was only 19 years of age, yet he accompanied the delegation as Creek interpreter.[6]

While in Washington City, the delegation stayed at the Indian Queen Hotel, its sign adorned with a painting of Pocahontas. The proprietor, Jesse B. Brown, had been described by Nathan Sargent as "the prince of landlords." It was reported that the Indian delegation was pleased with their accommodations and the sumptuous fare adorning the sideboards. Brown carved the joints of beef and served his guests generous portions. If anyone left the dining table hungry, it was their own fault, certainly not Brown's.[7]

The first order of business for the delegation was to meet and be welcomed by President John Quincy Adams who shook hands with each of them. When Adams commented about their long journey and an accident along the way, Opothleyaholo stated that a few of the members had been hurt in a stagecoach accident, but now were well. As all of the deputation had not arrived, Opothleyaholo believed there was nothing more to say until they were present.[8]

Although Thomas L. McKenney, superintendent of Indian Affairs, had provided them with new apparel upon arriving in the city, the Creeks had not conformed totally to the white man's costume. Adams observed their fantastic dress. They were beturbaned men, either using a brightly colored shawl or a fine material wrapped around their heads and accented with plumes.[9]

The president considered most of them good looking men, although their countenances were dark and gloomy, especially that of Opothleyaholo. A surprising evaluation due to the serious consequences that had brought them to the capital city.[10]

In preparation of a new treaty, Secretary of War James Barbour interviewed Opothleyaholo, on November 30, 1825. This dialogue, one of the many Opothleyaholo would have with government representatives through the years, shows his intelligence and his mastery of rhetoric.[11]

Barbour wanted to know if the Speaker was prepared to "enter upon the business of your mission." Opothleyaholo replied, "We are prepared, and I think it desirable to proceed to business, at once, as the Great Council of our Great Father is about to assemble, and we want to know, before the Great Council fire is lit, what are the views of the Government in relation to us. We do not think it necessary to wait the coming of our Brothers. We have power to proceed."

Barbour inquired as to "what power you have been appointed."

Opothleyaholo: "At the great council at the Broken Arrow, Gen. Gaines expressed a wish to see some of us here, and when at Tuckabatchee we were delegated by the whole nation to come on." Barbour asked for a written document showing their appointment. "We got our power from the mouths of the Nation, as is usual." It had been written, however, and sent to the government.

Barbour proceeded to correct a mistake "which it appears you labor under. You are here now at your own request which was made known to your Great Father by your agent, Col. Crowell, in April last. That request was granted. It is true Genl. Gaines said what you state, but it was only a repetition by him of what was granted before. I mention this only for the purpose of correcting an error in regard to the origin of this visit."

"It is true," Opothleyaholo agreed. "The Head Chiefs of the nation were talking last Spring of their distress before the agent. Our troubles bore hard upon us. We turned our eyes to our Great Father. He is our guardian. We said we want to see him. We asked the agent to say so. We got his answer, as you say. We heard the same thing from Genl. Gaines."

Barbour stressed to Opothleyaholo how deeply he and his people had grieved their Great Father. The Creeks had been given permission to visit him and yet "you took up the tomahawk and did the great violence with it which you have done. He expected you to seek your redress of him, and not to strike yourselves. But you did strike, and by so doing you have caused very general and deep dissatisfaction; made yourselves many enemies, embarrassed your Great Father, and filled him with deep regret."

"'Tis true, we did in our grief, strike. But it was an affair of the nation. In all cases of national concerns the consent of the Nation is first had. The names of its Chiefs are taken down—the names of the agent and the Interpreter also. In the late affair this was not done. A new way was attempted not known to the nation. The Nation could not walk in it."

Of course, both men were referring to the death of McIntosh and the Indian Springs Treaty, and the marks of the Creeks which were fraudulent. And Barbour explained that now "your Great Father" is in a difficult position. "The other party say they are aggrieved. They are coming on—at least the papers tell us so. What their object is, they will make known also."

"I expect all the transactions of the late disturbances have been laid before our Great Father," Opothleyaholo replied. The Speaker knew that writings had been entered into by both sides. "I doubt not the President has seen them all. He can judge. We are willing that he should judge. I wish our negotiation now begun to be in writing also. I wish it for my people. I look for protection to the United States. I expect the late Treaty to be cancelled."

When asked the number in the other party, Opothleyaholo informed that the number of McIntoshes was small. "They all lived near him. Since his death they fled—some to Georgia and others elsewhere. The Heads of the families, I do not think exceed Twenty. When the agent arrives with the Coweta part of our Delegation, he will be able to tell how many there were who undertook to sell our Country."

When asked his objections to the late treaty, Opothleyaholo answered:

I have objections to the manner of making that Treaty and to the substance of it. It was not made by the Muscogee Nation, and who else had a right to make it? But that is not all. The Muscogee Nation have objections to selling any more lands. They have parted from a great deal. The land that stands fast under the white people's feet, keeps slipping from under the feet of the red people. We have now hardly enough for our Women and Children to stand upon. Why cannot we be allowed to have land, and homes, and live like our white Brothers, and learn of them how to be comfortable?

Opothleyaholo, Creek speaker and leader, who fled to Kansas looking for the Union Army. McKenney-Hall 1837 litho after painting of Charles Bird King, Washington, DC, 1825. Archives and Manuscripts Division of the Oklahoma Historical Society.

Barbour inquired as to the number of people living in the ceded territory. "We do not understand any thing about lines that we can't see," Opothleyaholo said. "All the lands belong to all our people, the ceded and those that were not ceded. Here are four present as Delegates who live on the ceded Territory. Selocta—Mad Wolf—Ledagi—and Yoholo Micco. They have so little land, that they could not live upon it."

It appears that Barbour was having difficulty assimilating the meaning of Opothleyaholo's answer. If they did not understand lines, how then could they know about acreage? Yet, Barbour came back with the question of how many acres they had been left under the late treaty.

We do not know how to reckon by acres—but the Country left by the Treaty is so small that the nation could not live upon it. We have come here to make complaint—to tell our sorrows—to utter our grievances to our Great Father, to shew that the Treaty was made by fraud, by thieves, by walkers in the night. The Muscogee Nation would not object to a fair Treaty, honestly made, a Treaty that had no foul blots on it, and that should be made at their Council house where their Chiefs sit, and who should be properly authorized.

Barbour explained that their "Great Father in sending commissioners to you to treat for your lands did not intend to commit fraud. They were sent to make a fair Treaty." It was quite true, the president had not intended fraud, but the commissioners had. Naturally, this was not revealed to the Speaker but Barbour intended Opothleyaholo to understand that the treaty had been ratified, and if it was fraudulent, "your Great Father cannot cancel it. It can be done only by the Great Council of the nation who put their seal upon it and made it fast—if it is done at all." Their Great Father hoped they would at least "carry the substance of this Treaty into effect, in a new one made by yourselves as the heads of the Nation, and that you would be willing to occupy lands West of the Mississippi, away from the white man, to live in the future, and under some friendly helps for your improvement in peace and prosperity." Should the Creeks accomplish a reconcilement, they could name an additional sum of money and the "Great Father would consider the offer, and do all he could to settle this difficulty."

Opothleyaholo assured Barbour that the Creek Nation "are not unfriendly to the whites, and have no objection to live near the white people, and it is their wish to live near their Great Father the President of the United States." Taken as stated, it appeared removal was out of the question because they would no longer be "near their Great Father."

Barbour had Hambly read the agreement the Creeks had made and the names of the chiefs affixed to it. Opothleyaholo believed the paper to be correct and the names to be the chiefs of the nation.

"After the deepest reflection," Barbour said, "and beset with great embarrassment, your Great Father thought it best to direct Genl. Gaines to make you the proposal he did, and which has been read to you. I suppose you have no objection to carry the agreement into effect, according to the direction of your nation."

Opothleyaholo admitted the subject was embarrassing to the Creeks, also "it is of great importance. Clouds set upon it. Our Nation expects us to act under a clear sky. We must reflect well, and Counsel about what is to be done."

When pressed to settle the business that week and not wait for "your friends to arrive," Opothleyaholo said, "I have full confidence in the government of the United States. I am here as a suppliant. I am glad to be spoken to familiarly and kindly. The Delegation will reply in writing tomorrow, if possible, if not, as soon as they can." Opothleyaholo had expressed his belief in the federal government—it was a confidence that would remain with him despite all of the adversity and a confidence which would lead him into southern Kansas in the winter of 1861–62.

Chapter 10

A New Treaty

On December 9, Chilly McIntosh and 12 Creeks arrived in Washington, proclaiming themselves as delegates of the Creek Nation. They were sequestered in the Tennison Hotel.[1]

Back home in Georgia, the re-elected Troup, confident that the state was with him, received a resolution from the legislature upholding the validity of the Indian Springs Treaty. And as such, the ceded territory of the treaty, "within the limits of Georgia, is considered as an absolute vested interest." The state would, therefore, settle for nothing less than the whole ceded area. The resolution insisted "the right of entry" be effected at the time of the expiration in the treaty. Troup proposed not to accept an expiration date other than September 1, 1826.[2]

In Adams' address to the Senate, it is clear that President John Quincy Adams held the McIntosh party in disfavor. Adams reviewed the situation in Georgia, the murders of the three Creeks, and the flight of the party "for safety and subsistence from the territories which they had assumed to cede to our own." While living "on the bounty of the United States," they had advanced "pretensions" to have for themselves "exclusively" the monies "stipulated by the commissioners" for the cession of "all the lands of the Creek Nation." And the claim for protection by the eighth article was a ruse to use the United States as "instruments of their vengeance." The McIntosh party was "an impotent and helpless minority of their own tribe."[3]

While Adams and Barbour, who believed the McIntosh trouble had been fomented by the Georgians, overtly expressed their distrust of the Lower Creeks, McKenney distrusted the Cherokees Ridge and Vann. These Indians were not savages of the forest—they were educated and very keen when it came to dealing with the government. Opothleyaholo knew of their astuteness and with his naming them as secretaries of the delegation, he intended no subterfuge on the part of Washington.[4]

As promised by Opothleyaholo, the delegation's reply to the War Department was written by John Ridge and delivered to Barbour. The Creeks did not want to leave the graves of their fathers for the west. They would "surrender all claim and title to the lands east of the Chattachoochy (*sic*) River for money. We may as well be annihilated at once as to cede any portion of the land west of the river."[5]

Naturally, this would never do. The United States wanted all of the Creek lands within Georgia. Not ceding any west of the Chattahoochee would be unacceptable with the angered Georgians. Opothleyaholo and the delegation remained firm in their decision. They were not empowered to cede any lands west of the Chattahoochee. Barbour tried to reason with them; make them understand that if they did not accept ceding all the lands within the chartered limits of Georgia, negotiations might end and the Indian Springs Treaty be sustained and enforced.[6]

> It is ordained by the Great Creator that we are so reduced as to be dependent on your power and mercy, and if in the hugeness of Strength you determine to decide by power and not by right, we shall return to our friends and live there until you take possession of our country. Then shall we beg Bread from the whites and live the life of vagabonds on the soil of our progenitors. We shall not touch a cent of money for our lands thus forced from our hands and not a drop of white man's blood will be spilled. And as fast as we are knocked in the head—the throats of our wives and children are cut, by the first tide of population that know not law, we will then afford the United States a Spectacle of Emigration which we hope may be to a Country prepared by the Great Spirit for honest and unfortunate Indians.[7]

Barbour advised President Adams that negotiations were stalemated. The Creeks wanted to meet again with the president, to tell of their grievances, but Adams declined. If he were inflexible, "it would only increase their distress." If he were merciful and compassionate, it would be offensive to Georgia. The president would see them again before they returned home. He wished the delegation would "reflect" on another proposition agreeable to all concerned.[8]

The issue was the Chattahoochee River. It was implied to Adams that Gen. Gaines was the one who had suggested the Creeks take that river for a boundary. Although Gaines had no power to do this, Adams realized that if he had done so, then the government must consider their claims. Many believed the river as a boundary would be quite convenient. Barbour was to notify Georgia that the Creeks would cede only to the Chattahoochee. This was a safeguard to keep the state powerless from "reproaching" the government should the Chattahoochee not be obtained.[9]

At the cabinet meeting, Barbour once again brought up the subject of his plan to incorporate the Indians within the state, ending treaties and making the tribes liable to the government's laws. Adams dissented from the provocative idea feeling Congress' constitutional power in changing relations with

Indian tribes would be questioned by Americans. For now, they would be foreigners in their own land.[10]

The most blatant critique of the Indians in general came from Henry Clay, secretary of state, one who had been labeled "Chief of the War Hawks," as he had argued in favor of the War of 1812.

Clay believed no one could civilize the Indians, it would go against their nature. They were fated for extinction; as a race, they were not worth saving. No one could improve their breed. The human family would never consider their disappearance as a great loss to the world. Undoubtedly, within 50 years there would not be any red man alive.[11]

The New Year of 1826 found all involved in the treaty still at an impasse. Another treaty was drafted, all attempts made to have the Creeks cede their Georgia lands in entirety had failed. Feeling all negotiations were ended, it was reported Opothleyaholo tried to commit suicide. This news was passed on to President Adams. Opothleyaholo had demonstrated a strong character in all of his dealings with the government. Why, when his influential power was needed for the sake of his people, would he resort to such drastic means? Adams in his memoirs cites the report, but it is believed that it was nothing more than a vicious rumor.[12]

Finally, the Creeks compromised, and ceded all of their Georgia lands except for a parcel north of the Chattahoochee. Ridge and Vann advised Barbour that the chiefs would require their own reservations. Barbour rejected this and informed the delegation that "a fair equivalent in money might be added." They agreed, fixing $10,000 each as fair compensation but Barbour rejected this, saying $5,000 each was the limit and they agreed.[13]

On January 24, 1826, they signed the new treaty in which Article I declared the Indian Springs Treaty null and void. Article II took most of their lands within Georgia. Article VI gave to the friends and followers of the late Gen. William McIntosh the right for five persons, at the expense of the United States, to travel to Indian country west of the Mississippi and examine the terrain for possible settlement, as long as it was not in a state or territory, or possessed by Cherokees and Choctaws. Article XII provided that the Creeks must yield that country by January 1, 1827. However, the Alabama lands were not ceded.

The Creeks were to be paid in cash $217,600 "to be divided among the chiefs and warriors of said nation" with a perpetual annuity of $20,000.[14]

The McIntosh party was not allowed to sign the treaty; Opothleyaholo was adamant that they did not have permission of the full council. However, Barbour assured Adams a separate paper with their marks or signatures would be annexed to it. This separation of the two Creek factions would not be resolved until after the Civil War.[15]

After signing the treaty, Ridge and Vann presented a paper to McKenney with names showing their share of the $217,600. McKenney was assured this distribution was agreed to by all of the chiefs. Heading the list of 24 names was John Ridge, $15,000; Joseph Vann, $15,000; Opothleyaholo, $10,000; John Stidham, $10,000; Menawee (Menawa), $10,000; Charles Cornell, $10,000; Mad Wolf, $6,000; Paddy Carr, $500; Little Prince, $10,000; Major Ridge, John's father who was not in Washington, $10,000; and 14 others of the delegation, each receiving from $200 to $10,000, making a total of $159,700 to be paid to the individuals named.[16]

Although McKenney had told the Cherokees that these payments were their own affair, he was uncertain how this distribution of more than 70 percent of the treaty cash to 24 individuals would be taken by the nation. He discussed it with Barbour who believed it was the business of the Indians and no concern of the government.[17]

Ridge and Vann requested the payments in cash to be sealed in envelopes and given to the individuals named. McKenney stated such a transaction would have to be handled by the cashier of the branch bank.[18]

Barbour and McKenney met again to discuss the possibility of the less intelligent chiefs reactions to the sums allotted. McKenney called in Ridge and Vann and asked them if every member of the delegation "knew as well as they did, the mode which they had adopted for the distribution of the money." Ridge answered, "No—but that Opothle Yoholo and Charles Cornell knew and that was enough."[19]

Barbour endeavored to make the delegation understand that the nation might not submit to the distribution of funds. He was assured "that they would see that their people ratified the arrangement, as in the event of any dissatisfaction they had their annuity and this very money and would so apply as to satisfy all." Everything would be explained in council; all that had been written would be read.[20]

Yet the government was not convinced. They feared retaliation toward the delegation by their people. It could be as dangerous as the recriminations against McIntosh.

When the Georgians learned the Creeks were retaining a parcel of land north of the Chattahoochee, protests were lodged against the treaty's ratification. The treaty was referred to the Committee on Indian Affairs in the Senate where it was decided there would be no ratification. The annulment of the Indian Springs Treaty labeled it as illegal which condoned McIntosh's murder. The Creeks hadn't ceded all of their Georgia lands and none in Alabama. Only a supplemental article stating the cession of all the Georgia lands would assure the treaty's ratification. The ratification was set aside while Barbour negotiated once again with the delegation. It had been suggested to Barbour by Sen. Thomas Hart Benton of Missouri to allow gratuities to the chiefs involved as an inducement to their agreeing to cede the additional lands.

Benton believed this was the only way to deal with barbarians. Barbour would have nothing to do with what he considered bribes.[21]

Ultimately, an agreement was reached and appended to the treaty whereby the tract in question, the land north of the Chattahoochee, was ceded by the Creeks for an additional $30,000. At the behest of Barbour, the chiefs agreed that $24,000 of the money should be used to educate Creek boys at the Choctaw Academy in Kentucky. Col. Richard M. Johnson in 1825 had established the school five miles west of Georgetown. Johnson was a prominent figure who some credited with the shooting of Tecumseh in Canada in 1813 which led to the great Shawnee's death.[22]

Opothleyaholo enrolled an 8-year-old son in this school. He was given the name of the founder, Richard M. Johnson. The rest of the Creek boys received white men's names such as Henry Clay and Andrew Jackson. Obviously, this school was no different that any others that were established to educate the savage. The campaign to divorce the children from their heritage and make them white is a repugnant fact in this nation's history.[23]

Barbour did not present to the Senate the soon to become "notorious" paper about the individual payments until after the supplemental article was signed. There were leaks in government back then as now, and someone in the War Department already had passed along this information to Benton who disclosed the news to the Senate in a secret session.

The apportionment became a matter of debate. Barbour and McKenney were accused of being cognizant of this intended fraud upon the Creek Nation while negotiating the supplemental article. Ridge was castigated; everyone knew he "had been taught Christianity and morality among the whites." Was his act to defraud the Creeks a result of "the fruit of his education?" How was the Creek Nation to be protected from their own unscrupulous representatives? And what about the late McIntosh? He was accused as traitor for signing the Indian Springs Treaty. His accusers and executioners were now rewarding themselves.[24]

When the Georgians learned of the proposed payment to the Cherokees, they protested once again. They hated the Cherokees who still retained land in northern Georgia. And they feared them for they were quickly becoming an educated nation, more and more adopting the white men's dress and their lifestyles. The Cherokees, more than the Creeks, epitomized the degrading belief that an educated Indian was dangerous. And the Ridges and Vanns understood the machinations of the federal and state governments. The Georgians resented the insinuations and complained to Barbour at the War Department.[25]

Alabama resolved that their U.S. senators and representatives must "procure for this state" the lands "acquired" within the chartered limits according to the Indian Springs Treaty. Gov. John Murphy sought justice for his state.

"When chartered limits were assigned to the several states having Indian populations, it does not seem to have entered into the contemplation of any one that they would remain fixed and permanent." While Georgia had acquired property and jurisdiction of the soil from the Creek Nation at Indian Springs, Alabama had not received any land. In comparison to Troup, Murphy of Alabama, in his communication to Congress was resolute, yet seemed calm and thoughtful, and made no demands,[26] but his claims were not recognized and Alabama passed two acts. One gave the state, civil and criminal jurisdiction over the ceded Creek lands in Alabama. The second forbade the Creeks to hunt, trap and fish within the settled limits of the state. These acts gained the attention of the administration. President Adams cautioned Murphy that the acts would not be allowed to conflict with U.S. laws in regard to the Indians. The U.S. District Court in Alabama found the acts unconstitutional and Alabama abided by its decision.[27]

Troup, learning of the new treaty, refused to accept the right of the United State to declare the Indian Springs Treaty "null and void." He informed Adams that by the authority of the Georgia legislature, he intended to take possession of the Creek lands on September 2, 1826. And the Alabama–Georgia line would exist without relationship to the Indian Springs Treaty. Georgia had been given that authority by the Compact of 1802. The surveying would follow the boundary of the two states and the occupation of the Creek lands.[28] With the new treaty being ratified, Troup claimed that Georgia had "been defrauded of one million acres of her very best lands."[29]

McKenney, on behalf of the secretary of war, wrote to Opothleyaholo and others of the Creek delegation on May 20, 1826. "I am directed to reply, that, in the intercourse had with you in negotiating the treaty, the Secretary discovered nothing improper in your conduct, but esteemed you to be men of correct principles." He explained the apprehensions both he and Barbour had about the distribution. "As to yourselves individually, it will be much more flattering to you to receive at the hands of the assembled Chiefs of your nation the sums you had allotted, than to have anticipated their act, and afterwards ascertained by doing so, you had incurred the displeasure of even one of them."[30]

The distribution of the treaty money was not accomplished until August 1826 when the Creek council convened near the agency at Fort Mitchell in Georgia. In full council, the sum set aside for the individual Creeks was sustained, however, Ridge's and Vann's amounts were reduced to $5,000 each, while Maj. Ridge retained the $10,000.[31]

Surveyors moved through the country, establishing the Alabama–Georgia border. In September, Barbour received a protest from the Creeks conveyed by Crowell. They were "much disturbed" when surveyors entered their country before they could secure and remove their crops. The Native People had complied with the treaty's terms and asked the executive to intervene on their behalf and order the surveys stopped. They knew they had possession of the country until January 1, 1827. They enclosed an executive order by Troup, dated March 9, 1826, in which he had notified the surveyor general to send "circulars addressed to sectional surveyors."[32]

Barbour apprised Troup of the complaint. Adams sustained the Creeks' objection. There were only a few months left before Georgia could survey the land lawfully and Adams could "see no inducement on the part of Georgia to enter the territory of the Indians against their will, and in violation of the supreme law of the land."[33]

Troup replied on October 6, excusing his tardiness due to Barbour's letter having been delayed at Charleston. He discounted any objections as originating from the Creeks. Rather it was the usual intermeddling of Crowell. The survey was an accommodation to allow the Creeks to dispose more readily their "surplus commodities." Before the surveys, these crops had either perished, or could not be marketed so easily. Tacitly, Troup conveyed the idea that he was doing the Indians a favor. Most of the surveyors had completed their work and had not been accosted nor interrupted by the Creeks.[34] The Creeks were holding fast to their pledge of remaining peaceful with the whites.

The practice of the Americans to disregard any rights of the Indians granted through treaty was a disease so prevalent not one tribe of the hundreds in the United States ever escaped.

The Georgians were very selective in using both the early and new treaties. They took the date of possession from the Indian Springs Treaty, ignoring the Washington Treaty. Of the land acquired they accepted the Washington Treaty, believing they had at last received their just due.

Or had they? It was discovered in Washington that the boundary lines were in error. This error had left the Creeks still in possession of a tract in Georgia. "If the Government of the United States believed they acquired all the lands, when in fact they had not, the mistake was theirs, not ours," Troup boasted in his message to the Georgia Legislature in December.[35] Buoyed by such a grievous mistake on the federal government's part, Georgia continued with the surveying. And they became bold in their efforts, surveying the Alabama line past the latest Creek cession. Defying a tradition that precluded the running of state boundaries through Indian country where their title had not been extinguished, Troup challenged the federal government again regarding states rights.

On January 15, 1827, Crowell advised Barbour that several Creeks led by Little Prince had requested the agent to caution the surveyors in writing and require them to stop their work. The Creeks held the Treaty of Washington to be sacred and a protection for them against the encroachments of the Georgians. They reasoned that "if Georgia is permitted to violate that treaty with impunity, why may not Alabama?"[36]

Barbour learned that the Creeks had threatened surveyors James A. Rogers and Wiley Williams, the former being district surveyor. The Creeks had delivered a letter to Rogers signed by Little Prince. The Indians demanded that the surveyors "desist from stretching a chain over any of our lands not ceded by the said treaty." The "lusty" delegation had toyed with Rogers, confiscating his compass, then returning it to him and escorting him back over the new treaty line. Rogers halted his workers and notified Troup that if the governor intended to protect the surveyors, he hoped it would be soon "as provision is scarce and my hands uneasy to go home."[37]

Williams, likewise, sent a message to Troup, asking for protection.[38] A Georgia "troop of horse" was sent to the area where they intimidated the Creeks.

President Adams did not agree with Secretary of State, Henry Clay, when he deemed it necessary to protect, by force, the right of the Indians. Either the war hawk had changed his mind about the Indians, or a war could eliminate more of them under the guise of protection. The president thought "the civil process" would suffice for the time. The Georgia surveyors, he reasoned, were obeying the orders of the state. Should the federal government order the military against them, only violence would result. Before such "conflict of arms" happened, however, Adams would refer the matter to Congress.[39]

Barbour forwarded letters to U.S. Marshal John H. Morel, in Savannah; U.S. District Attorney R. W. Habersham also in Savannah; Gov. Troup and Agent Crowell to be carried to Georgia by Lt. J.R. Vinton, U.S. Army. Habersham was ordered to obtain "the proper process" to arrest the surveyors and deliver it to Morel who, upon "receipt of the process" was to promptly execute it.[40] Vinton's mission was to be accomplished "with least possible delay," to prevent violence "either by the authorities of Georgia or the Indians."[41]

Adams looked to Congress for a solution to the problem. A select committee, one chaired by Senator Thomas Hart Benton, the other by Representative Edward Everett, advised the president to purchase the remaining Creek lands in Georgia. Troup delayed any more confrontation awaiting the outcome.[42]

Crowell failed to make any headway with the Creeks, and McKenney, now Commissioner of Indian Affairs, was sent to see Opothleyaholo and Little Prince. Through accusations lodged against Opothleyaholo that he was in league with the Cherokees, McKenney secured most of the land. Little Prince signed the agreement and asked that a warning be issued to the Cherokees that if Ridge and Vann came to their country, it would mean their deaths.[43]

As to Troup and Georgia, they had been victorious in their conflict with the federal government. They had drawn national attention to their cause and, once on the bandwagon, their cries of Indian removal and states rights would not be forgotten by the southern states. The only thing that had prevented the civil war threat had been the forbearance of Adams.

On January 22, 1828, Adams submitted the agreements of November 1827 and January 3, 1828, to the Senate for their consideration and advice. The articles of agreement ceded all of the remnant of Creek lands in Georgia.[44] Their land had slipped again in favor of the Americans.

For a while, the result of McKenney's allegations had caused Opothleyaholo's power within the nation to lessen, but not for long. Little Prince died in 1828 and Eneah Micco was named his successor. Tuskinah had been chosen to replace the late Big Warrior. Both men lacked Opothleyaholo's qualities and although he had retained his office as speaker, he also became the recognized leader of the nation. But he never forgot the Cherokees. At the beginning of the white man's war, Opothleyaholo would seek counsel of their chief, John Ross.

The Indian question in the South had not been resolved with the Creeks giving up their land in Georgia. Now the great Muskogee Nation, wrenched apart by their own internal conflicts which had its beginning with unscrupulous Americans, was weakened and once more became the prey of the whites. Whiskey was easily obtained in their Alabama country and their crops became targets for unprincipled and lawless Americans. The Creeks wandered aimlessly, wretched and starving, quickly becoming degraded with the aid of the white man's whiskey. The chiefs and headmen sought Washington's help in becoming an independent nation in Alabama.

In October 1828, citizens of Montgomery County, Alabama met to take into consideration their relations with the Creek Indians. Alabama's rights as a state were examined and a preamble and resolution were drawn up.[45]

"As citizens of Alabama, they behold with astonishment a tract of country lying within their geographic boundaries, inhabited by a people who claim the right to exercise an independent government for themselves, who bid defiance to the laws of our state, and who are supported in their independence by the general government." The Alabamians questioned the right of the general government, or federal government, "to exercise a power which directly interferes with the internal regulations of Alabama." They saw as "dangerous and alarming" the general government's exercise of power within a state, unless constitutional, and they believed the general government's support of the Creeks "as founded in usurpation."

The good Montgomery County citizens resolved that Alabama, as a sovereign state and independent, had a "right to exercise over all persons, of whatever description within those limits, the authority of her laws." They resolved further "that the authority now exercised by the general government for the protection of the Creek Indians in their independent government, by which this state is deprived of jurisdiction over her chartered limits, as unconstitutional and against the rights of Alabama." The Alabamians wanted "passage of laws for the laying the country off into counties and bringing the Natives in subjection to the law."

Georgia was also back in the news. Although they had been relieved of the Creeks, they still had to contend with the Cherokees in the northern part of the state. They watched closely the Cherokees who were an example of how Indians could progress being ruled by their own laws within the state's boundaries.

In February 1828, the Cherokees began publishing a newspaper, *The Cherokee Phoenix*, its type font cast in the characters of the Cherokee alphabet invented by their own Sequoyah, George Guess. Later, the Georgia government would seize the press and use it to publish propaganda designed to destroy the Cherokees. The Georgians passed a law that December which declared Cherokee Nation's laws would be null and void after June 1, 1830.[46]

All efforts by the Creeks to form their own government was disregarded by Washington, the lawmakers quoting the Constitution which declared "no new States shall be formed or erected within the jurisdiction of any other State without the consent of the Legislature."[47]

Even President Adams was weakening in his support for the Indians. In his last annual message to the Congress, December 1828, he believed the government had been "far more successful in the acquisition of their lands" than in civilizing them. The taking of their hunting grounds had led to subsistence by the government, yet, "when we have had the rare good fortune of teaching them the arts of civilization and the doctrines of Christianity, we have unexpectedly found them forming in the midst of ourselves communities claiming to be independent of ours and rivals of sovereignty with the territories of the members of our Union."[48]

Festering beneath the states rights issue and Indian removal was the constant bickering on the part of the South due to the tariffs. They South was agricultural, and in the acquisition of Indian lands they had become a large tobacco and cotton exporter to the European markets. They purchased the European manufactured goods which they had found to be better in quality and lower in price than the Northern goods. However, with high tariffs on imported goods, the South was paying more. They wanted lower tariffs or free trade with Europe. The North, on the other hand, wanted higher tariffs so they might develop their own factories and be able to compete with Europe. The disputes between the North and the South had been caused through legislation. The North had allowed the South to expand in agricultural products and slavery, thus providing a substantial growth; simultaneously the North was punishing them for trading with Europe by passing high tariffs.

The 1828 tariff increased rates on foreign manufactured goods. As expected, it met opposition by the cotton states of the South, but the middle and free states of the west supported it. In New England, manufacturing had replaced agriculture as the economic base.

John C. Calhoun vehemently opposed the high tariff on the grounds that it would hurt his native state, South Carolina. Calhoun, who wrote, anonymously, the "South Carolina Exposition and Protest," believed if a state found a national law unconstitutional it could not be forced to comply and the state could block any federal intervention.

Through the efforts of Charles Pinckney, South Carolina had been a dominant power in developing the Constitution. Pinckney and the other delegates battled for strong state government as opposed to what they feared would become an omnipotent federal government.

In December 1828, South Carolina's legislature named the new law the "Tariff of Abominations" and adopted eight resolutions expounding its unjustness and unconstitutionality. These actions by South Carolina and Calhoun later caused an estrangement between President Andrew Jackson and his vice-president, and erased all hopes of the South Carolinian's succession to the presidency.

Henry Clay's "American System," its theme the economic theory of supply and demand, earned the support of the western territories. Protective tariffs for the eastern industries meant an increase in manufactured goods. This increase would demand a larger work force, the eastern population would grow which would provide a market for the agricultural products of the western territories. The South, if it could put aside its competitiveness toward the North, would benefit as well. Everyone would prosper. It would tie together the different sections of the United States. In Clay's opinion there was "no north, no south, no east, no west."[49]

The tariffs prompted debates in Congress, but it would be the Native People and their need for independence that would raise anew the Southern cry for states rights. Newspapers editorialized about dissolution of the Union and Civil War.[50]

Beyond the Mississippi in 1828, Chilly McIntosh and fellow Indians were prospering in their new country situated near Fort Gibson and the Grand, Verdigris and Arkansas rivers in the eastern part of present Oklahoma. Buffalo and deer were so plentiful that the Indians never had enough horses to bring back all they might have killed. They had gardens producing cucumbers, lettuce, radishes, beans, peas, beets, watermelons, potatoes and corn. Everyone was delighted with the country which "is rich and well calculated for our people who can live well by agriculture and farming." The Delaware Indians had visited them. They told the Lower Creeks that they are "the grandfather of all the Indian tribes."[51]

The so-called report of Chilly's was written by the Osage agent, Thomas Anthony. The conditions existing in what was to become known as Indian Territory had been pictured in words tantamount to the Garden of Eden. Whether this was written as Chilly saw it is uncertain, for it masked the true state of things.

Contrary to Chilly's report the Lower Creeks, for the time being known as the Western Creeks, were having a difficult time in their new country. Certainly there was plenty of buffalo, but they were located to the west where tribes roamed that might not prove amenable to these newcomers. At great risk they were killing buffalo, not for the thrill of the hunt, but rather in dire need for meat and skins for clothing. Their supplies had been slow in arriving. This dilatory tactic by the Indian Bureau echoed and re-echoed throughout all of the tribes that had ever signed a treaty with the federal government.[52]

As to the Delawares, Chilly had mentioned they were actually Lenape which meant "real men" or "native, genuine men."[53] They, too, were a confederacy and their nation at one time had dwelled along the basin of the Delaware River in Pennsylvania and New York, and the regions of present New Jersey and Delaware. Because they were the original political rank from which many tribes diverged, all of the Algonquin tribes, out of respect, gave them the title of "grandfather."

When the English discovered them on the east coast, they named them for the governor of their colony in Jamestown, Virginia, Lord de la Warr, Sir Thomas West.[54]

The Delawares made their first treaty in 1682 with William Penn. It was during this period of the 17th century that a Delaware chief gained celebrity with the whites as a wise, friendly man. His name was Tamanend meaning "affable." He was made "Saint Tammany" patron saint by the colonists in ridicule of the patron saints of the royalist societies. Saint Tammany did not become lost in American history, although it is questionable whether the Delaware chief would have been proud of his name's reputation.[55]

In May 1789 a fraternal organization was founded in New York City and called the Society of Saint Tammany. This organization strongly opposed the Federalists who supported ratification of the new constitution. Eventually, its headquarters would be called Tammany Hall and they would become the Democrat party's political machine.[56]

In 1872, William Marcy Tweed, "boss" of Tammany Hall, would be charged with siphoning off millions of dollars from the city of New York. Thomas Nast, artist, created the "Tammany Tiger" to represent this corruption. One widely publicized drawing in 1871 was of a self-contented tiger with a sign hanging from its neck with the legend "Republican Lamb, Inquire Within."[57]

In 1829, two major events greatly affected the Creeks. Alabama took the Creek land and divided it into counties and made the tribe subject to the local courts. Gen. Andrew Jackson became the seventh president of the United States, stepping all the way to Washington on the corpses of Creeks and Seminoles. This savior of the common man promised states rights protection. A fiery advocate of Indian removal, he promised an Indian policy that would be "just and liberal."[58] "Old Sharp Knife," as he was known by the Creeks and Seminoles, told the Creeks they would have to accept subjection to the Alabama laws. Should they refuse to agree, then the only thing left for them was to move across the Mississippi River.[59]

Jackson knew the South had to rid itself of the Indian population. Any large settlement of Americans south of the Mason–Dixon line would meet fierce resistance by the Southern tribes. For the sake of the Union's permanence, the red man had to leave. The alternative of a civil war because of savages was too odious to contemplate.

Chapter 11

Andrew Jackson and Indian Removal

As President, Andrew Jackson had not only vowed to be "just and liberal" with the Indians, but he would "give that humane and considerate attention to their rights and wants."[1]

In his first annual message he bragged that there were 24 sovereign states within the Union. As to the Southern tribes, by reason of association with the whites, "in the arts of civilized life have lately attempted to erect an independent government within the limits of Georgia and Alabama."[2] Jackson regretted the United States policy which left the Indian territory within a state's boundaries. Born out of the states' desires to see justice done, and in accordance "with the rights of the States," Jackson proposed a plan "to preserve this much-injured race."[3]

He suggested the government designate "an ample district west of the Mississippi and without the limits of any State or Territory now formed." Of course, this would require an assurance to the Indians that the area would be their's "as long as they shall occupy it." There they could have their own government and not be subjected to the United States' control unless "necessary to preserve peace on the frontier and between several tribes." Should the "aborigines" decline to leave their country, then they would be subjected to the respective state laws. "They will without doubt be protected in the enjoyment of those possessions which they have improved by their industry." Improvement of land was common to the whites, but not to the Indians. Certainly, many of them had cultivated the land and had homes and outbuildings, but their hunting lands had not been touched. Thus, it appears Jackson was covering all avenues when he noted they would be protected in what they had "improved." "It was presumptuous of Indians," Jackson said, "to claim tracts of country on which they have neither dwelt nor made improvements, merely because they have seen them from the mountain or passed them in the chase."[4]

General Gaines had a different opinion when it came to removing the Indians west of the Mississippi River. In his Inspection Report of the Western Department, Gaines had devoted considerable time to the Indian Department. He believed it was the duty of every U.S. citizen "to raise his voice, however feeble," in civilizing the Indians "and against their being driven from their homes." Those homes "possess the charm not less dear to them than to their civilized neighbors." The general believed it would be disastrous to "push them into the wide expanse of western prairie" there, perhaps, to face annihilation by "tomahawks" or "famine." The Indians' homes or villages, "miserable as they are," was "where the elements of civilization" was certain, and with less expense to "be imparted to them." It is to be wondered if Gaines' observations were ever considered or was his the proverbial voice in the wilderness?[5]

Jackson was successful in his proposal, and on May 28, 1830, he signed an act that was compulsory with regard to the removal of all Indians to the west of the Mississippi River. Appropriations in the amount of $500,000 for exchange or sale of territory were set aside, as were removal expenses.

That same year, the Cherokees were warned by the federal government to abide by Georgia state laws or remove to the west. Mississippi also passed a law that made the Indians within its borders subject to state jurisdiction.

In December, Jackson addressed his "Fellow Citizens" of the Congress. "The benevolent policy of the Government" was "approaching a happy consummation." The Choctaws and Chickasaws had accepted removal. These two important tribes would be an "example" in inducing the rest of the Southern tribes to remove.[6]

A speedy removal would mean money for the government. Yet, this was "the least of its recommendations." A "civilized population" would soon have country "now occupied by a few savage hunters." For posterity, Jackson revealed the paramount motive for hastening the departure of the Native People from the South. "It puts an end to all possible danger of collision between the authorities of the General and State Governments on account of the Indians."[7] With the bitter arguments over tariffs, something, anything had to be done to placate the South. The Indian, as a person, was valueless to the United States. His land was his only asset. Move them out of the South, and millions of acres of productive land for cotton would be available for the disgruntled Southerner. The Native People were sacrificed to save the Union.

Jackson knew that the "twelve million happy people" in the Union would not want their "country covered with forests and ranged by a few thousand savages" in comparison "to our extensive Republic ..." A Republic "studded with cities, towns and prosperous farms." The president related how the tribes that had occupied the land of the "Eastern States were annihilated or have melted away to make room for the whites." Such was the present situation facing the Southern Tribes. Perhaps it would "be painful to leave the graves of their fathers," Jackson said. But hadn't the white man done the same thing? Did the "wandering savage" have "a stronger attachment to his home than the settled, civilized Christian?" Of course not.[8]

In 1831 the U.S. Supreme Court found that the Cherokees were not a foreign nation within Georgia, and the federal government lacked jurisdiction over them. The tide was changing rapidly under the Jackson administration and the government's pledge to protect the Southern tribes. Then, the following year the U.S. Supreme Court reversed its decision in the case of Worcester vs. Georgia and found that the exclusive jurisdiction of Indian tribes within a state belonged to the federal government. Georgia, as usual, ignored the ruling and Jackson declared in favor of the state. The chief justice, "John Marshall has made his decision," Jackson said, "now let him enforce it."[9] Without the executive behind him, Marshall's ruling was ignored.

In the Creek country, depredations by the whites continued. A Creek delegation journeyed to Washington in January 1831 to protest to Secretary of War James H. Eaton. The Alabama laws were confusing to them and useless, as the white man was protected by them in killing and robbing the Creeks of their property. Even white army officers had come to their country and confiscated property in payment "for debts that were never contracted."[10] Eaton parroted what Jackson had told them before—abide by Alabama's laws or move to the west.

When Eaton resigned in April 1831, due to a personal problem, he was replaced in August by Lewis Cass, an Ohioan who as governor of Minnesota Territory in 1820 had organized an expedition to find the source of the Mississippi River. At Red Cedar Lake, Cass had documented wrongly that it was the source of the mighty river. With Cass's appointment, perhaps the Creeks felt a new person would listen more sympathetically to their grievances. Even newspapers described the condition of the poorer members of the nation.

The editor of *The* (GA) *Milledgeville Recorder* had witnessed the suffering and reported that most of the nation was literally starving to death. "To see a whole people destitute of food—the incessant cry of the emaciated creatures being bread! bread! is beyond description distressing." They were eating roots, tree barks and China tree berries.[11] "Nothing that can afford nourishment is rejected, however offensive it may be." The editor believed then was the time to remove the Creeks. "They would doubtless consent to emigrate for the purpose of preserving life." The cause of removal and humanities "would be subserved." Many of the Creeks on the Georgia borders had not planted corn "because they had none to plant."[12]

While some of the whites were openly sympathetic toward the Creek living conditions, others begrudged them the kill of the hunt. Whites were invading Creek country west of the Chattahoochee surveying off the lands they wanted for themselves. Cass was no different than his predecessor—abide or remove.

The status in the Creek country was becoming critical and in desperation another Creek delegation led by Opothleyaholo set out for Washington in December 1831. Along with the Creeks was a Cherokee delegation accompanied by Sam Houston. Houston, in his youth, had lived with the Cherokees and had become known by them as "The Raven." On their journey they stopped at Nashville long enough for Houston to show them through the Hermitage, Jackson's home, the ambience of which reflected the president's frontier personality.[13]

Jackson informed Opothelyaholo that at the expiration of five years from the date of the 1832 Removal Treaty, if the Creeks continued to live where they were, there would be no argument about state law—they would be Alabama citizens. If they did not obey, then "they must move beyond the bounds of the Mississippi and settle themselves in a new home—which course he thought would be most beneficial for them." In the Indian country they could govern themselves and no state or territory could enact laws for them.[14]

When the Removal Treaty was signed and ratified, the Creeks had ceded all of their lands east of the Mississippi which included 5.2 million acres in Alabama. Each principal chief was allotted a section of land; each family head one-half section with a guarantee of a deed at the end of five years. Orphan children were allotted 20 sections, to be kept or sold. In time, these sections were sold as the orphans were removed west. In addition, any interlopers on their allotted land would be removed for the five years. Assuring words, but worthless.[15]

The white man has the proclivity to make a racket out of most any situation. Learning that the Indians were rightfully retaining property, the chance had come to take advantage of them. The American knew he would not suffer any punishment since an Indian's word would never be believed in the courts. Full-scale frauds were initiated. And when the federal government informed them they would have to leave Creek country, they yelled loud enough for the politicians to hear them. At the same time, the Creeks notified Cass they were not protected and wondered why the president had not done what he had pledged to do. The Creeks were driven from their homes and sought shelter in the woods. They were hungry, their corn crops confiscated by the white men. They were facing death.

Requests were made to Jackson to prevent the sale of whiskey on their lands. Jackson replied the only power vested in him was to remove intruders from the public lands. Only Alabama had jurisdiction over that district "and only her Legislature can provide a remedy for this evil and her courts of justice enforce it."[16] Jackson and the politicians had no intention of interfering for the South might become disharmonized with the Union about the Indians. They could not allow the Native People and their rights to raise the states rights specter again.

In May 1833, Cass commissioned Gen. Enoch Parsons and Col. John J. Abert to bring about another treaty with the Creeks. Both men had been advised to seek immediate emigration of that nation.

After the ratification of the 1832 Removal Treaty with the Creeks, Jackson persisted in his campaign to send them west. It did not seem to matter that the nation had five years to make their decision. In his fifth annual message to Congress in 1833, Jackson described the Creeks as "ignorant, lazy and immoral." They had to disappear situated as they were "in the midst of another and a superior race."[17]

In 1834, Benjamin Hawkins, half-blood Creek, returned to Alabama. Hawkins, brother of the late Sam Hawkins, had removed to Arkansas Territory with the Lower Creeks, then on to Texas. He readily advised Opothelyaholo of the straitened living conditions in Arkansas Territory. The people were dying of smallpox, cholera and fevers. Hawkins knew of a grant to a Mexican named Brasores of 100 to 150 miles square north of Nacogdoches, Texas. In order to keep the grant, Brasores had to place 200 families on the land in a little more than two years.[18]

Opothleyaholo was appalled by the news of illness in the region where the government insisted they had to live. But he was greatly interested in the Texas land and remembered his friend, Houston, lived there. What Opothleyaholo did not know was that the Mexicans were averse to any intrusions of Indians such as the Seminoles and Shawnees. They maintained it violated the 33rd article of the Friendship Treaty between the two countries.[19] In 1832, Jackson had asked Houston to convince those tribes to return to the United States.[20]

John B. Hogan, later appointed superintendent for removal of the Creek Indians, believed Opothleyaholo was the dupe of three white men in the nation, and he was sure they had originated the Texas land scheme. The three men were Doctors Weir, Billingsley and Major Coules who operated stores in Tuckabatchee. Hogan was certain that Opothleyaholo was so frightened of the McIntoshes in the Arkansas Territory that he would attempt most anything to keep from going there.[21] Opothleyaholo, along with Hawkins, Tuckabatchee Micco, David Barnett and Jim Boy, journeyed to Nacogdoches to see the area in question.

The Creeks agreed to pay $60,000 for the grant with $20,000 as a down payment. In March 1835, Opothleyaholo called a council and explained the arrangement, obtaining the assent and signatures of the Upper chiefs to an agreement to purchase the land. The lack of money for the down payment was a problem but it was solved when a Mr. Carpenter of Montgomery County agreed to loan them $23,000. Carpenter, however, required them to furnish him with a draft in the amount of $32,000 signed by the Upper chiefs.[22]

On April 8, Opothleyaholo, Jim Boy, David Barnett and a New Yorker by the name of DuBois left Mobile by steamboat headed for New Orleans. Before their departure, Hogan had introduced himself to Opothleyaholo and had tried to learn why they were going to New Orleans. He was unsuccessful, and decided to use a new tack. He explained he was the special agent who would remove them to their new homes; "a country where they would be free and unmolested by bad white men." Their's would be a comfortable removal. They could not remain in Alabama as they had no jurisdiction. New rifles and blankets had been sent to their new home and would be waiting for them. The Creeks who had preceded them "had done well." They had plenty of corn, hogs and cattle. He, Hogan, would deem it "a great pleasure" to help them in their removal. "I had often heard of the great warrior Opothleholo (*sic*) and was anxious to be his friend."[23]

Opothleyaholo, speaking "with great feeling and energy," said he knew President Jackson and that Jackson had told him they "must remove." The Creek leader "did not like the Arkansas country; their women and children would all die there." The nation had held a talk. They "would not go to Arkansas; they were willing to remove to Texas." Should the Creeks be forced "away to Arkansas they might do so, but they must cut his throat before they could remove his body there." Most of his people's land had been stolen while he was visiting Texas. He asked Hogan to tell the president and the agent agreed to do so.[24]

Hogan warned Opothleyaholo that "Texas was a foreign State" with no U.S. jurisdiction. Should the government allow the Creeks to go to Texas it might offend the Mexican government and cause the Spanish to make war on them.[25]

Opothleyaholo wondered why a part of the Seminoles and Shawnees were there and why the Creeks could not go. They were not afraid of the Spanish, and they liked Texas better than "the Arkansas." In Texas they could keep their land. In Arkansas Territory they would be forced off the land by the whites.[26]

Before departing, Hogan had a conversation with DuBois and apparently learned from him that the Creek party was carrying $30,000 with them. At that time he only could surmise that the money was being used in regard to Texas. In his letter to Gen. Gibson, Hogan speculated about letting Opothleyaholo and the other "refractory chiefs" go to Texas. With them out of the way, the rest of the Creeks might be "induced to go to Arkansas." Hogan, like so many others, had underestimated Opothleyaholo's power in the nation.[27]

Whether Hogan was correct or not about the three men who were manipulating Opothleyaholo there is one indisputable fact: No one could explain what had happened to the $20,000 down payment that conveniently disappeared when the Mexican government denied Creek entry into Texas. Carpenter, of course, had the $32,000 draft and this, along with the investigations into the land frauds, would be stumbling blocks in the way of a Creek removal in 1835. The nation requested their annuity in order to settle all debts, contrived or not, as they would not be allowed to leave Alabama unless they were paid. Opothleyaholo feared his Negroes would be taken to pay part of the debts.[28]

Hogan had many visits with Opothleyaholo in 1835. The special agent sued for removal and let the Creek know that at the end of five years, 1837, if they stayed in Alabama they would no longer be recognized as the Creek Nation. They would be Alabama citizens without full privileges; they could never vote in any election. Only one Creek Nation would remain and it would be in Arkansas Territory.[29]

As to the people themselves, they continued to starve and stole and slaughtered Alabamans' stock. The citizens became alarmed when some Creeks shot a man and woman in Chambers County near the Fort Mitchell agency. People would not travel through the nation except in parties of three or four.[30]

In May, Gen. Gibson notified Hogan that if an armed force was necessary in Alabama, the president through Gov. Gayle would order a detachment of U.S. troops to be sent into the Creek country. At the same time, Gibson informed him "that the intercourse law is now inoperative" thus the Creeks were liable to Alabama laws two years ahead of time.[31]

Gayle notified Hogan that he needed the special agent's opinion of the alleged depredations.[32] Hogan responded that the murders had been committed by drunken, worthless Indians who had been arrested and incarcerated. As to the civil authorities handling arrests, the whites were frightened to do so for fear of retaliation by the relatives of the miscreants. The chiefs were hesitant in punishing "their bad men" as Alabama laws in turn would punish the chiefs. Hogan accused the Euchees of being vengeful toward the whites. Although Hogan knew the Euchees' grief had been caused by the whites, he nevertheless considered these Indians dissolute thieves and rascals.[33]

Gayle had questioned whether a proclamation to arrest "all Indians who might be embraced by our vagrant act" would be advisable. Hogan assured him that a proclamation addressed to the chiefs and "properly worded" might "have a good effect on the chiefs." However, he believed "all the proclamations in the world" would not make them remove unless the headmen said go. By this time, Hogan had been in the Creek Nation long enough to have changed his opinion of Opothleyaholo. "Opothleholo, although not the principal chief of the nation, is, in fact and deed, the greatest Indian in the nation ... I consider him the greatest obstacle in the way of emigration. He sends out his talks to the chiefs not to sell their land or go to the Arkansas until he gives the word."

Then they "will go 'en masse' and not an Indian will be left behind." Hogan believed that one company of infantry should be stationed at Fort Mitchell.[34]

The special agent was positive he could start the removal in September. When word reached the whites in June that the annuity would be disbursed, "it flew like wildfire" and whites on the council ground had their "pockets filled with accounts against the Indians."[35]

Opothleyaholo had hired a Kentucky lawyer, a Mr. Chilton, to write to Cass "complaining about Arkansas." Chilton's objective was to "induce" the War Department "to allow Opothleholo and his party a certain sum for emigration." Their plan was to take the money to Texas. Hogan described Chilton as a "petty-fogging lawyer"; "an open-mouthed, abusive opponent of the Administration."[36] But then, when had not a white person who tried to help the Native People been considered dishonest, unprincipled and even traitorous to his country?

When Opothleyaholo realized the move to Texas was not to be, he advised his people to go to Arkansas. In Alex Sommerville's report to Hogan about the decision, he is vague as to which came first, the decision about Arkansas Territory, or the devastating incident that involved Opothleyaholo's son, Richard Johnson.

On the night of July 8, Johnson got into a fight with the brother of David Barnett's wife. Johnson repeatedly stabbed the Indian in the chest causing his death. When the local sheriff came the next day to arrest Johnson, he learned that Opothleyaholo had banished his son. The Tuckabatchees noted the immediate change in Opothleyaholo's demeanor "since his son killed the Indian."[37] And why should he not be changed? The son who had been educated at the white man's Choctaw Academy was then a murderer, lost to his father, perhaps forever. There are no reports showing the aftermath of this murder, or whether Johnson was ever apprehended. However, in 1842 there was a curious notation by Maj. Ethan Hitchcock indicating that Opothleyaholo's son had been involved in the land frauds.[38] Was Johnson the son and is it possible the fight with the Indian was somehow related to the frauds? Johnson would have been 15 or 16 years of age at the time of the murder.

As to Johnson's banishment, it is possible that Opothleyaholo remembered the fate of Corn Tassel, a Cherokee, in 1831. Arrested, tried, and sentenced to death by a Georgia court for killing a fellow Indian, the Cherokees appealed to the U.S. Supreme Court. Before they could review the case, a Georgia sheriff was ordered to execute the sentence. No matter how Opothleyaholo felt about his son, obviously he could not bring himself to turn the lad over to the Alabama authorities.[39] Until now, the Muskogee Nation in Oklahoma has never known what became of Johnson since he attended the Choctaw Academy.[40]

There is another aspect of Opothelyaholo's decision to go to Arkansas

Territory, a knowledge held in high regard by the Creeks. Opothleyaholo would not have told his people to move to an area unless a certain root essential to their ceremonies was found there. He had sent scouts to Arkansas Territory to determine the living conditions and to look for the root. Obviously, he had found the root in Texas, otherwise why would he have remained adamant about buying the land?

Wherever the root is found the people may live. All of the suspicions that Opothelyaholo had been coerced into buying Texas land, and his fear of the McIntoshes in Arkansas Territory, were the ignorance of the white man. Rather he knew indubitably that the root was there. And when his scouts returned with vital proof of its existence, he gave his approval for the move. This root has been located west of Oklahoma, and the present Creek council, remembering Opothleyaholo's advice, knows the nation, if necessary, could move safely to that area.[41]

Cass wrote to Opothleyaholo in August answering a letter sent to Jackson in June about the land frauds, the Texas question and the removal.[42]

The secretary of war discounted the information as to the climate and soil in Arkansas Territory. "There is great abundance of land fit for cultivation and far more than your people will occupy probably for a century." The Creeks would never be dispossessed there by the "white people ... west of Arkansas no government is established." The U.S. had the jurisdiction there and "you shall forever be without the limits of any State or territorial government." Jackson would gladly issue a patent to the Creeks "expressing this pledge, and conveying to you the land as long as you may occupy it." White people, "except those in public employ, will be excluded from that region."

The "great father" could not give them permission to remove to Texas as it was a part of the Republic of Mexico. As to the land frauds, "your great father" had tried to dissuade the Creeks from "securing individual reservations to your people." How much better it would have been at the negotiations of the Removal Treaty had the delegation agreed to cede the whole country. The individual reservations "with the power to sell" had been sacrificed by the lack of the Indians' foresight "and by the anxiety of ours to possess them." The white offenders would be punished. Their great father would protect their rights and do them justice, contingent, however, upon "the treaty itself, and by the laws."[43]

The Creeks, particularly the Tuckabatchees, would not leave without making one last communication to the secretary of war in September. Opothleyaholo and others informed him that "the Tucabachies, with that of the Kialechies, Thloblocko–Clewalas, Autaugas, and Ottosees, who all burn the same fire and talk with the same tongue, forms all the Tuckabaches, and is the great leading town of the nation. They have agreed to emigrate to the country assigned them west of the Mississippi. We have set apart the 15th day of next month for our final departure. We repeat we talk to you with but one tongue. We shall at that time take our last black drink in this nation, rub up our tradition plates, and commence our march."[44]

The Tuckabatchees were adamantly opposed to any contractors being assigned to them for the removal. "We cannot consent to be carried off by strangers, who do it by contract at a price we believe too low for them to do us justice. We have heard of much complaint among those who have gone before us of the hard fare; that the allowance was far short of what they stood in need." They asked to be allowed to appoint some of their own people to organize the removal and suggested that the government agent Hogan be assigned to oversee the appointments. They believed that in doing it themselves there would be "ample justice to the United States as well as the red man."[45]

The Tuckabatchees were concerned about their elderly, the infirm and the small children. It would "require much time and patience on our march." They believed the contractors who would conduct them "at a low price" would force them to keep their time schedule, thus creating "much suffering" along the way.[46]

In November, Hogan met with Opothleyaholo in the leader's home. After amenities were exchanged, Opothleyaholo, regretfully advised him there would be no emigration that fall. The principal chiefs had accepted drafts given to them by the town chiefs for money their people owed and "to be paid out of the next annuity." Now the principal chiefs were responsible for the debts and if they tried to remove, the holders of these drafts, the white men, "would seize on their negroes and horses and ruin them all." Opothelyaholo was sorry to learn "the great father the President" would not pay any more annuities while they were in Alabama.[47]

Hogan rebutted that they had ignored the president's wishes and the war department had "lost confidence in them." The removal superintendent could not promise that President Jackson's orders about the annuity "would be countermanded," however, if they vowed "to go early in the spring" taking all of their people, he would notify the president of their complaints.[48]

All of their stock would have to be collected and sold, also, their land. "No corn should be planted by any Indian in Alabama."[49]

Opothleyaholo, and the others congregated in his home, solemnly pledged that when the time came, "they would all come into camp and be ready to move in a body" when Hogan gave the word.[50]

Hogan did write to Jackson explaining the difficulties and asked for the president's authorization to assure the chiefs that if they complied with their pledge they would receive another annuity in April, 1836.[51]

In December 1835, J.W.A. Sanford and Company was pleased to report that a party of about 500 Creeks had left for the Arkansas. They would join another party west of the Tallapoosa that would make nearly 800 in total. These Creeks would be superintended by Dr. S.M. Ingersoll and Benjamin Marshall, a half-blood Creek. Second Lieutenant Edward Deas was the disbursing agent and a medical man, Dr. Randall, was with the party. "The present party is intended more as an experiment than otherwise and as an inducement to further emigration next spring."[52]

In this letter, the contracting company lodged complaints against Hogan, alleging the superintendent had not assisted their company. The contractor was located in Columbus, Georgia. The fact that they were Georgians would arouse the Creeks' indisposition against them.

Ingersoll had reported from Tuscumbia, Alabama on December 22 that "appalling accounts of the Mississippi swamp" had been received and they had determined to go by boat. Unfortunately, the horse party would have to face the swamp. "It is said that hundreds of people are in the mire without a prospect of getting out ... Their bones may be found one thousand years hence by a different race of men than white men." Ingersoll believed it would be difficult and perhaps impossible to get the Indian horses through the swamp.[53]

By December 28, Deas reported that the emigrating party had reached the mouth of the Tennessee River at Paducah, Kentucky. Their next stop was Memphis, Tennessee where the steamboat Alpha and the two keels were landed on the opposite bank of the river on December 31. This was a preventive measure to keep the Indians from the whiskey shops of the town.

Aboard the Alpha, 26 miles above Little Rock, Deas wrote on January 9, 1836, that they did not stop long at Little Rock, presumably because of the whiskey. But no matter the precautions taken by Deas, enterprising white man managed to sell whiskey for Indian possessions. The Indians were healthy and quite satisfied thus far. They had averaged about 40 miles per day.[54] This first party did not reach Fort Gibson, Indian Territory until February 2, 1836.[55]

Chapter 12

West Toward Indian Territory

A resolution "On Opening a Military Road From Cantonment Des Moines to Fort Gibson" was communicated to the Senate of the 24th Congress on January 21, 1836. With the wholesale removal of the southeastern Indians to west of the Mississippi, legislators finally awakened from their stupor and realized there would be an estimated indigenous and emigrant Indian force of 244,870 people situated between the Rocky Mountains and the Mississippi. The western frontier's protection had to be updated because everyone knew all Indian institutions "have a tendency to war." All future difficulties would have to be "counteracted" by a military force to "overawe" the Indians of the white man's power. Also, Cass pointed out that the government had "promised protection to the emigrated tribes" and those Indians considered that an important guarantee.[1]

The length of the military road would be about 800 miles. At each end of the route and at an intermediate point, dragoons would be stationed while the infantry would occupy other posts. The Indians dreaded the dragoons and their "movement along the road would operate to restrain them."[2]

Thomas F. Hunt, major and acting quartermaster general, informed Cass that a cordon of posts along the road would not only increase the welfare and security of the frontier, but the road itself, outside of its military importance, would enable travel and communication to be established "between the several and various parts of our immense western frontier."[3]

It had been Gen. Edmund P. Gaines who, as commander of the army's Western Department, in 1823 suggested strengthening the Missouri frontier. There had been numerous Indian hostilities in that area. President James Monroe had approved Gaines's measure, but it would not be until 1827 when Fort Leavenworth was established on the western frontier.[4]

As usual the government was slow to act. Then in 1835 the citizens of Clay County, Missouri, applied to the U.S. Senate for the erection of posts and a road. The Missourians saw the necessity of building "a line of military posts" from the upper Mississippi extending to the Red River, all connected by a road. With government policy increasing the number of Indian tribes upon the frontier, the elk and buffalo retreating from their haunts, the Missourians believed that when the wildlife, so necessary for the sustenance of the Indian, had disappeared, then there would be a manifestation of bloody wars between tribes and an "invasion of our peaceful homes and firesides." "That a race of men, whose inveterate habits have withstood the contagious touch of civilization for centuries without any material and radical change in their modes of life, can be suddenly converted into peaceful tillers of the soil, we consider utterly impracticable and visionary in the extreme."[5]

While the senators were busy studying the feasibility of such an undertaking, in Alabama Opothleyaholo had met with Hogan asking for the annuity. Should Hogan be successful, he demanded that the Creeks be in camp for removal before the money was doled out and the leader agreed. Opothleyaholo wanted Hogan to advise the president about "the manner the white people were taking the lands of their dead relatives ..." Hogan was able to report to Gibson that in McHenry's district, which included Tuckabatchee, they had been able to reverse 600 cases of fraud—600 half-sections that had been obtained illegally by white people. With the sale of lands belonging to Opothleyaholo, Mad Blue, Little Doctor and Tuckabatchee Micco for $39,000, Hogan saw this as evidence "of their fixed determination to emigrate this spring."[6]

Later that month Hogan complained to Gibson about the people of Columbus, Georgia asking "for troops to save them from the Creek Indians." Deeming it a farce, Hogan believed the real alarm was the investigation into the frauds. The Columbus speculators were largely responsible for the fraudulent sales and Hogan accused Paddy Carr, the young interpreter who had accompanied Opothleyaholo to Washington in 1826, as being affiliated with them.[7]

There was no peace in the Creek country. Alarmed, Hogan wrote to Gov. C.C. Clay of Alabama describing the swift rise in hostilities commenced by the Georgians against the Creeks. Hogan had met Washington, an elderly Creek, who had witnessed an attack by a Georgia patrol on a small Creek party on the Georgia side of the river. That had necessitated a vengeful act by a larger party of Creeks who crossed into Georgia, killing two men. Georgians had fired on Creeks employed in picking cotton, one unfortunate soul being removed from the field and fired upon by several of the men. Now, Gen. McDougald had ordered out 1,000 men of his division with intentions of crossing into Alabama and starting "a war on this side of the river." Hogan believed Clay should come to the area and his presence might stop the troubles. Before

Clay could respond, however, a meeting was held at Fort Mitchell with McDougald and the chiefs involved. The chiefs agreed to restrain their young men, and should that fail they would surrender them to the authorities.[8]

Hogan had believed that the hostilities attributed to the Creeks was ludicrous. Yet, when he visited three towns considered hostile, "… not an Indian came to the council fire but was armed with his rifle, knife, pouch, horn, etc., ready for battle." And he charged that the emigration contractors were "among the heaviest speculators in Indian reservations."[9]

The Sanford Company countered by accusing Hogan and Dr. McHenry of inciting the Creeks' wrath against the company. By March, the company was proposing that Capt. John Page replace Hogan.[10] The charges and rumors between the removal company and Hogan, reminiscent of the earlier conflict between Troup, Gaines and Andrews, only fueled the discontent that was building in the Creek Nation.

And in the southwest, another disagreement was building toward a showdown. At a deserted mission, once called Mission of San Antonio de Valero, renamed the Alamo, near the village of San Antonio, a small group of volunteers led by Col. William Travis fought to the death against Gen. Santa Anna and 4,000 men of the Mexican Army.

Davy Crockett, who had been against an Indian removal undoubtedly because his enemy Andrew Jackson championed it, and Jim Bowie and Travis, calling themselves "Texans," lost their lives on March 6, the last day of battle. It had been Crockett who, under Gen. Coffee in November 1813, had helped kill 200 Red Sticks. "We shot them like dogs," he had boasted later in his reminiscences.[11]

In the Creek Nation, the Upper Creeks who were in favor of removal were now considered friendly and the Lower Creeks under Eneah Micco who resisted removal were the "hostiles." A complete reversal of the situation existing in the 1820s, yet so transparent; if the Indian was complying with the government he was "friendly." Hogan, in a lengthy letter to Cass in March, delineated the conditions, past and present, in the nation. He requested that Page be ordered to accompany him to every town for investigation purposes and to become acquainted with the chiefs. Page needed to hear from the Creeks in council the many reasons for their bitterness toward the whites. As an example, Hogan related a recent visit to a Lower Creek town.

An old chief who had had his land stolen from him said: "He would stay and die here, and the whites might have his skull for a water cup; they wanted everything, and when he was dead, they might have his skull, too." The old man apparently had been referring to whites who had dug up Indian skulls a few months earlier and carried them out of the nation. Typically, there had been nothing done to alleviate the Creeks' anger.[12]

Sanford and Hogan were requested by Cass to discharge their "respective duties and disregard all private feelings."[13] But Sanford could not quit his complaints against Hogan and the "worse then useless investigations" that was stalling the removal.[14]

In April, Page was appointed as disbursing agent and was directed to cooperate with Hogan. By early May, Page was reporting that the Lower Creeks were raiding plantations. "The war whoop has been sounded among them."[15]

Page had been invited to Tuckabatchee. Opothleyaholo complained that "the white people have ploughed and planted around our houses; none of my people have planted anything; you told us not to plant." Hogan had promised the investigations would stop shortly but now he was gone to Mobile. Opothleyaholo said: "His hand was hardly cold from the greeting of one agent before another was presented to him." He was "tired of hearing the name of investigation." The leader wanted to know when the business would be closed. Page could not give him an answer. Opothleyaholo asked for rations for his people. "I am endeavoring to keep my people together as much as posssible," he said. "I talk to them but they have nothing to eat and what can I do? They must eat; they cannot live on air." The contractors had been feeding some of the poor, but unless they enrolled in the camps that generosity would cease.

Opothelyaholo unveiled a plan adopted by the Upper Creeks in regard to the disputed lands. "A company of gentleman have seen nearly all the companies who purchased our lands and they have agreed to raise a sum of money equivalent to the value of the lands we claim to have been defrauded of." All of the transactions would be overseen by two principal chiefs of each town and a U.S. agent. As the chiefs knew well the frauds and the injured persons, the difficulties could be settled and the government relieved of all further trouble with the Creeks. Page felt strongly that Opothleyaholo feared his people, driven to desperation by lack of food, would "scatter and commit depredations." Already about 2,000 of them had gone to the Cherokee Nation hoping to be fed.[16]

Soon after his meeting with Opothleyaholo, Page was dismayed to learn that the Euchee bridge and the buildings "only two miles" from Fort Mitchell had been burned. He had sent word for the friendly Indians to come to the agency where he intended to feed them. He hoped the government would sanction this. "It is impossible to see them in a starving condition."[17]

Page had believed the Lower Creeks were threatening only the area around the agency, but he soon learned that the hostilities were more widespread. About 65 miles from the agency, the Creeks had killed a white family, including seven children, and had decapitated them. One child had been thrown into the yard where the hogs had eaten on it. Another bridge on the Euchee River on the first route to Montgomery had been burned; a tavern and plantation houses had also been burned and corn and provisions stolen. A steamboat above the agency had been attacked, killing four of the crew. At Roanoke, Georgia, about 20 miles from the agency, another steamboat was taken and the little town torched. Stagecoaches were stopped and some of the drivers were killed.[18]

Page conceded that the hostiles were in possession of the country surrounding the agency. They had emptied corn cribs, confiscated all the meat, stock, clothing and even some money. Hostile patrols were watching all movements and Page wished for two or three military companies as the 35 men sent from Augusta "were hardly enough to protect ourselves inside the pickets." Should the hostiles choose to attack Fort Mitchell with a large force, "in five days we should have to open our gates for water as it is all outside, about twenty yards from the pickets." One major had decided to dig a well inside the pickets.[19]

The ferry to Columbus was being watched and Page feared all communication would be cut off.[20]

All emigration proceedings were suspended because of the hostilities. Sanford notified Gibson that two camps in the Tallapoosa and Coosa districts had been opened with nearly 2,000 ready to march when they received word from Opothleyaholo "telling the Indians not to move until he could go with them." Despite all efforts to the contrary, "go they would not, without this chief."[21]

"Opothelholo has been detained by a bail writ for a debt for which he is as much responsible as he is for the national debt of Great Britain," Sanford wrote. He accused Abbott, government certifying agent and prosecuting attorney in the case, as "the pliant tool of Col. Hogan." Abbott knew of "the great influence which this chief possesses over the action of the whole nation..." He also knew that in "detaining" Opothleyaholo the removal of the Upper Creeks would be stopped.[22]

Columbus was under military law "expecting an attack every night."[23]

Sanford appealed to Gibson for help in replacing Hogan, openly charging the man with trying to bribe the contractors.

The politicians and the military soon labeled the disruption in the nation as another "Creek War." With the Seminoles warring in Florida, and the Upper Creeks asking for their annuities in advance, the government and President Jackson saw how they could use the present situation to the advantage of the United States.

The first indication of a scheme afoot came in a letter to Hogan from Gibson. A directive from Cass had ordered Gibson to inform Hogan that due to the hostilities, the Creek removal would be a military operation. Gen. Thomas Jesup would be in command and Hogan's duties as superintendent of the removal would cease.[24]

President Jackson had used the hostilities as a pretext in order to satisfy the contractor's demand that Hogan should be eliminated from the affair. The dissimilarities between Jackson and John Quincy Adams are patent. Adams had refused to suspend Agent Crowell on the word of Chilly McIntosh. Rather he had believed justice could be better served by investigating the allegations. Yet, Jackson had believed the contractor and without any forewarning, Hogan was dismissed. The belief that while he was in office it was Jackson's law and not U.S. law that prevailed, can be substantiated by the decisions made to use the existing tragic conditions in the Creek Nation to the government's gain.

After Opothleyaholo was released from jail, and before Jesup's arrival, he had taken "a decisive stand against the war, as also his people." The leader had killed one chief and put 13 more in irons "for showing a hostile disposition." His actions had effectually checked the movement of Indians wanting to join the hostile party.[25]

And on May 30, Gov. Clay, who had come to the nation, had a lengthy interview with Opothleyaholo. The leader explained that the Creeks had been given five years from the 1832 Removal Treaty to decide whether they would stay in Alabama or move west. But "the whites had come in great numbers among them, and henceforward there had been much trouble and confusion."[26]

When Opothleyaholo had returned from Texas he discovered that the whites were continuing to swindle his people out of their reservations. Immediately he contacted Dr. McHenry, certifying agent, "to forebear from certifying contracts for the sale of them, and he had discovered that it was not an uncommon thing for one Indian to be persuaded to assume the name of and personate another, and sometimes to sell and stand up to be certified to several tracts of land, not one of which he was in reality the owner." The Creek leader had appealed to Jackson for an investigation into the situation and requested "the president not to permit of certifying to contracts, except in the presence of discreet chiefs."[27]

A meeting had been called to be held at Dr. McHenry's about the frauds. Land speculators had not been stopped and had counseled various Indians "if the chiefs attempt to restrain or interfere with you, kill them." They sold pistols, powder, knives and lead to them. Tuskinah, Big Warrior's heir, was prompted at this meeting to make the Creeks "believe that those among them who went before the agent to make complaint about the fraudulent sale of their lands, could be the very persons who would be taken and sent immediately off to Arkansas."[28]

Opothleyaholo had been ill and unable to attend the meeting but he had "sent word that the chiefs, generally, and for the most part were apprised of the affairs of their people and therefore knowing who among them had actually sold and who not, could assist in making a proper report of them."[29]

Opothleyaholo had warned Tuskinah about "the evil course he was pursuing." He knew that the Tuckabatchee chief "was the dupe of others and if he persisted in such course it must necessarily end in consequences that would be ruinous, and that all would be afflicted with sorrow for."[30]

There had been a paper circulated among the people. The leader was certain "it could not have been the work of Indians, for they cannot read and write ... white people must have been at the bottom of it." And he was correct. A footnote to the interview explained that the paper had been written by Sir George Cockburn, commander of the English fleet during the War of 1812. An Englishman, who was a silversmith in Columbus, had recently taken the paper and had ridden among the Indians. He read and explained that it was "highly inflammatory." The man claimed to have been born in London, the natural son of the Creek prophet, Francis who had visited England. When Francis returned home, he was hanged by Jackson for his participation as a Red Stick during the Creek War.[31] Perhaps this paper played a small part in inciting the Creeks, but pertinent documents indicate it was not the primary reason.

Opothleyaholo called Clay's attention to the claims made against the people for debts not made. And he was deeply disturbed about the "ardent spirits" that were easily obtained by his people. He did not want the whiskey dealers coming into their removal camps. "Such floods of liquor amongst them" had caused "their debasement and misery."[32]

They had been "gathering up their cattle" in the woods to sell them before their departure when news of the hostilities reached them. Immediately they had quit "hunting their cattle and hastened to the relief of their white friends." They had not ceased until the depredators either were made prisoners of the whites or had been "expelled [from] the neighborhood through fear." Clay asked him if he would be willing to continue his aid to Maj. Gen. Patterson who was present at the interview. Opothleyaholo charged Eneah Micco and Tuskinah as being responsible for the "disseminating of the red people." The authorities should demand that these two men deliver the murderers and other depradators. Should they refuse, if "the general called upon him" although their horses were much fatigued by their recent service, still they would "cheerfully turn out to his assistance" in capturing them.[33]

In June 1836, an act by Congress provided for the extension of Missouri's western boundary to the Missouri River. The Sac and Fox Indians had to be treated with in order to gain the land they had just acquired forever. And, as the area was free due to the Missouri Compromise of 1820, it would have to become slave again. Later, in March 1837, President Martin Van Buren proclaimed the Indian title to the lands was extinguished, opening it for settlement.[34] Six counties were organized in northwestern Missouri out of the "Platte Purchase." This act could never have been accomplished without the active support of the Northern politicians at a time when the American Anti–Slavery Society was using the mails to send propaganda throughout the United States. In his 1835 annual message to Congress, President Jackson had recommended a law that would ban sending such publications through the mail.

By 1836, the abolitionists were swamping Congress with petitions pressing for the abolition of slavery.[35] Yet, Congress allowed Missouri, one of the largest states in the Union, to become even larger and a slave-holding state as well.

Arkansas was admitted as the twenty-fifth state with slavery legalized. Sam Houston, Jackson's protege, became president of the Republic of Texas. The Upper Creeks were removed from Alabama, in this last year of Jackson's second presidential term, but they were called to serve again.

On June 9, General Thomas Jesup assumed command of the frontier. On the 17th, Opothleyaholo, at the head of 1,150 warriors, joined him. By the 27th, Jesup reported to secretary of war Lewis Cass that with the capture of hundreds of hostiles, he considered "the war at an end."[36]

By July, the hostiles led by Eneah Micco and Eneah Emarthla, an 80-year-old Red Stick, had been arrested, chained together, and with their women and children were deported to the west—destitute, naked, adrift in a strange land. Eneah Micco died in 1837 near Fort Gibson.[37]

However, the government was not through with the Creeks. Jesup asked them to send warriors to Florida to fight the Seminoles. Opothleyaholo told Jesup his people were ready to leave and they could not send any men to Florida. The general would not be swayed, however, and urged them to go, promising payment for their time. Jim Boy, who had recently served under Jesup, demanded "a paper" stating he would be paid the promised $2,000 for his services in command of the warriors. He explained he had a large family to support and "there would be nobody to take care of my children." Jesup resented the Creek's insinuation about the paper and declared "he was a United States officer and did not talk with a forked tongue." Jim Boy would receive the money, Jesup assured him, but there would be no signed paper. The Creek received only half of what Jesup had promised.[38]

The general brought up the subject of the Creeks' debt to Opothleyaholo. Should they know anyone who owed the white people, they "must send them to Florida and the government would pay their debts."[39]

With Creek men gone to Florida, the removal of the Upper Creeks had ceased. It would not be until August 6 that Page could report he had turned over to the Alabama Emigrating Company, Opothleyaholo's party of 2,700 Indians who would be in the charge of Lt. M.W. Batman.[40] Yet, Jesup reported on September 5 that Opothleyaholo had departed for the west with 2,300 of his people.[41]

Opothleyaholo and his people left behind, for the wealthy land grabbers, acres and acres of cleared rich, black soil well suited for the short-fibered cotton that, with the aid of the cotton gin, would increase the South's production, economy and most of all, power. A power that had to be maintained in the political echelon of the federal government.

The painful story of this mass exodus may only be found in the emigration files of the Office of Indian Affairs, American State Papers, the Library of Congress and the Muskogee Nation.

The Indian van had carried the five sacred brass plates which had been removed from under the council house in their beloved "Tuckabatchy" square.[42] The brass plates are extant.[43] Uprooted from their homes, driven like cattle into the pens of a concentration camp before departure, they were allowed but few possessions. Before reaching Tuscaloosa, "the white people levied upon our negroes upon those old accounts" which Opothleyaholo later declared the sheriffs had been paid $8,500 by them to free the negroes.[44]

Menawa had not wanted to leave his home, even consenting to become an Alabama citizen. He implored the officials to let him stay, and considering his service in the recent "Creek War," it was decided to exclude him from the emigrating party. But something went awry. And despite the declaration of his intent to become a citizen, he was ordered to emigrate. The Great Warrior, in his heart, had known he would never see his homeland again. All he wanted in the future was peace, and never to see a white man in his new country.[45]

Opothleyaholo had recounted how the whites had followed them, confiscating "a great many of our ponies." Whether the supposed debts were legitimate or not, the Americans seemed determined to rid the Creeks of their property. There had been whiskey available to those who had money or anything of value. Batman seemed helpless to overcome these problems, and the worst one, inadequate provisions. Whenever possible, the starving people would take hogs, chickens, and other edibles from the white man's land they were passing through. There had been great consternation that this was being done to the settlers.[46] Babies and small children were dragged from the line of march by those in authority and killed, their skulls crushed against tree trunks.[47] Obviously, this was done in order to eliminate the Creeks' thievery of the whites, and to save on provisions.

At Memphis, Tennessee, the mighty Mississippi had to be crossed. Some of the Creeks were put on keelboats, others on a steamboat, but when the supply was depleted, the rest would have to face the powerful river on foot. The order all the way from Alabama had called for an expedited arrival. But now, Opothleyaholo, clutching his staff, stood still on the bank and would not allow the people to be pushed into the water. The leader prayed to the Great Spirit for help. Facing the swirling waters, Opothleyaholo put his confidence in his God. The people were forced to swim across.[48]

On their last overland trek through Arkansas, the weather had turned bad, with rain nearly every day and the roads, which were rough in dry weather, became nearly impassable.

Arkansas newspapers reported the unforgettable sight of thousands of bedraggled Creeks, some naked, their unshod feet cut and bleeding, as the vast line extended from Little Rock to Fort Gibson in Indian Territory. Many

Arkansasans had been touched by the piteous cries of the women and the hungry cries of the children who, in their infantile wisdom, could not understand what was happening to them.[49]

The Creeks slogged through the muddied ruts of the roads, or over sleet-hardened ground. They had had to leave their dead without ceremony as they were ordered to keep going. Hurriedly, they had covered the bodies with a quilt or sheet, knowing the carcasses would be devoured by the packs of wolves which, like the greedy whites, followed them incessantly. Today, at a traditional Muskogee funeral, a quilt is placed over the casket, or folded at the foot of the bier in memory of those who had perished along the way. Inside the casket is the person's favorite food. It will be fed to the spirits which, the Muskogee's believe, dwell above earth and beneath Heaven.[50]

The Creeks had left a temperate climate, braved cold rain, sleet and snow and arrived at Fort Gibson in December. Their baggage had become separated from them, and therefore, they were inadequately clothed for the plains winter. There were no rifles and blankets waiting for them as the government had promised. Hungry and homeless, it would not be until the spring of 1837 that they would be able to begin their lives in the new land. That same year, Michigan was admitted as the 26th state, a free-soil state, balancing the admission of Arkansas.

In 1838, Secretary of War H.R. Poinsett was officially advised that the total of Creek Indians that had emigrated was 14,609, of which 2,495 were considered hostile. There was nothing in the report to indicate Creek losses. Of the 77 towns that had emigrated, only 44 towns were left when the Creeks reached Fort Gibson[51]

The cognomen, "The Trail of Tears," originated with the Cherokees when they were forcibly removed from their lands in 1838. Under the command of Gen. Winfield Scott, soldiers with bayoneted guns hunted them down, and any sign of resistance meant death. The Cherokees called their trek to the west Nuna-da-ut-sun'y, "The Trail Where They Cried," which became "The Trail of Tears." Today,when one hears about that trail it automatically brings to mind the Cherokees. Yet, the title, Cherokee in origin, sufficiently described all of the Five Civilized Tribes forced removal to the west.

Chapter 13

Resettlement and Recovery

The Creeks received fish hooks, little white pipes and hobbles for horses in 1840 in payment for property lost during the removal. Money was what they had expected to receive according to the Treaty of 1838. They wanted their money in silver instead of paper which depreciated in value and they in turn lost on it.[1]

In November 1838, Creek chiefs had met with Capt. William Armstrong, acting superintendent of the Western Territory, and Brevet Brig. Gen. Matthew Arbuckle, U.S. commissioners at Fort Gibson. This meeting was called in order to adjust the Creek claims "for property and improvements abandoned or lost, in consequence of their emigration west of the Mississippi." First, the Creeks had to relinquish all claims for those items. Their payment for this property was $50,000 in stock animals as soon as practicable after the ratification of the treaty." Also, the Creek Nation was to have invested by the United States $350,000 at five percent interest. "The interest for the first year to be paid in money, the interest thereafter to be paid in money, stock animals, blankets, domestics or such articles." The president was empowered to direct the distribution.[2]

The Creeks had not yet recovered from the horrendous removal in 1836 and they needed money for provisions and clothing. Trying to understand the reasoning behind the articles that were sent in 1840 is impossible. The fish hooks were obviously for fishing. This exemplifies the disdain or ignorance of how the Creeks fished. They used a particular root, mashed, which then was put into the water. As it bubbled, it attracted the fish, stunning it, sending it to the top of the water, where it could be retrieved by the Indians. The little white pipes and hobbles for the horses are ludicrous. How were these items to be used to sustain the Creeks through the winter?

Opothleyaholo had become concerned about the time of year when they received their annuities. It would be the wintertime when travel was difficult. They had complained about it, but thus far nothing had been changed. The annuities were sent to New Orleans in the summertime, there to be picked up by the superintendent of the Southern Superintendency assigned to the Creeks and others in Indian Territory. However, that was the time in the South for the yellow fever; no sensible person would go there for the sake of the Indians. It did not matter that the Creeks had asked for the payment in September when they could prepare for the cold weather. Rather, they were having to travel to the agency in harsh winter weather.[3]

The Creeks had been promised a school in their country, but that promise had not been honored. They asked for the $3,000, a provision of the 1832 Treaty, to be sent to them so they might have a school, schoolmaster and even a doctor in the nation. They wanted a school in their own country, not in Kentucky.[4]

Another problem troubling the Creeks were white men who were in their nation without their consent. Opothleyaholo remembered that they had been assured there would be no white men in their country except those in authority.[5]

Wandering hostile tribes were stealing Creek horses and other property. Usually it was the Osages, who were as impoverished as ever.[6] Their annuities of cattle to raise livestock were used to feed the tribe instead. Their thievery was not because of any honor that might be attached to the feat, but, they had seen their lands, a part of Indian Territory, reduced, and the sale bringing in hardly any money or provisions for them. The Osage were noted as thieves, and their custom before robbing white settlers who were interlopers on their land, was to blacken their faces and cry after entering the house. They felt sorry for the people they were going to rob.[7]

In January 1839 the Osage had signed a treaty which removed them from Indian Territory to their reduced lands in Kansas. However, this had not stopped their bedevilment of the immigrant tribes.[8]

Soon after their arrival in the late 1820s, the McIntosh faction had established communities along the lower Verdigris River valley and west along the Arkansas River.

Opothleyaholo and his party had distanced themselves from the Lower Creeks. The Canadian and Little Rivers became their domain.[9]

North Fork Town, situated near the north fork of the Canadian, became an active settlement in trading. The Great Osage Trail, coming from the north, junctioned with the east-west California Road at North Fork Town. The Osage Trail became known as the Texas Road due to its use by pioneers heading for the new area called Texas.

There were many stores opened for trade at North Fork Town. Here, in this fertile region, trade flourished with the outside world. For a time, Opothleyaholo was a partner with J.R. Taylor who was a trader, operating a small store. Taylor was a New Yorker and had spent two years at West Point. He had married a Creek woman. It was at this time that Opothleyaholo became well-known as "Old Gouge."[10]

Opothleyaholo's people had selected one of the best areas in the territory for raising livestock. Soon, herds were growing; they raised sheep, hogs and domestic fowls. They cleared parts of the rugged land, cultivating the soil, and planted fields of corn, oats, tobacco, cotton and rice. There were gardens of assorted vegetables and fruit orchards. And they built their modest houses. By the year 1846, the were exporting corn, which was eventually sent to foreign countries. People from the midwestern states traveled to their nation to purchase hogs and horses.[11]

The Creeks became attached to the land, and truly felt it was home. They had faith that finally all they saw and roamed over was theirs forever. Yet, they were plagued by the trespassing white man. At a council held at North Fork Town, Opothleyaholo, his powerful form draped by a blanket, his head beturbaned with a brightly colored shawl, and wearing deerskin leggings, spoke about the age-old problem.

He presented an analogy between the continuous obsession of the white man to take the Indians' land and a beautiful island in the Chattahoochee River which floods had reduced in size through the years.

"My brothers, we Indians are like that island in the middle of the river. The white man comes upon us like a flood. The Great Spirit knows, as you know, that I would stay that flood, which comes thus to wear us away, if I could."

He likened the long-rooted grass that could have saved the island's erosion to that of education. He believed education was the key to survival among the whites. Although he was adamant about not wearing white man's pants, condescending only to the wearing of a frock coat, he perceived that if the Creeks were to survive, the children had to be educated. "Then they may be planted and deeply rooted about us and our people may stand unmoved in the flood of the white man."[12]

In 1842, two frontier posts were established, and both would have great significance for the Five Civilized Tribes in the years ahead.

Fort Scott in Indian country, west of the Missouri state line and midway between Fort Leavenworth and Fort Gibson, was built near the military road that paralleled Missouri from the north to the south. Fort Washita, on the Washita River, was established as protection for the Chickasaws and Choctaws, claiming their treaty right. The war-like Comanches, Kiowas and other plains tribes, had been threatening these nations.

It would be Fort Scott, initially garrisoned by two companies of the First Dragoons, that would have a dramatic role in the lives of the Indians, the

Mexican War, border warfare days in Kansas Territory, and the subsequent Civil War. Fort Scott became a trading center for the Osage Indians. Actually, the fort was situated on ancestral Osage lands which, by treaty, had been ceded to the United States, then to the New York Indians. The federal government had no legal right to be there.

The dragoons, who erected log houses to the northeast of the later fort site, had come from abandoned Fort Wayne in Arkansas. They had been romanticized as fearless fighting men, either on foot or horseback. Heavily armed, their primary purpose was to maintain peace between the relocated Southern tribes, the aggressive Plains tribes, and the whites, inexorably moving toward the west. The name dragoon came from the French word "dragon" for the soldier's short musket. Indeed, in earlier times these soldiers had been called "the dragons of war."[13]

Although Gen. Gaines had recommended certain forts to be established on the frontier, this particular fort, situated on a bluff amidst rolling hills and prairies and near the site Gaines had selected, would be named for Winfield Scott. Gaines and Scott had alternated the command of the Eastern and Western Departments of the U.S. Army during the years 1821–1831. By 1842, however, they were nearer enemies than friends.

Fort Washita (Wah-shuh-tah) had been established by Col. Zachary Taylor. He was a veteran of the War of 1812 and had earned the nickname "Old Rough and Ready" as a colonel during the Seminole War of 1835–42.[14]

Although both of these forts were primarily for protection, they would become posts, particularly Fort Washita, in training and experience for such later officers as Stephen W. Kearny, John B. Hood, Jefferson Davis, George McClellan, Robert E. Lee and Ulysses S. Grant.[15]

Fort Washita not only helped safeguard the Chickasaws and Choctaws, it provided an opportunity for the soldiers to purchase quantities of corn, meat, butter and eggs from the Indian farmers.

James K. Polk of Tennessee, who championed the annexation of Texas, in 1845 became the 11th president of the United States. He had supported Jackson for president and during Jackson's second term he was Speaker of the House of Representatives. The two men became friends, so much so that Polk earned the sobriquet "young Hickory." Texas and its proposed annexation had propelled Polk, a slaveholder, into office defeating Henry Clay. Clay had believed "Annexation and war with Mexico are identical."[16] The North as well as the South had succeeded in electing Polk to office. However, the resolution for Texas annexation had been signed by President Tyler, Polk's predecessor, March 1, 1845. Then it had been up to Polk to work for its fruition.

France and England had long been associated with Texas. When annexation seemed imminent, England had been prepared to fight, if necessary, to keep the Southwest out of U.S. hands. The European and other foreign powers knew that in peacetime, the U.S. standing army consisted of 10,000 men. They believed they could overwhelm the United States with superior forces. They had not considered the volunteers of the citizenry.

The Democratic National Convention, which had nominated Polk, had resolved in their convention "that the reoccupation of Oregon and the reannexation of Texas at the earliest practicable period, are great American measures."[17]

Sen. Thomas Hart Benton, in a Senate speech, had proposed the resolution, "That the incorporation of the left bank of the Rio De Norte (Rio Grande) into the American Union, by virtue of a treaty with Texas, comprehending, as the said incorporation would do, a party of the Mexican departments of New Mexico, Chihuahua, Coahuilo and Tamaulipas, would be an act of direct aggression on Mexico; for all the consequences of which the United States would stand responsible."[18]

Despite Clay and Benton's apprehensions, when Polk, a devotee of the slave power, took office, the Texas annexation became a certainty. And the erroneous claim on the part of the United States to the Rio Grande was guaranteed to bring about a war with Mexico. But the true winners would be the slaveholders, one southern gentleman declaring, "It (Texas) will give a Gibraltar to the South."[19]

The legislatures of Mississippi and Alabama had been in favor of annexation. A Mississippi legislature report stated "Your committee are fully persuaded that this protection to her best interests will be afforded by the Annexation of Texas; an equipoise of influence in the halls of Congress will be secured, which will furnish us a permanent guarantee of protection."[20]

Secretary of the Navy, Thomas W. Gilmer, of the Tyler administration, had favored annexation. "The institutions of Texas, and her relations with other governments, are yet in that condition which inclines her people (who are our own countrymen) to unite their destiny with ours. This must be done soon, or not at all. There are numerous tribes of Indians along both frontiers, which can easily become the cause or the instrument of border wars."[21]

Polk had four goals for his administration: reduce the tariff, re-establish an independent treasury, settle the Oregon boundary dispute with Great Britain, and acquire California.

It had been Andrew Jackson's wish to buy California so that the North and the East would not oppose the annexation of Texas. For quite some time the fishing industries on the east coast had wanted a harbor on the Pacific Ocean. Texas claimed that the annexation of California would provide such a base.[22]

Although Jackson no longer held public office, he held sway over many political issues. His death on June 8, 1845, would not diminish his influence over future administrations.

Yet, Mexico had seemed to watch all the political wrangling in Congress about annexation without alarm. United States commerce still was allowed in Mexican ports. All of this unconcern apparently was vexing to the administration. Polk had tried to buy California, but the offer was rejected. Mexico was in a dispute with the U.S. about the boundary of Texas. As things stood, the Nueces River was considered the southern boundary of Texas.

This dispute had its beginning in 1819 at the time of a treaty with Spain for the Florida cession. A settlement for the western boundary of Louisiana had been agreed on to be the Rio Grande. A mix-up occurred between Washington and the U.S. Minister to the Court of Madrid. A new treaty was negotiated by John Quincy Adams, secretary of state, and Luis de Onis, Spanish minister, whereby Spain ceded Florida and its claim to the Oregon country. What would become an important reason for a war with Mexico was the establishment of the Sabine River as the new boundary. France had agreed to the right of the U.S. to the Rio Grande, as did Spain. And it was Andrew Jackson who discovered that Washington had withheld the true boundary, thus depriving the U.S. of the large area lying between the two rivers.[23]

Henry Clay was of a different opinion. He had always believed that Texas was included in the Louisiana Purchase and had opposed the 1819 treaty. In a letter to the *National Intelligencer* with a dateline Raleigh, North Carolina, April 17, 1844, Clay had defined his position. "It is therefore perfectly idle and ridiculous, if not dishonorable, to talk of resuming our title to Texas, as if we had never parted with it. We can no more do that than Spain can resume Florida, France Louisiana, or Great Britain the thirteen colonies now comprising a part of the United States."[24]

In regard to the extension of slavery, Clay wrote: "I conceive that no motive for the acquisition of foreign territory could be more unfortunate, or pregnant with more fatal consequences, than that of obtaining it for the purpose of strengthening one part against another part of the common confederacy. Such a principle, put into practical operation, would menace the existence, if it did not certainly sow the seeds of a dissolution of the Union."[25]

Polk and his cabinet, eager to bring about an end to the boundary dispute with Mexico, ordered the Army of the Southwest Department to Texas.

Correspondence was begun between Secretary of War Marcy and Gen. Zachary Taylor, then stationed at New Orleans, in which it was hoped that the general and his army would occupy the east bank of the Rio Grande in Mexican territory. This, of course, was done subtly, but Taylor refused to take such risky action without explicit instructions. Finally, in July 1845, he was directed to take position in defense of the new acquisition "to the extent that it had been occupied by the people of Texas." His army landed early in August at Corpus Christi near the mouth of the Nueces River where it remained. Washington was not satisfied, however. They hinted that they expected him to advance to the Rio Grande, but "Old Rough and Ready" was too shrewd not to realize that if he did go to Mexican territory, Washington could maintain that he had acted without its authority. Accordingly, should the Mexicans attack, the blame would be placed on Taylor.[26]

Gen. Gaines, who was on the inactive list in New Orleans and superseded by Winfield Scott, was more vociferous when he wanted to place 50 battalions on the Rio Grande. He was ignored.

The winter spent in occupying the Nueces area passed without incident and Taylor continued to disregard any hints from Washington about the Rio Grande.

Gaines continued to request that the war department authorize him to put 50 battalions on the Rio Grande. Sounding like the 20th Century Gen. George S. Patton, this 19th Century general was confident he could end the war in six months. But as yet there was no war to end. Gaines biggest faux pas was to attack Winfield Scott and accuse him of "sacrificing the interests and honor of the service at the shrine of that morbid thirst for the presidency."[27]

Texas was admitted to the Union as a slave state on December 29, 1845, the 28th star in the flag. In March 1846, Polk issued the order for Taylor to advance across more than 100 miles of desert to the Rio Grande.[28]

Early in May 1846, after repeated requests by the Mexican government for Taylor to retreat to the Nueces, the Mexican army of 6,000 men crossed the river, and attacked Taylor's 2,300 men at Palo Alto on the eighth. Finally, what the administration had hoped for had started. On May 11, Polk, in a special message to Congress, said that the Mexicans "at last invaded our territory and shed the blood of our fellow-citizens on our own soil." On May 13, Congress declared that a state of war existed between the Republic of Mexico and the United States and asked for 50,000 volunteers and an appropriation of $10 million to sustain the war machine.[29]

Gen. Gaines was relieved of his command after forming volunteers to march to the Rio Grande. Ordered to Washington by President Polk, he was found guilty of doing what the administration had intended Taylor to do. His verbal attack on Scott obviously strengthened the case against him. He was not punished, however. Gaines resumed command of the Western Department. He died June 6, 1849 in New Orleans. It is remarkable that Congress would ask for 50,000 volunteers, the same amount that Gaines had requested prematurely.[30]

Gen. Taylor had dominated the Mexican War. Winning battles made him popular with Americans. It was drawing near to the presidential election of 1848 when the Whigs were looking for a candidate. Taylor became the Whig candidate on the fourth ballot. Polk, a Democrat, viewed this with alarm. He transferred the main theatre of war to Winfield Scott, usurping Taylor's power and increasing Scott's prestige for the election.[31]

Taylor, noted for his sloppy appearance, rugged manner and combativeness, had to surrender most of his army to Scott who intended to land at Vera Cruz. Taylor, in a defiant mood, disregarded Polk's orders to let Scott take the upperhand, and with his much reduced army defeated Santa Anna at Buena Vista on February 22, 1847. Scott, meanwhile, had marched through Mexico City, establishing military rule, and accepted the surrender of the Mexican government on September 14, 1847. With the Treaty of Guadulupe Hidalogo ratified March 10, 1848, the Mexican War ended.[32]

With the capture of Mexico City Col. James H. Lane, a lawyer from Indiana, became provost marshal of the American forces. This would be the start of Lane's political career. He would go on to become the leading force in Kansas Territory politics and be with Opothleyaholo at the start of the Civil War.[33]

President Polk tried to justify ordering Taylor to Corpus Christi in July 1845 by addressing the issue in his second annual message to Congress, December 1846.

"That the Congress of the United States understood the State of Texas which they admitted into the Union to extend beyond the Nueces is apparent from the fact that on the 31st of December 1845 only two days after the act of admission, they passed a law 'to establish a collection district in the State of Texas' by which they created a port of delivery at Corpus Christi, situated west of the Nueces and being the same point at which the Texas custom-house under the laws of that Republic had been located." A surveyor had been appointed by the President to collect the revenue "by and with the advice and consent of the Senate." The surveyor "has been ever since in the performance of his duties. All these acts of the Republic of Texas and our Congress preceded the orders for the advance of our army to the east bank of the Rio Grande."

Polk admitted Taylor's army was ordered to Texas and he stated that "Corpus Christi was the position selected by Taylor." Yet, this was accomplished four months before Texas was admitted to the Union.[34]

Scott, who had triumphed in the war, would lose in his bid for the presidency. Taylor, who was designated the "hero of Buena Vista," became the 12th president. Polk made his place in history by being the president who added approximately one million miles to the United States. The newly acquired territory included Texas, California, present day Arizona, Colorado, Nevada, New Mexico, Wyoming, Utah and a corner of later southwest Kansas. In this, Polk was second to Thomas Jefferson who, through the Louisiana Purchase, had acquired the most square miles for the United States.

On December 28, 1846, Iowa, north of Missouri became a free state; Wisconsin, a free, 30th state, on May 29, 1848. Gold was discovered in California August 19, 1848, and California was admitted as the 31st state on September 9, 1850. Like Iowa and Wisconsin, it, too, entered the Union as a free state.

At this time the balance of power had shifted to free soil. Congressional debates ensued in regard to all of the new territory that had come into the United States. "Manifest Destiny," coined by an editor in 1845, became a slogan for those who believed it was their duty to provide space for America's growing population and extend it to the Pacific Ocean.

But what of the Indians whose last domain lay in between?

Chapter 14

Kansas Territory's Border War

Jefferson Davis was a senator from Mississippi and the son-in-law of President Taylor when Henry Clay was composing the Compromise of 1850. Davis believed that slavery was inevitable in the new territories. "I hereby assert, that never will I take less than the Missouri Compromise line extending to the Pacific Ocean, with the specific recognition of the right to hold Slaves in the territory below the line."[1]

Clay's compromise allowed California to be a free state, since servitude, termed peonism, was already established there. New Mexico and Utah were to be organized as territories with or without slavery, as their constitution might provide when appointment for statehood was made. And statehood of New Mexico was imperative. It was an area known as fertile land with rich mines of precious metals. And it linked the U.S. possessions in Texas with those on the Pacific coast. A strict fugitive slave law was enacted, which by itself would help to destroy the Whigs, Taylor's party.

Clay's compromise, fortuitous for the Americans, was the warning bell for the Indians in the "Platte Country." After the 1836 annexation to Missouri, the trimmed area of Platte Country extended from Texas and the Missouri River to the summit of the Rocky Mountains and to the borders of British America. As early as 1844, William Wilkins, secretary of war under President Tyler, had proposed a new territory "Nebraska" be organized in the country between the states of Missouri and later Iowa, and the crest of the Rocky Mountains. Stephen A. Douglas, a member of the House Committee on Territories, introduced a bill in December 1844 to establish the territory of Nebraska. It was tabled, as were future ones, until it became a necessity to establish communications with the west coast by rail.[2] Men had flocked to California in the quest for gold. The government and the entrepreneurs knew that the only feasible way of conquering that vast area between the frontier and the coast would be the extension of the railroads across the Great American Desert and the formidable mountains.

President Franklin Pierce foresaw the need for railroad expansion. He believed that ... "the heavy expense, the great delay and at times, fatality, attending the travel by either of the Isthmus routes have demonstrated the advantage which would result from interterritorial communication by such safe and rapid means as a railroad would supply."[3]

The South had a different route picked for the first transcontinental railroad. It would follow the border line of the U.S. and Mexico. But here was another dispute as to the true boundary between El Paso and San Diego.

During the Mexican War, Lt. William Emory, a West Point graduate, leading a small topographical detachment, had marched with Gen. Stephen Watts Kearny's Army of the West to California. Although this movement was to wrest California from Mexico, Emory in his "Notes of a Military Reconnaissance," was able to provide Congress with reliable data about the Southwest. In this work was a detailed map of the region.

Later, Emory was appointed astronomer for the demarcation of the boundary line between California and Mexico in 1848. He was breveted to major and served in this capacity for five years.

Although the actual boundary line had not been settled by the politicians of both countries, Emory and his men surveyed the ends of the borders of California and Texas. It was a horrendous assignment. The heat was intolerable and Indians harassed the surveyors. Many men deserted the ranks.

It was Emory who discovered that John Bartlett, head of the U.S. Boundary Commission, had ceded the land south of the Gila River to the Mexicans. Emory knew this contained the best right of way for the South's railroad to southern California.

The major had important Washington friends, among them Jefferson Davis. Davis and Emory had been classmates at West Point. It was from Davis and Henry Clay, Jr. that the nickname "Bold Emory" had originated, signifying the young cadet's courage. Now "Bold Emory" knew to whom he would lodge his protest. Whether he knew that Davis and other Southerners were pushing for the railroad line is not known; all Emory wanted was to correct a serious error.

With the South pressuring Congress to buy this region from Mexico, and Emory angrily protesting the ineptness of Bartlett, President Pierce sent James Gadsden to Mexico as minister. Gadsden, a railroad magnate, was instructed to buy the land for the southern line. Finally, in June 1854, Mexico agreed to the purchase price of $10 million for close to 30,000 square miles.

Emory was given the title of Commissioner and Astronomer to run the boundary under the Gadsden Treaty between the U.S. and Mexico from

1854–57. Afterward he was major in the 2nd Cavalry and was breveted Lt. Col. in 1857 for his valuable service with regard to the boundary line.

And Emory, long in the middle of disputes, having served at Charleston harbor, South Carolina during that state's threats about tariff nullifications, and in the Creek Nation during its strife in 1836, was fated to be part of the troubled Kansas-Nebraska Territory and later, the Civil War.[4]

By 1853, the South, realizing the Compromise of 1850 had shut the door on slavery in the territories, decided to repeal the Missouri Compromise. When California was admitted as a free state, the old objective in balancing the political power in the Senate by admitting one free and one slave state was in trouble. Where was the land for the South to offset the development of free states in the Northwest? The slave states had to come from the proposed territory of Nebraska. The area was extensive and some members of Congress had proposed three territories instead of one—Nebraska, Cherokee and Kansas.[5]

No one considered what a debilitating affect this new territory would have on the Indians who had been guaranteed the country "as long as the grass grows and the waters flow." The extension of slavery was the priority.

The author of the repeal was David R. Atchison, U.S. Senator from Missouri. As president pro tempore of the Senate in 1849, when Zachary Taylor's inauguration fell on Sunday, March 4, it had to be postponed one day. In this capacity, Atchison was next in line for the office, and many people claimed he had been President of the United States that Sunday.

Atchison had opposed Sen. Benton when the latter had changed his views about slavery. Benton had come home to Missouri in 1850, only to face political defeat. He had favored the expansion of the railroads to the Pacific, but when "Old Bullion," Missouri's hero, had dared to oppose the slave powers his time in the U.S. Senate was over.

"Staggering Davy" was the nickname Atchison earned for himself having been "in his cups" more and more as he propounded his views on Nebraska Territory. He was crude, spitting randomly as he spoke and then wiping his mouth on his sleeve, and weighed almost 300 pounds, but no one had trouble understanding his views about the new territory. And he had an ally in the person of Judge William C. Price, another Missourian. Price opposed any settlement that had been set aside as Indian country. If slavery could not be part of that area, then no one could be there except the Indians.

Had there not been such controversy about Nebraska and the South demanding the usual two states, Kansas might never have become part of the plan. Atchison had said in regard to slavery, "I am willing that people who may settle there and who have the deepest interest in this question should decide it for themselves."[6] Time would prove that Atchison did not believe this, and out of his blistering, bawdy speeches would come men who, falling under his spell, would create havoc in the area.

Atchison had vowed he "would sooner see the whole of Nebraska in the bottom of hell than see it a Free State." As to Kansas Territory, if he could have his way, he would hang every Abolitionist who dared to settle there.[7]

He crowed about his association with the Border Ruffians which was made up of several groups denoted by the area in which they originated. Atchison commanded the Platte County Rifles or Regulators and in Easton, Leavenworth County, was formed the Kickapoo Rangers. Taken collectively, they were known as Border Ruffians.[8]

Atchison chided the South for not heeding the calls for help in establishing slavery in Kansas. "If we secure Kansas as a slave state, Missouri is secure; New Mexico and southern California, if not all of it, become slave States. In a word, the prosperity or the ruin of the whole South depends on the Kansas struggle."[9]

The "Popular Sovereignty" principle of letting the people make the decision free or slave, had first been adopted in New Mexico and Utah territories. The crusade to wrest the land from the Indians started when George W. Maypenny, Commissioner of Indian Affairs, toured Indian Reserves in the proposed territory. During the weeks Maypenny spent in the area, he counseled with 17 tribes, estimating their population to be 14,384 and their holdings to be 13,220,480 acres. The commissioner did not have time to visit with the other six tribes, among them the Osage, but he determined these tribes to have a population of 11,597 and their land estimated at slightly more than 18.3 million acres. On April 11, 1854, two delegations of Delawares and Shawnees left for Washington to make land cession treaties to be followed on the 21st by the Iowa, Sac and Fox and Kickapoos. No sooner had these Indians stepped on the boat, when many Missourians rushed to their lands, laying cabin foundations, and marking trees with their names. But they did not stay. They returned to the slave state and waited for word about the treaties.[10] This rushing onto Indian land recalls the actions taken by the whites in Alabama and Georgia.

President Franklin Pierce approved the Kansas–Nebraska Bill on May 30, 1854. At the end of 1854, it was estimated that 8,000 Free–State settlers were already in Kansas. Despite Atchison's avowal that the people should decide, the South expected Kansas, the southern section of the territory west of Missouri and extending to Pikes Peak, to be a slave state. After all, that area should be slave as it fell south of the line the Southern Democrats had drawn clear to the Pacific. They would gladly let Nebraska be free.

Dr. George A. Cutler had no political aspirations when he moved to Kansas from Gentry, Missouri soon after the passage of the Kansas–Nebraska bill. He had studied medicine at the University Medical College, New York, and following graduation in 1853 had emigrated to Gentry where he hung up his shingle.

When Cutler lost a close friend who was shot in an argument at the first election for a delegate to Congress in the Free–State party, the doctor decided to actively favor Kansas as a free state. Cutler was chosen as a candidate for the first Territorial Legislature in the spring of 1855. His opposition was Gen. J. H. Stringfellow of the Pro-Slavery party. Stringfellow was, also, what had become known as a Border Ruffian. And he hated Abolitionists, vowing to kill them whether it be man, woman or child.[11]

It was James Redpath, a native Scotsman and newspaper correspondent espousing the Free–State cause, who had coined the appellation "Border Ruffian."[12] Most of them were men from Missouri's western border who had been freighters and bullwhackers along the Santa Fe Trail. From their description given by Dr. Gihon, secretary to Kansas Territorial Gov. John W. Geary, to gentler souls it seemed they had been weaned on whiskey and cut their teeth on revolvers.

Gihon depicted them as roughly dressed, in dusty, mud-spattered long boots drawn up over coarse, fancy colored cloth trousers that were equally dirty. They wore red or blue shirts and old slouch hats adorned with a cockade or brass star pinned to the front or side, topped off with a turkey, goose or chicken feather. Their hair was long, greasy and tangled, faces bearded, hands grubby. They were rough spoken, bragged after killing abolitionists and consumed quantities of whiskey without the appearance of drunkenness.

The Border Ruffians were armed with large Bowie knives, the handles protruding from at least one or both boot tops. A rifle or carbine was slung over a shoulder. A wide leather belt encircled the waist with a large revolver fastened on each side while a sword hung from the left hip.[13]

These were the Missourians who almost to a man had no inclination to build cabins or mark trees. Their headquarters was Westport, Missouri and they approved their title "Border Ruffian," which was painted on the hack they drove in that area. Soon many Missouri border towns changed their store names to "Border Ruffian Store," or businesses to "Border Ruffian Companies."

They believed there was only one way to make Kansas a slave state. Nearly 5,000 in strength, in 1854, they crossed the border and, armed with their Bowie knives and Navy Colts, they voted in every district and prevented many legal voters from exercising their constitutional rights. This election produced the bogus pro-slavery legislature. Out of this legislature came the formation of 35 counties including, Wilson, Woodson and Greenwood.[14]

The "bogus laws" of the territorial legislature needed to be enforced, compelling the Free–State people to accept them. Even President Franklin Pierce and then Secretary of War Jefferson Davis had proclaimed that refusal to obey was rebellion. Backed by the chief executive of the United States, at a pro-slavery meeting in Leavenworth in October 1855 the situation was discussed and eventually resolutions were drawn up and presented to the people of Kansas in November. Resolution number 12 designated their name to be "the 'Law and Order party,' the 'State Rights Party of Kansas,' the opponents of Abolitionism, Free-soilism and all other isms of the day."[15] With these resolutions, terrorism was unleashed in Kansas Territory.

As an example of how votes were garnered, there is the story about one Missouri man known only as "Shanghai." When the election for the Lecompton Constitution was held in December 1857, Shanghai was in Marshall County, Kansas, where three or four log cabins served as proof of settlement.

In one cabin a hole had been made in the ceiling where a soap box, as a ballot receptacle, had been placed on a whiskey barrel. Up the narrow staircase climbed the patriotic Shanghai with a ballot in his hand. He yelled out his name, an alias, and dropped his vote into the soap box. The more whiskey Shanghai drank, the bolder he became and bet $100 that by the time the polls closed he would have outvoted all of them. He was challenged and lost to a man who had cast ballots 100 times. Shanghai had come to the election equipped with a St. Louis business directory and had managed to use about half of the surnames in the "A" listing. From the 30 men present that day came nearly 1,000 votes for the Lecompton Constitution.[16]

Into this tumultuous region came James H. Lane, former lt. gov. of Indiana, who had just completed one term in the House of Representatives. Lane would become the leader in the Free–State cause whipping with his oratorical talent the Free–Staters into retaliation against the Border Ruffians. Murders, vandalism and thievery had been committed on Kansas soil by the pro-slavery advocates. What the Free–State men perpetrated under the banner of justice and freedom was as heinous as their adversaries.

Political affiliations brought Lane and Cutler together. Cutler had suffered much physical cruelty at the hands of the Border Ruffians. In 1855, Cutler had been elected as a delegate to the Constitutional Convention which met at Topeka in October. He became ill with typhoid fever after the convention's adjournment, and was kept at Dr. Charles Robinson's home in Topeka until he was able to return to Doniphan. He secured the services of a George Warren to take him back home, carefully avoiding Atchison, Kansas, a pro-slavery stronghold named for the senator. However, Warren was less wary of the opposition and rode through Atchison on his return home. He was arrested, searched, stripped of his clothing, and roughed up. In time, the Border Ruffians made him disclose where he had been.

Immediately, men climbed a wagon and, accompanied by a considerable number of horsemen proceeded to Doniphan where they found Cutler alone and in bed. At Cutler's capture, a courier was dispatched to Weston informing those pro-slavery men that the Free–State delegate was their prisoner. They wanted reinforcements, fearing an attack by Free–State men.

Cutler was returned to Atchison where in the early morning hours the

Weston mob arrived, very drunk, very noisy, and threatening to hang Cutler at once. Secretly, the sheriff slipped a loaded pistol to the sick man, and warned him to defend himself. Later that morning the Law and Order Party held a trial. Cutler was tried for high treason and convicted. The self-proclaimed judge gave him the choice of sentence—hanging or a trip to Lecompton where the pro-slavery army was collecting, preparatory to taking Lawrence, the headquarters for the Free–State Party.

At that moment, Cutler believed he would not recover from the typhoid, and he chose to be hanged. Arguments erupted among the men. Instead of a noose, the doctor was placed in a wagon and started under guard for Lecompton. Once there he was housed in a tent and was drenched during a hard rain. He had a relapse, and one night delirious with a high fever he attempted to escape, crawling about 100 yards and fainting. He was found the next morning and returned to the tent where he remained and eventually was exchanged.[17]

Why Cutler was never killed is a mystery. Perhaps he was viewed as a dying man and no longer a threat. The doctor was one of the fortunate ones. In many instances Free–State men were literally hacked to death with hatchets. Avenging such horrible deaths, the Free–State men would mutilate Pro-Slavery men by cutting off their hands, noses and ears before slitting their throats.

Cutler became a member of Lane's Army of the North. Free–State emigrants crossing Missouri for Kansas Territory were turned back at the Missouri River, thus denying them entrance into Kansas. Lane devised a plan to bring emigrants from Wisconsin, Massachusetts, Indiana, Illinois and Ohio across Iowa. Most of the emigrants were able to travel by rail to its terminus at Iowa City. From there to the Missouri River they rode in stagecoaches or in hired wagons. The trail had been marked by cairns on rises and had been appropriately called "Lane's Chimney." By August 1856, the first emigrants had crossed into Kansas. Although Lane insisted they were people who wanted to settle in Kansas Territory, there were those among them who had vowed to take up arms against the pro-slavery men.[18]

The Border Ruffians feared no one except Lane. Many had fought with him in the Mexican War and remembered his derring-do. Cutler and Lane, who eventually settled in Doniphan, would be associated in territorial politics which, eventually, would lead to Cutler's appointment as agent for the Creek Indians in Indian Territory.

Chapter 15

Secession Begins

Robert J. Walker was appointed the fourth territorial governor of Kansas on March 26, 1857. Long in politics, Walker had made the speech nominating Andrew Jackson as a candidate for the presidency. He was a U.S. Senator from Mississippi who had favored the removal of the southern tribes to the west.

Walker and President James Buchanan had two objectives in regard to Kansas. First, all Kansans must submit to the bogus legislature laws. Second, a constitution had to be formed under which Kansas should be admitted as a slave state.

Walker delivered his inaugural address at Lecompton, May 27, 1857, in which he urged the Free–State men to take part in the election of delegates to the constitutional convention. He assured them the election would be a fair one. He did not limit himself in his speech to the perilous affairs in Kansas. He took time to view the Indian situation in Indian Territory.

"Upon the south Kansas is bounded by the great south western Indian Territory. This is one of the most salubrious and fertile portions of this continent. It is a great cotton growing region, admirably adapted by soil and climate for the products of the South." That Walker looked upon Indian Territory as another slave state in addition to Kansas, or a replacement should Kansas be free, is clear from his lengthy description of the area.

"It ought speedily to become a State of the American Union. The Indian treaties will constitute no obstacle, anymore than precisely similar treaties did in Kansas ..." Walker, while extolling about the Indian lands which he considered the majority of acreage was useless to them, became charitable in how the territory would serve both white and Indian. "This territory contains double the area of the State of Indiana, and, if necessary, an adequate portion of the western and more elevated part could be set aside exclusively for these tribes and the eastern and larger portion be formed into a State and its land sold for the benefit of these tribes (like the Indian lands of Kansas) thus greatly promoting all their interest."[1]

The only interest Walker cared about was how the area would benefit the South. This inaugural address became a part of the Annual Report of the Commissioner of Indian Affairs, 1857.

Although Walker came to realize that the Kansas question could not be so easily solved [he resigned his office in 1858] he does seem to have been a forerunner in citing Indian Territory as the next land to be set aside for the white man.

Picking up where Walker left off, Elias Rector, superintendent of the Southern Superintendency, in his 1859 report to Greenwood, the commissioner, said: "The country that lies between Arkansas and Missouri, on the east, and the ninety-eighth parallel of longitude on the west, and between nearly the parallel of thirty-seven north latitude, and Red river, is certainly not excelled, if it is equaled, for beauty, fertility and agricultural capacity, for soil, mineral wealth and climate, by any portion of the United States of equal extent." Rector cited the fact that "these Indians actually occupy and use not a five-thousandth part." His opinion was that since they did not use all of the land, therefore, despite treaties which guaranteed all of the region to them, they had no need for it.

"I have already spoken, in a previous report, of the certainty that this fine country must ultimately, and at no distant day, be formed into States. Not only the remorseless flow of our population, but stern political necessities, make this decree as fixed as fate."[2]

Douglas H. Cooper, agent for the Choctaw and Chickasaw tribes, pointed out in his report that "the Indian territory west of Arkansas is rich in minerals, in water power and in lands of unsurpassed fertility, and blessed, too, with a salubrious climate."[3]

Even the Cherokee agent, George Butler, commented on the excellent raising of cattle and that the slaveholding Cherokees had profited by owning slaves who had taught them how to cultivate the soil. Butler believed the answer to civilizing the "wild roving tribes of Indians" was to make them slaveholders, also.[4]

All of these men were southerners. And they were appointees during the administration of James Buchanan, a pro-slavery president. Buchanan had made his views of the Kansas strife known to Congress in his annual message of 1858. "It has been solemnly adjudged by the highest judicial tribunal known to our laws that slavery exists in Kansas by virtue of the Constitution of the United States. Kansas is therefore at this moment as much a slave State as Georgia or South Carolina." Buchanan wanted Kansas admitted as a slave state which "would restore peace and quiet to the whole country."[5]

The president delineated the effect the Kansas question was having on the rest of the country. "The dark and ominous clouds which now appear to be impending over the Union I conscientiously believe may be dissipated with honor to every portion of it by the admission of Kansas during the present session of Congress, whereas if she should be rejected I greatly fear these clouds will become darker and more ominous than any which have ever yet threatened the Constitution and the Union."[6]

The clouds would continue to darken and become more threatening, not only for the Union but the Indian as well.

In 1842 the Sac and Fox of the Mississippi ceded their Iowa lands to the United States. In exchange the tribe was given a tract of land 34 miles long and nearly 20 miles wide on the Marais de Cygnes River and its tributaries west of Ottawa, Kansas.

In 1858, John P. Usher of Lawrence and Robert S. Stevens, who had connections with the Indian Bureau, devised a plan to build 150 wood and stone houses along the river for the Indians' benefit. The contract was let to Stevens who received payment in Indian scrip.

The Indians protested to Washington that they didn't want the houses, but all of their pleas went unheeded by the government. The tribe of 1,500 lived in wigwam villages across the reservation. They had no need for the houses.

The units were cheaply constructed and consisted of two rooms and a porch built along one side. The Sac and Foxes, victims of another fraud by the white man to relieve them of their money, reluctantly tried to live in them.

It was not long, however, after tearing up the floors and breaking out the windows, that the Indians returned to their wigwams. They left charcoal drawings on the walls of the little houses depicting the objects of wonder they had seen in the east such as steamboats, trains, and the different wild animals of the plains.[7]

Then in 1859, the tribe made another treaty with the U.S. whereby about 300,000 acres in the western part of the reservation would be sold for their benefit. The Sac and Fox retained close to 153,000 acres. Quenemo, in the Marais des Cygnes River valley in the southeastern part of Osage County, was the agency.[8]

Not content with duping these Indians out of their money by constructing houses, another profitable scheme was devised to buy up the land that had been put in trust in 1859.[9] The 300,000 acres were put up for sale under sealed bids in 1860. Kansas residents presented their bids but lost out to the Washington insiders, namely Hugh McCulloch, John P. Usher and William P. Dole. These three men became the owners of the best land available. Not surprising is the fact that McCulloch, a banker in Ohio, would become Lincoln's secretary of the treasury in 1865; Usher, secretary of the interior in 1863, and Dole, commissioner of Indian Affairs in 1861.[10]

The remaining lands were awarded to Stevens, Perry Fuller, who was a trader at the Sac and Fox Agency, and John McManus. These men had amassed large amounts of Indian scrip and in turn used it at its par value to pay for the former Sac and Fox lands.[11] Stevens, later, would defraud Kansas of money in a bond scheme during Gov. Charles Robinson's term of office. It seems ironic that treaty money due the Sac and Fox built the houses, and then purchased their land.

Farther south in Indian Territory, a small fort named Cobb was erected in 1859 and located in the Leased District. This area was common country belonging to the Choctaws and Chickasaws. For approximately 40 years Wichitas, Kickapoos, Shawnees and Delawares had inhabited the area on the upper Washita River.

By the ninth article of the 1855 treaty between these two tribes and the U.S., this land was to be leased to the United States in perpetuity "for the permanent settlement of the Wichita and such other tribes or bands of Indians as the government may desire to locate therein." Excluded were the New Mexico Indians and those whose ranges were north of the Arkansas River and those whose permanent locations were north of the Canadian River.[12]

In 1858, agent Douglas Cooper informed Elias Rector that these tribes felt the Kickapoos, Shawnees and Delawares could not remain. They were considered intruders, and Cooper vowed to remove them with the aid of the military if necessary.[13]

To complicate matters, in October the Wichitas "had arrived at Fort Arbuckle in a destitute and almost starving condition." Why the Wichitas were at Arbuckle was, as usual, the result of the ineptness of the U.S. Army.[14]

As explained by Supt. Rector, Comanches from Texas had stolen Wichita horses. Asked to return them, the Wichitas also invited the Comanches for a friendly talk with them and the Choctaws and Chickasaws. The Comanches agreed, returning part of the horses "and were encamped in peace, some of the Wichitas being with them."[15]

One officer at Fort Arbuckle knew they had been invited to the area. Major Earl Van Dorn had not been apprised of the situation. Van Dorn had believed the Comanches were there "for hostile purposes." A forced march ensued and reaching the "camp in the night" Arbuckle troops slaughtered "some sixty of them, including four Wichitas."[16]

The Comanches felt they had "been treacherously dealt with by the Wichitas as well as the United States." Rector feared a "border war on the Choctaw, Chickasaw and Seminole frontier." He envisioned "all surveying operations" being suspended; "the overland mail to California cease to run, and its stations broken up."[17]

The killing of the Comanches and Wichitas was reprehensible, but it was made worse by the fact that "the troops, or their auxiliaries, foraged for several days on the fields of these poor Indians, to their ruin."[18]

To relieve the starving Wichitas, Rector had contracted with Charles B. Johnson "to furnish them with beef, bread and salt."[19] Then he contacted their agent Blain to go to the Leased District and set up his office. The superintendent requested "the immediate posting of a military force in their country and the speedy erection of a fort and agency there."[20]

By 1859, all disagreements had been settled. Reserves in the Leased District had been assigned by Rector and besides the original tribes, Comanches from Texas and Caddoes, and bands of Kechis had been added.

Rector was pleased that a "permanent fort shall be established near the site of the old Kichai (*sic*) village."[21] He suggested an additional post at Frozen Rock, a few miles from the former Fort Gibson in the Cherokee Nation. And he entertained the possibility of abandoning Fort Washita and surrendering it to the Choctaws.[22]

With the passage of the Kansas–Nebraska Bill, disenchanted Whigs, Democrats and Free–Soilers who wanted to keep slavery from the territories formed a new party called Republican. John C. Fremont, son-in-law of Thomas H. Benton, was their first candidate in the presidential election of 1856. Buchanan, pro-southern Democrat, had won the election, but this had not discouraged the Republicans.

They had the man who could win the presidential election of 1860. He was Abraham Lincoln and despite his loss in the senatorial race to Stephen A. Douglas in 1858, the Republicans knew that from the well-publicized Lincoln–Douglas debates, the Illinois lawyer had emerged as an anti-slavery champion. He intended to preclude slavery from the territories, and would not interfere where it existed. Lincoln had actively opposed the Mexican War and the Kansas–Nebraska Act. He was anti-expansionism, yet, because of his stand on the slavery issue, he was elected President in 1860.

The strife in Kansas and the impending presidential election, with its attendant campaign speeches had not gone unheeded by the Five Civilized Tribes in Indian Territory. When Lincoln declared he would not allow slavery in the territories, the Indians had become alarmed. Although the land they were to have in perpetuity was never officially declared "Indian Territory," still it wasn't a state. Being slaveholders, they had become apprehensive that the government would confiscate their property. But that was only one of their fears.

They knew the white man saw how the Indians had improved the untamed lands. And when William H. Seward, in a Chicago election campaign speech in Lincoln's behalf, had said, "And Indian Territory south of Kansas must be vacated by the Indians" they became frightened and suspicious of the president-elect and his soon to be secretary of state, Seward.[23] Seeds of distrust were broadcast across Indian Territory.

Then the weather changed and Kansans and the tribes in Indian Territory were to experience a natural calamity. From June 19, 1859, until November 1860, there was very little rain, creating a drought that gripped the countryside. Streams dried up, and vegetation died, except for the prairie grass along creeks and ravines which survived during the spring and summer, to be cured by the hot winds and become hay for the cattle. It was estimated Kansas lost 30,000 people who left the territory unable to cope with the dire conditions.

In the reports of the Indian agents of the Southern Superintendency for 1860, they cited the failure of the corn crop due to the drought, which meant many Native People would be starving unless relief was sent. Word of the disastrous condition in Kansas reached the people back east. The New England Relief Society, representing many states, dispatched their agent, George W. Collamore, to Kansas and make the necessary arrangements for dividing the territory into two districts. S.C. Pomeroy was placed in charge of northern Kansas with W.F.M. Arny, a former captain of the steamboat Lightfoot on the Kansas River, in charge of southern Kansas.

The aid amounted to more than eight million pounds of provisions and clothing, $85,000 in money and 2,500 bushels of seed wheat. Sacks that had been marked "W.F.M. Arny, Army Agent" could be seen in most communities after the distribution, mainly on the persons of men and boys. Pants and coats had been made from them and the logos of "W.F.," "Army," or "Agent" became part of the apparel.[24]

As for the starving Native People, little was done to relieve them. In December 1860, Secretary of the Interior Jacob Thompson discovered bonds and coupons were missing from the Indian Trust Fund. Unscrupulous politicians and entrepreneurs had been willing to use these monies to further their own gain. How the bonds came to be missing is a provocative story.[25]

In Kansas, the freighting concern of Russell, Majors and Waddell, transplanted Missourians, had, since 1855, held contracts with the government to move stores to outlying posts in the west. Headquartered in Leavenworth, the company employed, annually, more than 1,700 men, 500 wagons and 7,500 head of cattle. The three men had been freighters for many years, at times working separately and then together. William H. Russell had been quite active in Kansas Territorial days, and in 1856 was treasurer of the executive committee to raise money to make a slave state out of Kansas.[26]

In 1858, the company acquired a government contract to transport 16 million pounds of freight over the Oregon Trail. This was twice the amount of the 1855 contract. With such a large undertaking the company had to purchase an additional 3,500 wagons and 40,000 oxen.[27]

Arriving at Salt Lake City too late in the year to return to Leavenworth, they had to leave wagons, oxen and cattle on the outskirts of the city. Wagons that had cost $150 each sold for $10 and most of the animals starved to death. The firm lost $150,000 but still netted a profit.[28]

Russell traveled to Washington in the winter of 1859–60 in regard to contracts. While there he was approached by U.S. Senator William McKendree

Gwin, a California Democrat, with his idea of making communications more rapid within his state. It was Gwin who first proposed the Pony Express. Russell, Majors and Waddell were then running a daily stage from the Missouri River to Salt Lake City and as stations had been established along the stage line, it would only be a matter of providing facilities from Utah to Sacramento.[29]

Although Russell was hesitant, believing the concept would not be profitable, he did contact Majors and Waddell and he was turned down. Gwin was persistent, however, and promised government subsidy if the express proved to be a failure financially. With the government subsidizing the project, the partners agreed.[30]

The Pony Express was opened for business in April 1860. It had been necessary to purchase more than 400 horses, hire 80 express riders, and 200 station agents.[31]

The new line soon had the freighting company in financial difficulties. Russell returned to Washington in late fall of 1860 to secure more money. After conferring with Secretary of War John B. Floyd, freight line company drafts drawn on the War Department were given to Russell in expectation of future service. They amounted to nearly one million dollars. The promises to pay were not customary but could be negotiated.[32]

A clerk, Godard Bailey of South Carolina, knew Russell and more importantly, Bailey was in charge of state bonds belonging to the Indian Trust Fund. Russell, using Floyd's acceptances, prevailed upon Bailey to give him a substantial amount of the bonds. Russell then mortgaged them on Wall Street, and raised the money.[33]

At this time, with talks of secession and importations at a standstill, the federal government was practically broke. The bonds depreciated in value and the lenders notified Russell they needed more collateral. Once again, Bailey supplied more bonds. The Indian Bureau in the meantime had requested the coupons of the bonds, payable January 1, 1861. Bailey realized he could be implicated and notified Floyd of the transactions, explaining he had taken the bonds to save Floyd's honor. Approximately $870,000 belonging to the Indians had disappeared.[34]

On December 30, a Grand Jury at Washington returned an indictment charging Floyd with two counts. One, malfeasance, and the second, for conspiring with Bailey and Russell to defraud the government.[35] Floyd escaped trial, returning to his native Virginia to promote secession. The indictments against Bailey and Russell were dismissed by the criminal court in March 1861.[36]

It has been estimated that the backers lost $200,000 during the 18 months that the Pony Express operated. However, the Express was credited with saving California for the Union. Lincoln's inaugural address sent from St. Joseph,

Missouri reached Sacramento in 17 days, 17 hours. Eventually, the telegraph, stretching across the country east to west spelled doom for the enterprise. And as the Indian Trust Fund figured heavily in the Russell, Majors and Waddell company capitol, it is certain the true losers were the Indians themselves.

On January 21, 1861, the day that Gov. Seward called up a bill admitting Kansas as a free state under the Wyandotte Constitution, Jefferson Davis, Clement C. Clay and others abandoned their seats and the Capitol to take part in the Southern Rebellion.

Following Lincoln's election, South Carolina, long the forerunner in the states rights declarations, passed an Ordinance of Secession on December 20, 1860. "And that the Union now subsisting between South Carolina and other states, under the name of the United States of America, is hereby dissolved."[37]

Not all of the southerners felt inclined to leave the Union because the "Black Republican" Lincoln had gained the office. Alexander H. Stephens had appealed to the Georgia Legislature convened at Milledgeville in November to weigh all consequences of the issue. "In my judgment, the election of no man, constitutionally chosen to the high office, is not sufficient cause for any State to separate from the Union."[38] Stephens believed "the greatest curse that can befall a free people is civil war."[39] Yet, he had advised that a convention should be called and then "should Georgia determine to go out of the Union ... I shall bow to the will of her people."[40]

Georgia held that convention January 18, 1861, and Stephens went on record in regard to secession as being one of the nays. The yeas had it and Georgia followed South Carolina in secession. Later, Stephens became the vice-president of the Confederate States of America.[41]

The Augusta (Georgia) *Chronicle and Sentinel* for January 1, 1861, watched the secession movement gaining strength and wondered about the South's future. "A sad thing to observe is, that those who are determined on immediate secession have not the coolness, the capacity or the nerve to propose something after that ... South Carolina considers it her policy to create a collision with the Federal authorities for the purpose of arousing the South from her slumber. Never was there a greater mistake."[42]

Out in Texas, Governor Sam Houston had argued against leaving the Union. At one time, most of the people would have listened to the "Hero of San Jacinto," but those days were over and Houston was an old man. A convention was assembled at Austin on January 28, and overwhelmingly passed an Ordinance of Secession. It was submitted to a popular vote and, not surprisingly, ratified by a considerable majority. The consensus was "it being very much safer, in most districts, to vote Secession than not at all and not to vote at all than to vote Union."[43]

The governor of Maryland, Thomas H. Hicks, a slaveholder and southerner by birth, appealed to the secessionists in that state. "I am yet compelled by my sense of fair dealing, and my respect for the Constitution of our country, to declare that I see nothing in the bare election of Mr. Lincoln which would justify the South in taking any steps tending toward a separation of these States."[44] Maryland, a Border State, remained in the Union.

On January 29, 1861, Kansas was admitted as a free state. The last hope of the South had been defeated. The Wyandotte Constitution was for freedom, the rights of man, the protection of the home and the establishment of justice. It, also, fixed the permanent boundaries of Kansas. The western boundary became the 25th meridian, cutting off the territorial counties of Arapahoe, Oro, Montana, Fremont, El Paso and Broderick. The politicians foresaw two different taxes for the state. The western part they believed would be strictly mineral as opposed to the rest which was agricultural. This area subsequently became part of the Territory and eventually the state of Colorado.[45]

When the news reached Kansas that she was the 34th star on the flag of the Union, Free–State men of Lawrence hurried to Capt. Thomas Bickerton's farm to disinter "Old Sacramento," one of the cannons the Mexicans had placed on the heights of Sacramento Pass. This brass six-pounder and 15 others had been captured by Col. William Doniphan at the Battle of Sacramento in the state of Chihuahua in northern Mexico during the war. Doniphan's army had marched from Santa Fe to Chihuahua, covering 3,000 miles, and this achievement still is considered the longest march in the annals of military history. Doniphan returned to Missouri and for a time was a Border Ruffian and this cannon was used to bombard the Free–State Hotel in Lawrence. Then it was taken to Franklin and put in a blockhouse. Eventually, it was confiscated by the Free–State men and used for a time, then was removed to Bickerton's farm where it was buried. Bonfires were lighted, public buildings in Lawrence were opened and despite the snow-covered ground jubilant people thronged. "Old Sacramento," brought into the territory by the Border Ruffians and confiscated by the Free–State men, symbolized the struggle for statehood. It was fired in Lawrence all night, heralding the good news that she was a free state at last.[46]

Although Kansas did not have a vote in Lincoln's election, the state provided the "Frontier Guard," which for 15 days from April 18 to May 3, 1861, guarded the White House and Mr. Lincoln until troops reach Washington. The body of men was commanded by Gen. James H. Lane.

Less than a year later, southern Kansas would become a questionable shelter for the most unfortunate victims of the Civil War, the Five Civilized Tribes in Indian Territory.

Chapter 16

Southern Emissaries in Indian Territory

The South had been preparing for war quite sometime. During his tenure as secretary of war, John B. Floyd had, at different times, managed to move muskets, rifles and ammunition from the arsenals in the North to those in the South. According to E.A. Pollard in his Southern History of the War "it was safely estimated that the South entered the war with 150,000 small arms of the most approved modern pattern and the best in the world."[1] Floyd persisted in the preparations by sending the greater share of the army to Texas and he saw that the navy sailed to faraway seas.[2]

When Maj. Robert Anderson, commanding Fort Moultrie in the harbor at Charleston, South Carolina, realized the fort could not long withstand an invasion due to its poor structural conditions, he moved his command by ferry boats at night to Fort Sumter on December 26, 1860. Then a domino effect followed with the seizure of arsenals and posts in the South.

In South Carolina, the federal arsenal at Charleston was taken by volunteers. Castle Pinckney, Fort Moultrie, and Sullivan's Island were all occupied. The custom house and postoffice at Charleston was seized without resistance. Lighthouse lights in the harbor were extinguished, and buoys were removed from the channel so that a special pilot had to be used before entering or departing.[3]

Near the date Anderson moved to Sumter, Floyd sent an order to the Allegheny Arsenal at Pittsburgh, Pennsylvania, for the transfer of 46 cannons to Ship Island near Balize, Louisiana, and 78 cannons to Galveston. With secession on most everyone's mind, the Pittsburgh authorities sensed treason and dispatched messages to Washington. The order was cancelled. Had it not been voided, the South would have had in its possession 44 ten-inch Columbiads, 69 eight-inch Columbiads, and 11 iron thirty-pounders. The Columbiads had been used in the War of 1812. The later ones were used as seacoast cannon. They were bronze and fired a 50 pound shot close to 600 yards.[4] Even the U.S. Revenue service cutter "William Aiken" at Charleston harbor was delivered by its Capt. N.L. Cost to the state authorities.[5]

In January, the state of Georgia took possession of the federal arsenal at Augusta. Savannah, Forts Pulaski and Jackson, which were also taken, commanded the seaward approaches.[6]

The federal arsenal at Fayetteville, North Carolina, along with Fort Mason and other posts were seized. Fort Morgan near Mobile, Alabama and the federal arsenal there were taken as was the arsenal at Baton Rouge, Louisiana, together with Forts Jackson, St. Philip and Pike. In Florida, the navy yard at Pensacola, and Fort Barrancas were taken followed by Fort McRae. The federals managed to remain at Fort Pickens. The revenue cutter *Cass* at Mobile was turned over to Alabama.[7]

President Buchanan determined that there would be no reinforcement of Fort Sumter although the South Carolina commissioners sent to Washington had demanded its surrender. Buchanan refused. Realizing Sumter was vulnerable, he decided to provision the fort. With his term near its end, the president wanted the two sections to negotiate and, hopefully, if he could not obtain a solution, perhaps Lincoln could.

On January 5, 1861, the steamer *Star of the West* left New York bound for Fort Sumter with reinforcements and supplies. Southern spies learning of her destination, as it had not been announced publicly, notified the authorities in South Carolina, who were waiting when the ship with 250 soldiers on board appeared off the bar at Charleston. Steaming up the harbor toward Sumter, she was fired upon by forces at Fort Moultrie and on Morris Island. Without communicating with Sumter, she headed back toward New York. Anderson and his men would have to fend for themselves.[8]

In February, an important strategic location was taken by the South.

It was 4 A.M. February 16, 1861, when 90 men on horseback dismounted in the suburbs of San Antonio, and were ordered by Col. Benjamin McCulloch to enter the city on foot. Backed by some 310 Texas volunteers, the men were determined to seize the federal forces under the command of Georgian, Maj. Gen. David Twiggs of the Eighth Military District. The rest of the Texans galloped in at daylight, and finding no resistance from the near 160 Union men, were in position around the arsenal, the ordnance, the Alamo and the quarters in the commissary buildings by 5 A.M.[9]

As early as February 5, J.C. Robertson, chairman of the Committee of Public Safety of Texas, had notified T.J. Devine, Samuel A. Maverick, P.N. Luckett and James H. Rogers of their appointments as commissioners. They were to visit Twiggs in the name of Texas and demand "receive and receipt for all military, medical, commissary and ordnance stores under his control."[10]

On February 3, the committee, fearing Twiggs might not surrender without a fight, appointed McCulloch colonel of cavalry. He was to hold himself "in readiness to raise men and munitions of war" whenever called upon by the state.[11] McCulloch, a former Texas Ranger and Mexican War veteran, had been U.S. Marshal for the Texas coastal region at the time of his commission in 1861. He was a Tennessean who had followed his older friend, Davy Crockett, to Texas, but not to the Alamo. He had fought in the Battle of San Jacinto.

The 49-year-old McCulloch had been able to raise an adequate force when ordered to do so. "To Texans a moment's notice is sufficient when their State demands their services" he had assured Robertson in his report following the successful mission to San Antonio.[12]

In actuality, Twiggs had never intended to resist, declaring he would not fire on fellow Americans. Uppermost in the military minds of the South was for Texas to claim all of "that which now belongs to Texas." Concern centered on Forts Bliss and Quitman. They believed "the men and munitions in those forts could be moved without delay to New Mexico, giving the Federal Government at Washington a large body of troops to hold that country against the Southern movement ... it will be unwise to permit a single company of U.S. troops to march from any portion of Texas into New Mexico ... We repeat it, we must not let a single company from Fort Bliss to Fort Brown leave the State by the Kansas, New Mexico or any other route save the coast."[13]

By nightfall of the 16th, Union forces had marched out of San Antonio and encamped at the San Pedro Springs, there to await transportation to take them to the coast. And on the 18th, Twiggs surrendered all of the federal posts to the Texans.[14]

Lt. Col. Robert E. Lee of the Second Cavalry was assigned to the Texas frontier. He had received orders to return to Washington and coming into San Antonio after the surrender was dismayed to learn the news.

Eventually, the Texans turned their thoughts to Indian Territory and on February 27, James E. Harrison, James Bourland and Charles A. Hamilton were appointed commissioners and left for "the Chickasaw Nation about 30 miles southwest of Fort Washita." The commissioners, accompanied by J.A. Echols of Waco, were acting upon "an ordinance to secure the friendship and cooperation of the Choctaw, Cherokee, Chickasaw, Creek and Seminole Nations of Indians."

Gov. C. Harris and others of the Chickasaws "appreciated our views and the object of our mission," the commissioners reported. Attending a convention of Chickasaws and Choctaws at Boggy Depot, which had convened on March 10, Harrison addressed the assembly two days later. He pointed out the wrongs the South had suffered by the U.S. Government which "had ceased to protect us or regard our rights." Harrison said the South's "patience had become exhausted." They had had no recourse but to sever all relations with the U.S. and organize "a new Government of Confederate Sovereign States of the South, with a common kindred, common hopes, common interest and a common destiny." The Confederacy was powerful, influential and wealthy, he explained.

The commissioners believed "the Choctaws and Chickasaws are entirely Southern and are determined to adhere to the fortunes of the South." The two nations were "embarrassed by the absence of their agents and commissioners at Washington."

Moving across the Indian Territory, the commissioners met with the Cherokees, Creeks, Seminoles, Quapaws and Sacs. "The Creeks are Southern and sound to a man, and when desired will show their devotion to our cause by acts. They (the Indian Nations) feel themselves to be in an exposed, embarrassed condition. They are occupying a country well suited to them, well watered and fertile, with extensive fields of the very best mineral coal, fine salt springs and wells, with plenty of good timber, water powers which they are using to an advantage. Pure slate, granite, sandstone, blue limestone and marble are found in abundance."

The report continued that the Indians felt the North would invade their country and they were not properly armed to repel the aggressors. "They declare themselves Southerners by geographical position, by a common interest, by their social system and by blood, for they are rapidly becoming a nation of whites."

The commissioners recommended the nations "to the fostering care of the South." "Twenty thousand good fighting men could be raised and under a good Southern officer's direction, repel any Northern invasion of Indian Territory. Convinced that the South and not the North would protect them, one of the Indian men had said: "Lincoln may haul his big guns about over our prairies in the daytime, but we will swoop down upon him at night from our mountains and forests, dealing death and destruction to his army."

Gaining the loyalty of the Indians, the next step was to enter into treaties with them, and in that there should be no delay. The commissioners warned that "the Administration of the North is concentrating his forces at Fort Washita about twenty-four miles from the Texas line, and within the limits of the Chickasaw Nation." The report was dated April 23, 1861.[15]

Chapter 17

Lt. Averell's Secret Mission

When Second Lieutenant William W. Averell, dressed in a coarse civilian suit and black overcoat, boarded the Baltimore and Ohio Railway in Washington City on April 17, 1861, he was unaware of the role he would be playing in the future of the Native People in Indian Territory. He only knew that he must reach Lt. Col. William H. Emory, commanding the First U.S. Cavalry at Fort Arbuckle, Indian Territory, posthaste, with the orders entrusted to himself from the General-in-Chief, Winfield Scott.

The incongruity of Averell's attire with the rank he held in the Regiment of Mounted Riflemen, and his alias, were indicative of the highly secretive orders he carried in an oilskin packet, and the horrendous conditions of the country through which he must travel to accomplish his mission.[1]

Averell had been in Washington on sick leave almost two years. He had been stationed in New Mexico at Forts Craig and Defiance. He had engaged in skirmishes with the Kiowa Indians, and in 1858 was severely wounded during a nighttime attack on his camp at the Puerco of the West. Finally, he was given sick leave. In the interim, the 28-year-old West Point graduate had watched, with growing apprehension, the disuniting of the United States, with many southern states seceding and joining the Confederate States of America.[2] The federal Fort Sumter in South Carolina, where Maj. Robert Anderson had commanded, had surrendered on April 14 to more than 4,000 Confederates.

In his report written on board the steamship *Baltic* on April 18, Anderson had described events leading up to his decision to surrender. After 34 hours defending Fort Sumter, with quarters "entirely burned, the main gates destroyed, the gorge wall seriously injured, the magazine surrounded by flames and its doors closed from the effects of the heat, four barrels and three cartridges of powder only being available, and no provisions but pork remaining, I accepted terms of evacuation offered by Gen. Beauregard." It had been a valiant effort on the part of Anderson and his men to try to save the fort for the Union. Anderson was a realist and knew there would be no help coming from the North. While Charleston men and their ladies, dressed in finery, had watched and cheered the rebels, the garrison marched out of the fort that Sunday afternoon of the 14th "with colors flying and drums beating, bringing away company and private property and saluting my flag with fifty guns."

There had been a premature explosion when the last gun was fired and one gunner was killed and several wounded.[3] At any rate, with Fort Sumter now in the hands of the South, Lincoln knew he must act immediately. On April 15, he declared a state of insurrection and called up 75,000 militia for duty.

Lt. William W. Averell, Union Army, who carried the secret order to Col. William Emory to abandon the forts in Indian Territory. *Special Collections, United States Military Academy, West Point.*

Averell could no longer nurse his wound and suppress his obligation to his country and the uniform he wore. Although his wounded limb was not yet back to normal, on April 16 he wrote to Col. E.D. Townsend, assistant adjutant general, volunteering his services. "A sense of duty to the United States Government, now that it is in danger, impels me to forego the benefits which might arise by availing myself of the unexpired time." Averell's sick leave was due to expire in June.[4]

The next day Townsend responded to Averell. "You will by order of the General-in-Chief proceed at once to Fort Arbuckle and deliver the accompanying letter to Lieut. Col. W.H. Emory, or the senior officer present."[5]

In March, Emory had returned from Indian Territory to Washington to give his intelligence report directly to Gen. Scott. Indian Territory was rife with secessionists and feelings were strong for the South.

Emory was a native of Maryland with many southern friends, yet, army headquarters was confident of his integrity. Unlike Lee who felt his duty belonged to Virginia, Emory agreed to return and "take post at Fort Cobb in

Indian Territory." He was given command of the 1st U.S. Cavalry at the three remaining posts in Indian Territory, and, also, at Fort Smith, Arkansas.[6]

Emory was not a stranger to the area, having served on the Indian frontier since 1855 with Fort Riley, Kansas Territory as his central point. He had been posted at Fort Arbuckle, 1858, and had established Fort Cobb in 1859.[7] All of these forts in Indian Territory were the result of the treaty conditions for tribes in that region.

However, before leaving the city on March 18, the order was rescinded. Emory was to go to Fort Washita, "concentrating the troops at Forts Cobb, Arbuckle and Washita at or in the vicinity of the latter post." With only two cavalry companies at Washita, Scott wanted them reinforced with two additional companies of cavalry and five of infantry from the other forts. Only 24 miles separated Fort Washita from the Texas line. "Fuss and Feathers" Scott considered it to be "a highly important military point." Later, when Averell was sent to find Emory at Fort Arbuckle instead of Washita, the confusion reigning at army headquarters was manifested.[8]

In the same report directing Emory to Fort Washita, Gen. Scott referred to the "friendly Indians on the reservation near Fort Cobb." Scott believed the government should act "in good faith" to notify the Delawares, Comanches, and others of the withdrawal of the troops to Washita.[9] But there was no indication that the nations of Creek, Cherokee, Seminole, Choctaw and Chickasaw, who had been promised protection by the federal government, also, were advised of events which clearly would affect them in the future. They knew at headquarters from listening to Emory's report that the South had sent emissaries to visit these tribes.

It had been 35 years since the South, particularly South Carolina, Georgia and Alabama, had been ready to secede from the Union unless these Indian nations were removed to the west. Now, the audacious South wanted these Indians to align themselves with the Confederacy, not only for the resources, but they believed, as the late Gen. Gaines had, that Indians would make excellent fighters. Indeed, Rector had cited this very thing in his 1859 report. The South intended to muster Indian troops to protect the territory from federal invasion, which they believed would come from Kansas. With Texas in their possession, a Confederate-held Indian Territory would increase their chances of holding the West. They wanted New Mexico Territory which had passed an act in 1859 to provide for the protection of property in slaves. Most of the federal officers stationed there were slaveholders. It was crucial for the Confederacy to control Indian Territory and New Mexico, which would lead to the federal gold and silver mines.

En route back to Indian Territory, Emory left Memphis for Fort Smith on March 24 aboard the steamer *Arkansas*, but was delayed by low water in the Arkansas River. While aboard the steamer, 60 miles below "the Dardenelles" on April 2, he ordered the commanding officer at Fort Arbuckle "to commence the movement upon Fort Washita."[10]

Reaching Fort Smith, Emory on April 10 advised the commanding officer at Fort Cobb that Indian agents had informed him the Choctaws and Chickasaws did not want the "Cobb" Indians in any closer proximity to them than they were at the time. These Cobb Indians needed protection from hostile raids of their own tribes and to keep in check any raids on Texas.[11]

With Texas seceding, the War Department was no longer interested in protecting that state. However, they were quite concerned about the Cobb Indians and the fact the little post, about 160 miles northwest of Fort Washita, "is at such a distance from the base of co-operation as to leave it unsupported." Supplies and forage were difficult to obtain. The fort would need to be powerfully garrisoned.[12]

This situation put Emory in a quandary. In January the Choctaws had formally resolved to ally themselves with the South. Texas had seceded in February. The commander at Fort Washita had reported to army headquarters that Texans were threatening to attack the post. The conditions in Arkansas were unsettled. The Cobb Indians could not be left unprotected against the hostile Indians. Yet, the government knowing that Texas intended to invade the territory, felt that the strength of three federal garrisons totaling 500 men gathered at Fort Washita would help forestall the inevitable.

Gen. Scott, at the behest of Sen. Charles B. Mitchell, Arkansas, had recommended that Emory retain only one company at Fort Cobb. Although Matthew Leeper, agent of the Cobb Indians, had not yet arrived at Fort Smith, Emory had met with the contractors Johnson and Grimes who told him the "Indians are hutted and planting and without means and could not move at this time."[13] Actually, these food contractors feared the Indians would be out of their reach at Washita, hence their price gouging sales would plummet and their competitors would gain by their losses.

In his report Secretary of the Interior Caleb Smith had said: "The practice of licensing traders to traffic with Indians has been productive of mischievous results. The money received by them in payment of their annuities, generally passes immediately into the hands of the traders. They are left to depend upon their annuities from the government and their subsistence and these find their way into the hands of the traders, while the Indians receive from them goods at a profit of from one to three or four hundred per cent."[14] As time would show, although Smith and the Interior Department were quite knowledgeable about the exorbitant prices, it would only become worse within a very short time.

Thus, Emory, having been given discretionary powers as to the changing atmosphere in the area, left two companies at Fort Cobb and simultaneously, decreased the strength at Fort Washita. Both he and Scott had succumbed to the self-interest parties of that day.[15]

Emory's difficulties were just beginning. Maj. Sackett and Capt. Prince at Fort Arbuckle did not want to abandon that post. He dissented from their request. Arbuckle's troops were to move to Washita. One company of the First Infantry at Fort Arbuckle was already in place at Washita, having been ordered there on March 19 by Brig. Gen. William S. Harney at Headquarters, Department of the West in St. Louis.[16]

While Averell, the messenger, was wending his way to St. Louis, Emory was on the road to Fort Washita as cited in his April 18 report. His primary concern at this time was the supplies for the troops in the district. A year's supply was "expected around by the Arkansas River." He knew the risk existed of their being confiscated by the secessionists along the river. Already ammunition destined for the three forts had been seized by the rebels at Napoleon, Arkansas. With the present stores expected to run out by May 31, he proposed they be supplied overland and sought authority to "withdraw the troops toward Missouri where it will be convenient to do so."[17] Emory did not specify a particular point, but the abandoned Fort Gibson in the northeastern part of Indian Territory would have been a logical site. Supplies would have been transported along the old military road from Fort Leavenworth south to Fort Scott and then to Gibson.

Averell detrained at Rolla, Missouri, on April 20, and found the slave state in an uproar over the events transpiring in the east. Rebel flags were flying from windows of recruiting offices and homes.[18]

Despite voting to remain in the Union in March 1861, Missouri continued to be divided in politics. With Civil War declared, the roving bands of Missourians would come to be known as guerrillas and bushwhackers, and the avenging Kansans would bequeath their sobriquet of "Jayhawker" to the Kansas soldier. This was the climate Averell rode into, and from Rolla south to Fort Smith his mission would become more perilous.

> Leaving Rolla by the first stage coach at 5 a.m. the 22d, with several prominent Southern gentlemen as fellow-passengers, I proceeded, with changing horses, mails, and passengers, toward Fort Smith, through towns wild with secession excitement and rumors of war. The unruly temper of the people and their manifest readiness to embrace any pretext for violence made it necessary for the safety of my dispatches and their successful delivery, that my name and character should remain unknown. Having assumed a name and purpose suitable to the emergency, I experienced no great difficulty in passing safely through several inquisitions.

Somewhere along the route, Averell's male passengers left him. When it became apparent that the driver was drunk, the lieutenant drove the stage most of the way between Cassville, Missouri and Bentonville, Arkansas. At Evansville, Arkansas, he learned that Fort Smith had been captured by 800 Secessionists commanded by Col. Solon Borland of Little Rock. That night on the southern side of the Boston Mountains, the rumor became fact when his stage met another heading northward from Fort Smith.

Ferrying across the now rain-swollen Arkansas River, Averell reached Fort Smith on the morning of April 27. He had been ten days on his trip from Washington. And it was here he needed supplies and a horse to take him into Indian Territory. On the back of Emory's sealed order was an endorsement signed by F.J. Porter, assistant adjutant general, instructing the post quartermaster at Fort Smith to facilitate Averell's needs in order to reach Emory as quickly as possible. When Porter had written the endorsement, Fort Smith was federal territory. Now it was in the control of the South and alive with political frenzy. Secessionists were training and target practicing on the parade ground and the greatly needed quartermaster was in the guardhouse.

Capt. Samuel Sturgis and four companies of the First Cavalry had left the fort four or five days before, headed west, undoubtedly to meet up with their commander Emory. Additional intelligence indicated "that pursuit up the Arkansas and from the direction of Texas was on foot." Streams were flooding and bridges had been burned.

Surely Averell was discouraged with the news. Fort Arbuckle, his final destination, was 260 miles from Fort Smith. He needed food, but a horse was the priority. He found a man who was willing to "trade a horse, saddle and bridle for my gold watch and a bit of money." Possible confiscation of the man's horse by the rebels prompted the transaction.

Averell's wounds had kept him out of the saddle for two years, and the laborious, bone-crushing stagecoach journey of 300 miles had left him in a weakened condition. Amidst the clamor on the parade ground, Averell mounted the horse. "The horse was unbroken to the saddle, and after a fierce but unsuccessful effort to throw me, ran wildly away through the successive lines of drilling troops, but I managed to guide him in a westerly direction and mastered him before reaching the Poteau River." Once across the river, Averell would be in Indian Territory. "This steam, 100 yards wide, was bank full and the bridge destroyed. Removing my heavy black overcoat, I swam the horse across, after a fearful struggle, in which I lost my overcoat and also suffered some injury from being struck by the horse."

Drenched, cold and exhausted, Averell followed the California Road in the Choctaw Nation west of Fort Smith until the road forked, tracing the northern and southern slopes of the "volcanic protrusions called San Bois Mountains," which "rise in several ranges about 1,500' high and gradually sink to the level of the undulating prairie seventy-five miles west of the fork." The San Bois had been named for the French trappers in their quest for more and more furs. The northern route led to Fort Arbuckle, while the southern trail went to Fort Washita. Sturgis's retreating command from Fort Smith had deepened the ruts, showing Averell they were headed south toward Washita. He did not question why Sturgis would go to Fort Washita instead of Fort Arbuckle where his commander Emory was. Averell followed the Northern Trail toward Arbuckle for about a mile in the hopes of confusing any would-be pursuers, and then he returned to the Washita road. He knew the Texas Road, or the Great Osage Trail, crossed both routes of the California Road at the western end of the San Bois. There he could head north toward Perryville and pick up the Arbuckle road once again. Not until he reached "Holloway's Overland Station, fifty-four miles west of Fort Smith" did Averell realize he was being followed.

His black overcoat had been replaced by a "light-blue overcoat of a private solder." The four "mounted desperadoes" had overtaken him at the stage stop, and the different overcoat persuaded them that Averell was not the man they wanted. They were seeking "a rancorous secessionist like themselves who was going to fetch a sister from the army on account of the prospective troubles."

Averell was allowed to continue on his way. A few hours later, leaving the road to let his horse graze, he watched as the same four men passed, following his trail. "Resuming the road after them, a friendly wayfarer, who had met them and heard their inquiries, informed me of their wrathful purpose to shoot me on sight."

"With the intention to reach the trail crossing of the Arbuckle road at the western end of the mountains" Averell proceeded cautiously forward. Soon, however, he saw the four men backtracking and "took to the woods." Upon seeing their prey, they fired, ordering Averell to stop.

The lieutenant struck a course across the mountains toward the north. He moved with difficulty through hills thick with pine trees and rocky streams and canyons. That night, packs of howling wolves challenged him in the woods, spooking his horse until Averell had to walk and lead the frightened animal. Not until 2 a.m. did he reach the Arbuckle road on the San Bois' northern slopes.

With daylight the four men came on in pursuit. "After another troublesome night in the woods among wolves and impassable ravines, I found a Cherokee cabin, some food for myself, and horse and a guide to the Arbuckle road ten miles west of Perryville." Averell was mistaken about the Cherokee as their nation was farther north, and likely the man was Choctaw or Chickasaw.

At any rate, from there the weary courier rode for another day and night before reaching Cochrane's ranch. It was at this point that Averell discovered Emory's troops were concentrating at Washita 40 miles to the south.

"Obtaining a fresh horse and an Indian guide, we set out for Washita, but toward night were overtaken by a blinding storm of wind and rain, in which the Indian lost the way and I lost the Indian. Making my way to the Big Blue River, I swam it in the dark and unsaddled, tied my new horse to one stirrup, and running my arm through the other, lay down and slept till morning. Upon awaking, the Indian, who had found me, informed me that we were not far from the road between Washita and Arbuckle and about ten miles west of the former place."

Reaching the road once again, Averell, upon seeing the deep, double trail in the mud, knew a heavy body of mounted troops was headed west toward Fort Arbuckle. Resolutely, he followed, and six miles later he found the First U.S. Cavalry and a company of the First U.S. Infantry. More importantly, he found Col. Emory. It was May 2.

After reading the orders, Emory conferred with his officers. The colonel was ordered to evacuate all three posts in Indian Territory and march men and supplies to Fort Leavenworth.[19] Now, the Union hierarchy believed these forts and their small body of troops would be overwhelmed by the Texas Confederates. With war plans escalating in the east, and with Arkansas likely to secede, the need for able-bodied troops elsewhere was a high priority. Perhaps loyal Arkansas volunteers could be used in the territory later, but for now, it would be propitious to abandon Indian Territory even though the South was trying to occupy it. The Union desertion of Indian Territory was a blatant violation of the treaty some Indian leaders were striving to keep in the face of Southern overtures. At this time Washington was willing to let the Indians supervise and protect themselves.

With the needed supplies seized by Arkansas Secessionists on April 18, Emory had had no choice but to abandon Fort Washita. The troops from Arbuckle and Cobb which he had ordered to Washita failed to arrive. When it was obvious they were not coming and the Texas militia was, he began the retreat to Fort Arbuckle. The next day, Washita was taken by the South without a struggle.

The violent spring storm, of the kind so prevalent on the southern plains, and which prevented Averell from reaching Washita, also, saved him from capture and Emory's orders being confiscated.

Averell, obviously weakened by his long journey, rode in an ambulance as Emory's forces proceeded north along the east bank of the Washita River. On May 3, the troops from Fort Arbuckle and the two infantry companies from Fort Cobb finally heading south toward Washita at Emory's orders met them five miles from Arbuckle. At Arbuckle the trains were loaded to capacity, and on May 4, with military honors, the U.S. flag was lowered and the post was officially abandoned. Emory left Sgt. Charles A. Campbell, Co. E., First U.S. Infantry, in charge of the remaining U.S. property. The troops headed for Fort Cobb.[20]

"On the 5th," Emory wrote in his official report, "finding myself followed, I halted and sent Capt. Sturgis with his company and Lieut. Averell to the rear to bring into my camp the advance guard of the pursuing forces which he did happily without having to shed blood."[21]

On the same day, a dispatch reached Emory from Campbell that a large force of Texans had taken possession of Fort Arbuckle. Being disarmed, Campbell and his men could offer no resistance. The command and their families, along with the private property, were promised "safe passage" to Fort Leavenworth by the Confederates.[22]

The following day, the captured Texas guard of 30 men was allowed to "retrace its steps." Emory, who had sent orders ahead for Fort Cobb's remaining infantry to meet him, was now concerned for their safety. Not until May 9 did Emory meet up with those troops 35 miles northeast of that post. The men, on foot, were being guided by the Delaware Indians Black Beaver and Possum.[23]

Black Beaver had been used by the army as scout, interpreter and guide during their explorations of the west. He had served as captain of a Delaware company fighting for the United States during the Mexican War. John J. Audubon, the naturalist, had depended upon Black Beaver as a guide in his westerly travels. Throughout all of his career, Black Beaver was considered the most intelligent, trustworthy guide and scout. And it was Emory's good fortune that he was at Fort Cobb.

In his report for 1860, Matthew Leeper had said: "The best improvement found on the reserve is a private enterprise of Black Beaver." Beaver's home was a "pretty good double log-house, with two shed rooms in the rear, a porch in front and two fire-places, and a field of forty-one and a half acres enclosed with a good stake-and-rider rail fence, thirty-six and a half which has been cultivated."[24]

Black Beaver, properly Suck-tum-mah-kway, would be overlooked by many future historians with regard to the route he used to take Emory and his command to Fort Leavenworth in 1861. This retreat of 11 companies, 750 fighting men, 150 women and children, teamsters and other non-combatants, would take them across the Canadian, Cimarron, and Arkansas rivers, the Seminole and Creek Nations and the Cherokee Outlet before reaching Kansas. The trail would come to be called the Black Beaver Road. During the post Civil War period, the route would become well-known, however, by another name. Jesse Chisholm, half-breed Cherokee, while driving Texas longhorns to the railheads in Kansas, followed the deep ruts made by Emory's retreat and it became part of the historic Chisholm Trail.[25]

Emory, in a report to Lt. Col. Townsend on April 13, had asked to be relieved of his command, wanting to return to Washington. Embarrassed to be an officer from a southern state in command of Union troops, he believed it was impairing his efficiency. "If these reasons should prove unsatisfactory, I am prepared to resign my commission."[26] Despite his request, he executed his duty and went on to Fort Washita.

Army headquarters found his reasons to be satisfactory, however, and on

May 9 accepted Emory's resignation. Communications being sporadic, on his retreat to Fort Leavenworth, he was incognizant that he had no military rank and was simply a citizen in command of the First U.S. Cavalry due to a misconception at headquarters. Upon hearing the true facts about Emory's request, Lincoln restored him to Lt. Col. of a new regiment, the Sixth Cavalry on May 14.[27]

Averell left Emory's train at El Dorado, Kansas, arriving in Washington City on May 30, where he wrote his report about the mission. His report today is considered the most colorful of all contained in the *Official Records of the War of the Rebellion*.[28]

That same day, Commissioner of Indian Affairs, William P. Dole, sent a letter to the Department of the Interior. "I desire again to call your attention, and through you that of the War Department, to what seems to me the necessity of sending a military force into the Indian country west of Arkansas." Apparently, Dole had suggested this necessity previously but without success:

> I again repeat that my conviction is, that a military force of two or three thousand men located in the Indian Territory, near the borders of Arkansas and Texas, would have the effect to secure the neutrality of the Indian tribes in our southern superintendency, besides having a salutary effect upon the States mentioned; and that unless this course is adopted by the government we shall soon find it impossible to maintain our agencies with the Choctaws, Chickasaws, Creeks, and other tribes on our southern borders, and incur the danger of having many thousands of these savage warriors in arms against our people. Our duty under treaty stipulations requires that we protect these tribes from the mischievous intermeddling of white persons without their borders, and our interest as well as that of the Indians, it seems to me, demands that steps should be taken to secure peaceable relations with them.[29]

Dole's prescience would be evident in the coming months. His protestations were lost somewhere in the political maze.

Communications in the 19th Century were often delayed and a number of them were transmitted verbally, if at all. As previously discussed in those early days of the Civil War, the War Department in Washington issued and rescinded orders over and over again, depending upon any facts received.

The South was also not immune to false rumors. A handbill and an appeal for arms had been sent to Gov. Thomas L. Moore of Louisiana from men in Shreveport. The handbill with a dateline of May 7, Marshall, Texas, read:

"An express has just reached this place that Montgomery of Kansas, at the head of 2,000 or 3,000 men, has taken possession of Fort Washita and Cobb on our northern frontier, and threatens the invasion of our State and the desolation of our country. Col. William C. Young at the head of 600 men was holding him in check and has dispatched runners calling upon the people for help."[30]

Where or how this story started cannot be explained. It was Col. Young who had taken Fort Washita in April after Emory had withdrawn from the area.

Gov. Moore quickly notified Confederate Secretary of War Leroy P. Walker of these developments. On May 14, Walker responded from Montgomery, Alabama, the site of the Provisional Government of the Confederacy. He assured Moore that he had "foreseen the probable movement of the enemy in the directions of Forts Cobb and Washita." To meet that risk, Walker had appointed Ben McCulloch brigadier-general with full authority of the Confederacy to guard the Indian Territory.[31]

Clearly the South believed the North would strengthen its forces in that area, a move the Confederacy did not hesitate to do in the months ahead. The South's campaign with the Indian Nations was self-seeking, still, they did appreciate the area, something Winfield Scott and the northern warlords failed to perceive.

By May 14, the date of Walker's letter to Moore, federal troops on their retreat were close to the Arkansas River in northern Indian Territory.[32]

Then Moore contacted Walker again on the 14th to the effect that northern Texas gentlemen were in New Orleans begging for arms, something everyone in the area would be doing in the months ahead. "Fort Washita occupied by one company of Texas troops. Fort Arbuckle is occupied by 1,500 U.S. troops. Colonel Young is besieging Arbuckle."[33]

Col. William H. Emory, Union Army, whose task was to move men and equipment to Fort Leavenworth in Kansas from Indian Territory. *Special Collections, United States Military Academy Library, West Point.*

Another report on the 14th from Capt. S.T. Banning of the Fannin County Company at Bonham, Texas, to Walker described the actions at Fort Arbuckle. The goods and property had been "turned over to the Chickasaw Indians by order of William C. Young." Banning disapproved of Young's treaty of peace with the Reserve Indians wherein conditionally "the Southern Confederacy feed and protect them as heretofore done by the United States Government at a very heavy expense." Very few Texans approved the treaty believing that "here was a worse than needless expense."[34]

On May 13, McCulloch was

ordered to proceed by way of Arkansas to Fort Washita to capture the 800 Union troops there. The Adjutant and Inspector General Samuel Cooper stated that the Confederate War Department had learned that Union troops were preparing for a retreat to Kansas. McCulloch was to intercept them if they had already left Washita.[35]

On the 23rd, McCulloch reported from Little Rock to Walker that Emory and the federal forces had retreated to Leavenworth. "I have learned that the notorious General Lane is rapidly organizing a force in Kansas to march into the Territory. Montgomery is no doubt hovering near the border."[36]

On May 25 the former major of the U.S. Army, Col. Earl Van Dorn of headquarters troops in San Antonio, ordered Col. H.E. McCulloch, Ben's brother, commanding the First Regiment of Texas Mounted Rifles, to march to the Red River. There he would assume command of the Texas State troops "in that vicinity under Col. Young." His mission was to take POWs "or defeat and drive off U.S. troops in vicinity of Forts Cobb and Arbuckle." This order was rescinded on May 28 when Van Dorn was advised that U.S. troops "had fallen back towards Fort Leavenworth."[37]

Emory, upon reaching Fort Leavenworth, May 31, reported to Townsend that he had "turned over the command to Major Sackett in good condition, not a man, an animal, an arm, or wagon has been lost except two deserters." He signed the missive "Late Lieut. Col., First Cavalry."[38]

Chapter 18

Alliance with the Confederacy

Albert Pike, Arkansas lawyer and editor, had been appointed by Jefferson Davis on March 5, 1861, as "commissioner of this Government to all the tribes west of Arkansas and south of Kansas."[1]

On March 12, Davis recommended the formation of an Indian Bureau. A bill was quickly enacted organizing that department and was passed on the 15th. On the 16th, David Hubbard was nominated by Davis to be Commissioner of Indian Affairs which became a part of the Confederate War Department.[2]

Pike had become well-known to the Five Civilized Tribes, particularly the Creeks, as they had retained him to represent them in the U.S. Court of Appeals. They had never been paid for their cessions of land in Georgia and Alabama contained in the Fort Jackson Treaty of 1814. In 1857, $800,000 was awarded to the Creeks for their 8,849,940 acres of land.[3]

Creek chiefs and leaders, such as Opothleyaholo, had become quite familiar with Pike with the passage of years. He had been through their country many times as he headed toward the plains to hunt buffalo. And he had sojourned with them, learning about their culture and fascinating history while waiting to pay them claim monies.[4]

A veteran of the Mexican War, Pike had welcomed the opportunity to convince the Indians to join the Confederacy. Well aware of his past dealings with the Creeks, Choctaws and Chickasaws, the Southern lawmakers knew he was the most logical emissary for the treaty transactions that they sought. However, he aspired to the command of troops in that region, and even suggested it to R.W. Johnson of Arkansas when he detailed the organization of troops, white and Indian, before meeting with the tribes. "My plan, if I were put in command, would be to proceed instantly to raise the regiments."[5]

Jefferson Davis had intended to cover all avenues of an alliance with the Indians, and he appointed his old friend, Douglas Cooper, agent to the Choctaws and Chickasaws, "to cultivate the most friendly relations and the closest alliance with the Choctaw Nation and all of the tribes west of Arkansas and south of Kansas."

The agent was well-liked by his charges and they would believe him. He was empowered "to raise among the Choctaws and Chickasaws a mounted regiment, to be commanded by yourself, in cooperation with Gen. McCulloch." Cooper's regiment of ten companies, 64 to 100 men each, was to be enrolled for a year.[6]

When Pike learned McCulloch was to be in charge of the Indian country, he was greatly disappointed. He did, however, carry out his duty, and along with McCulloch left Fort Smith on May 30 for Indian Territory. Their first stop was Tahlequah in the Cherokee Nation.[7]

McCulloch had anticipated the necessity of enlisting John Ross "to get a force into the nation that will prevent any force from the North getting a foothold" in their country. When the Texas commissioners had visited Indian Territory in February, they had reported that Ross declared the Union was not dissolved. He had, however, sympathized with the South and if Virginia and the other border states seceded, his people "would declare for the Southern Government."[8]

Some of the Cherokee Nation extended northward into southeastern Kansas. Previously known as the Osage "buffer" zone, these lands had been set aside for Osage half-bloods and their children in the 1825 treaty. Ten years later, the New Echota, Georgia, Treaty with the Cherokees, was approved. Under the terms of this treaty, the Cherokees relinquished all claim to their country east of the Mississippi and agreed to remove west of Arkansas. In addition to the lands in Indian Territory, 800,000 acres at a cost of $500,000 to the nation was set aside for the Cherokees. It was the "buffer" zone, the rectangular area between the Osage reserve in Kansas and Missouri's western border. The government had extinguished the Osage title to the land before the sale was made to the Cherokees. It then became known as the Cherokee Neutral Lands.[9]

Very few Cherokees settled in the area, but when Kansas Territory was established and the bogus, or Pro–Slavery Legislature was in power, the neutral lands were formed into one county named McGee with a six mile strip extending northward into Bourbon County. Today, McGee is composed of Cherokee and Crawford counties.

White settlers had staked claims to these lands, and during the Border Warfare years, much of it became ground for intermittent battles between the Free–State men such as James Montgomery and his band called "the Osages," and Pro–Slavery forces, most of them from Missouri.

In his 1859 report, Rector had cited the Neutral Lands as then being worth one million dollars to the Cherokees, and they wanted to sell it. He blamed the United States for permitting white settlers in the area. Rector was indignant that despite this area not originally being included in Kansas Territory, but now, that with the forming of the county, it was being "treated, for all practical purposes as part of the Territory of Kansas."[10]

Finally, the Cherokees complained about the intrusions, and even the Osages were embittered by the settlers' actions. Washington was notified of the conditions and in early 1860, U.S. troops from Fort Scott, commanded by Capt. Samuel Sturgis, were ordered to the area to burn out the settlers. Empty wagon trains escorted by the soldiers were driven on to the Neutral Lands, then loaded with the settlers' belongings and returned to the fort. With their homes in ashes, the families retreated to the fort, also.[11]

McCulloch knew of these neutral lands in southeastern Kansas and planned, after effecting a treaty with the Cherokees, to post troops there and eventually capture Fort Scott to use as a base of operations for his command.[12]

He was cognizant of the two rival factions within the Cherokee Nation; one side in sympathy with the South, the other, the largest, headed by John Ross, was certain to remain neutral.

Pike had informed Secretary of State Robert Toombs about the two rival factions that were "bitterly hostile to each other." The feud dated back to the 1835 treaty when it was made by "unauthorized persons against the will of the large majority of the nation and against the chief, Mr. Ross." In 1839, Maj. Ridge, John Ridge and Elias Boudinot, brother of Stand Watie, three signers of the treaty, were assassinated in Indian Territory by Cherokees, allegedly by the order of Ross. Watie, another signer, managed to elude the assassins and had survived. Pike, knowing Ross favored neutrality, was prepared for the chief's refusal and intended to inform him that his country would be occupied anyway. Ross, who was one-eighth Cherokee, had the support of the full-bloods. "The half-breeds or white Indians (as they call themselves) are to a man with us," Pike had said.[13]

Although both Pike and McCulloch foresaw difficulties with the Cherokees, neither man believed the Creeks would give them any trouble. Pike was sure the nations would be with the South "and those who are not will be unimportant."[14]

Ross assured McCulloch and Pike that "in the event of an invasion from the North," his people, with him in the lead, would repel it. McCulloch decided to abide by Ross's position of neutrality at that time. In a letter to Ross dated June 12, he gave him that assurance, yet he informed the chief that those "who are in favor of joining the Confederacy must be allowed to organize into military companies as Home Guards." Ross dissented from McCulloch's "demand" believing it "would be a palpable violation of my position as a neutral." Ross did not intend for "organized companies not authorized by our laws but in violation of treaty" to be formed. He believed domestic strife would ensue and create "internal difficulties among the Cherokee people."[15]

McCulloch felt Ross was merely "waiting for some favorable opportunity to put himself with the North. His neutrality is only a pretext to await the issue of events." McCulloch was confident that in order to compel Ross to join the Confederacy he must take Fort Scott, and "subjugate that portion of Kansas. I am satisfied that Lane has no force yet of any importance." The occupation of Fort Scott would place "Kansas in my power," bolster the morale of the Missouri border counties, "and accomplish the very object for which I was sent here, preventing a force from the North invading Indian Territory." McCulloch's plans had not stopped at Fort Scott. He had believed that with Missouri's cooperation with him, he could take "a position on the Kansas River" as he desired.[16]

McCulloch had not thought it wise to march the Indians into Kansas. "They are willing to organize for its defense [Indian Territory] but want to remain in it." Thinking the Indians would revert to savage conduct in a fight, he felt he could not restrain them once engaged and "I should much fear the censures that would be heaped on our Government by employing them." His foresight would be borne out in the Battle of Pea Ridge and the fire Pike would endure for having used Indians in that contest.[17]

The grandiose plans of the former Texas Ranger were only one of the many the South had received that spring and summer of 1861. Francis J. Marshall, the veteran major general of the Kansas militia, the Law and Order men during the Border Warfare days, had written to Davis in May about "that portion of country west of the Mississippi River to the summit of the Rocky Mountains and south of the Platte River in Nebraska, and northern Missouri to the northern line of Arkansas and Texas." Marshall told of the displeasure of the people in this area with the federal government "in removing the U.S. troops from the Western Frontier." The citizens, particularly those of Colorado Territory, were apprehensive about hostile Indians on the warpath. "With six regiments of cavalry from Arkansas and Texas and the forces that can be obtained from the Indian Territory, I can seize and hold Forts Laramie and Wise and Fort Union, if necessary."

The Kansan planned to confiscate "all military stores and munitions of war" of Kansas and Colorado forts. His headquarters was to be established "near the Cheyenne Pass." With Laramie and Wise in his possession all communications would be cut off "between the Northern States and the Pacific Coast."

Forts Leavenworth and Riley, with help from Missouri, would be seized and the expulsion of "the Northern vandals" from Kansas would ultimately "declare Missouri, Kansas and Colorado a part of the Confederate States."

Marshall had intended to seize "the daily overland express mail to California," and use it to move mail to and from the South. "A majority of the owners of the capital stock of this company entertain warm Southern views and would willingly acquiesce therein." The mail was the Pony Express and the company was Russell, Majors and Waddell. As to whom the real stock owners were, Indian treaty money initially had funded the concern.[18]

Dole had received a letter from Augustus Wattles, special agent of the Central Superintendency, in May concerning the former Pro–Slavery party's active participation in arousing the Kansas Indians. Wattles, an Abolitionist from Ohio, had helped found Moneka, a hamlet west of Pleasonton, Kansas, in 1857. Wattles told of the "lawless white men" who were raiding the Osage Nation and stealing their ponies. When the Osages took chase they killed several of the thieves and retrieved their ponies. "A company of men is now getting up here and in other counties, to go and fight the Indians." The Osages, through Wattles who was not their agent, appealed to the Great Father for protection.

Elsewhere, Robert B. Mitchell, former Maj. Gen. of Kansas, was "raising volunteers to fight the Indians." Wattles believed Mitchell would attempt to make a treaty with the Osages that in the end would lead to Michell's acquisition "of a large quantity of land for himself and followers." The agent requested the "Indian Department" act immediately to stop the pro–Southern sympathizers from breeding discord among the Indians.[19]

The Confederacy's attempt to incite the Osages and the Cherokees in southern Kansas "to bear arms against the U.S. Government" was reported to Dole by William Brooks, residing in Newton County, Missouri. Brooks had named a John Mathis, who lived in the Osage Nation, and a Robert Foster, a Cherokee, as the ones who had made inflammatory speeches against the Union. Mathis actually was John Matthews an Osage trader living at Little Town in southern Kansas. He was the son-in-law of "Old Bill Williams," the mountain man. A "Secession Company" had formed at "McGhee's (*sic*) residence" in the Neutral Lands. Twenty-five men had joined at that time and Brooks asked for help either in removing the men from Indian country or taking measures that will restrain "them from exciting the Indians in Southern Kansas." A.J. Dorn, Osage agent, was an avowed Secessionist "and consequently would favor, rather than suppress the move."[20]

By late June, McCulloch had received approval by the War Department to take Fort Scott, but was cautioned not to infringe on Cherokee neutrality as "the great object of your command being not only to conciliate the Indian nations, but to obtain their active co-operation with us in prosecuting the war."[21]

After his interview with Ross, McCulloch had returned to Fort Smith while Pike remained in Indian Territory. And for all of his strategic planning, McCulloch was hampered by the non-arrival of supplies. He complained to the War Department that regiments arriving in Fort Smith were "without tents or camp equipage of any kind." On June 29, McCulloch reported that federal forces were in Springfield, Missouri, and would soon be joined by Gen. Nathaniel Lyon "with the intention to enter this State and Indian Territory." The general was greatly embarrassed by the lack of transportation and arms and still, the expected Texas regiment had not arrived. "We are much in need of arms and ammunition. Is it not possible to send me a supply?"[22]

If McCulloch was having trouble being supplied, just where did Marshall believe the supplies would come from to provision the troops he would need to carry out his plans? Obviously, he planned to use Union's supplies after taking the forts. Possibly, Marshall had intended to use supplies from the storehouses and warehouses he had built. He had obtained a government contract in 1852 whereby he was allowed to provision army men returning from the western forts in the winter.[23]

A Charles Wagner in Montgomery had been queried about a supply of arms there. His answer had been, "None but a box containing seven rifles."[24]

In the meantime, Cooper had been successful with the Choctaws and Chickasaws and a regiment of mounted rifles from both nations had begun. Here again was the need for arms and ammunition. "I could not arm over three companies from all the guns in the regiment," Cooper said.[25] McCulloch verified that Indian Territory had "very few arms and I am continually applied to for a supply."[26]

On July 10, Pike concluded the first treaty in Indian Territory at North Fork village in the Creek Nation. Opothleyaholo's signature was not among the Creek names on the treaty. It read like its predecessors with the United States. Their lands were to be held "so long as grass shall grow and water run." The Confederacy had the right to build and establish forts, military and post roads within the nation. The institution of slavery was legal. Article 37 agreed that the Creek Nation, upon President Davis's requisition, would raise and furnish troops "for the defense of the Indian Country and of the frontier of the Confederate States as he may fix." It also promised that the Indians would "receive the same pay and allowances" as comparable troops in service to the Confederacy. The Creeks were assured in Article 38 that they would not "be required or called upon to pay, in land or otherwise" Civil War expenses or for any war "waged by or against the Confederate States."

Due to their relationship Creeks and Seminoles were to be allowed a "delegate to the House of Representatives of the Confederate States of America." Their privileges and rights would be the same as those of the other delegates. Annuities were guaranteed naming arrearages in prior treaties with the United States and upon ratification of the current treaty, the Confederacy would pay $71,960 for annuities and annual payments due July 1, 1861.[27]

When the treaty was ratified by the Confederate Congress, amendments were made, the most notably being rights and privileges of an Indian delegate.

As amended, these rights and privileges would be determined by the House of Representatives. It appears the Creeks and Seminoles, although allowed a seat in the venerable House, were not to be accepted by the Confederacy as their equal.[28] Although the Southern politicians were glad to have the Indian Territory's rich domain in the Confederacy, they considered the Indians themselves as troublesome and worthless allies.[29]

McCulloch and Pike had been confident that the Creeks would come into the Confederacy. Yet, the Upper and Lower Creeks were not in concert about the white man's war. Opothleyaholo and Ross had counselled about remaining neutral. The two men had sent delegates to Antelope Hills in the western part of the territory to meet with the Plains Indians and discuss neutrality. Bolstered by Chilly McIntosh, Pike determined to end the talks without the absentee members of the Creek council. He knew Ross was advocating a neutral position. Also, he believed, as he reported to Richmond, that Ross was attempting to bring into a confederation the Plains Tribes along with Cherokees and Creeks to form an Indian State. Such a state would be a formidable foe to the South and the North. Pike bragged that he had defeated Ross and in turn, Opothleyaholo and the plan for an Indian State by concluding the treaty while the delegates were at Antelope Hills.[30]

The Creeks in council with Pike had insisted that the colonel of their regiment to be raised should be elected by the men. Pike had recommended that agent William H. Garrett be appointed colonel.[31] The Creeks objected. McCulloch, reporting to Richmond, found objection to the selection of Garrett. "From what I know of his habits, I am satisfied that a worse appointment could not be made."[32]

In August, Daniel N. McIntosh, youngest son of William, was commissioned colonel of the Creek regiment. Chilly became lieutenant colonel of a Creek battalion. Pike reported vaingloriously "two thousand Creeks and Seminoles against Lane's and Montgomery's marauders will be a force not to be despised."[33] Pike either had ignored the dissension among the Creeks or was unaware that some were charging their names had been fraudulently signed to the treaty.

On August 5, a Creek council was assembled in which Opothleyaholo called the attention of the nation to the treaty signed in July. The Creeks who had met with Pike had done so without benefit of the national Council, and were in disobedience of tribal law.

Ouktahnaserharjo, commonly known as Sands, Tallise Fixico and Micco Hutki had gone to Antelope Hills. On their return they had been dismayed to find their names on the treaty. Motey Kennard, principal chief of the Lower Creeks and Echo Harjo of the Upper Creeks were censured for their complicity in making the treaty. No longer would either man be considered chief.[34]

The remembered days of the Indian Springs Treaty were brought to the forefront. A Non–Treaty Party was formed, the plurality being Upper Creeks. Although Sands was elected as acting chief of the nation, it would be the steadfast Opothleyaholo who would remain the leader.[35]

Since coming to this wild land in 1836, it had only been the past decade in which the Creeks had become comfortable in their new home. The acrimonious feud that had existed between the Upper and Lower Creeks had seemed to dissipate with the passage of time. Roley McIntosh, half-brother of William, had been the Lower Creek chief, and despite the Upper Creeks having a chief, McIntosh was accepted by the entire nation.

In 1859, an election had been held. Kennard was elected principal chief of the Lower Creeks with Jacob Derrisaw as second. Echo Harjo was elected principal chief of the Upper Creeks with Sands as second. "With this election," Agent Garrett had reported to Rector, "the late principal chiefs of the Lower and Upper Creeks, Roley McIntosh and Tuckabatchee Micco, retire from public life."[36]

With the abandonment of Fort Gibson in the Cherokee Nation in 1857, the Cherokees and Creeks had no immediate post in their region. "The growing up of a vicious little town there" had given an increase in the whiskey trade for the two nations, Rector complained. He urged that a post be established or "the attempt to suppress the traffic in liquor will be futile."[37] Rector's critique of the Cherokees was not optimistic, blaming their lack of "visible improvement" on drunkenness and gaming.[38]

The Creeks were also vulnerable to the whiskey and the game of "faro" played openly at an annuity payment meeting held just inside the Cherokee country. Gamblers from Arkansas and elsewhere had congregated for the usual ploy to separate the Indians from their money. Rector saw the Creek fullbloods as "orderly, honest and industrious."[39]

There were schools and churches in their nation. In 1860, Garrett cited a constitution that was adopted at the general council, which provided for an "election by the people of one principal and one second chief." The two districts were to become four with appointments of judges for them "with five supreme judges for the entire nation." The Creek police called "Light Horse" had been given more authority "to destroy all spiritous liquors brought into the nation." The Light Horse could levy fines and penalties upon the miscreants.[40]

Several bands of Shawnees, Kickapoos and other Indians had been allowed to settle on the Creek southwestern border, adjoining the Seminoles. These settlements were viewed favorably by the Creeks, who had adjudged these Indians would guard them from Comanches and other prairie Indians who made raids to steal their horses.[41]

Without military escort, Rector had conveyed $400,000 from Fort Smith to the Creek Agency with only nine men as guards. He told of the plan of "near twenty Cherokee desperadoes to rob the Creek agent of a large sum of money," and deplored the lack of military escort in the region, blaming the transfer of the Indian Bureau from the War Department to the Interior Department as the culprit.[42]

These pre-existing conditions would bear heavily on the treaties Pike was desperate to obtain. He had no trouble concluding treaties with the Choctaw–Chickasaw nations. He would, however, meet with dissension among the Seminoles and those who protested the treaty such as Billy Bowlegs, Alligator and Haleck Tustunuggee.

It was Rector who had reported in 1859, that "Bowlegs, fortunately for his people is dead; but others survive, who are inclined to create difficulties, and may need a salutary lesson." Samuel Rutherford, Seminole agent, did not cite the death of Bowlegs in his report; thus, another error in history.[43]

Billy Bowlegs, the last Seminole chief to emigrate to the territory, was alive. When Opothleyaholo resolved to stay with the Union, Bowlegs was one of the many Seminoles who journeyed to the leader's home where the present Eufaula is now located. Bowlegs, along with Haleck Tustunuggee, and Alligator in the months ahead would align themselves with Opothleyaholo and with Euchee Little Captain they would take an active part in the stand for the Union.

Chapter 19

Indian Territory Isolated from Union

Evan Jones, aged Baptist missionary to the Cherokees, had alienated himself with the Secessionists who were becoming more prominent in the Indian Territory. Jones, who was anti-slavery, had been with the Cherokees in Georgia and had emigrated with them. He is credited with the Cherokee organization of the Keetowahs, a secret society, which became known as the "Pin Indians" due to the pins shaped like a cross they wore on their clothing. Jones and the Pins were considered Abolitionists and were supporters of John Ross.

In June 1861, the missionary had retreated to Kansas for personal safety reasons. He was firm in his conviction that Ross and the Cherokees could never be coerced into succession. The full-bloods remembered only too well how the Georgians had treated them and they would never trust their former enemies to abide by any treaty. And Jones was certain that since the Cherokees, Creeks and Seminoles were not considered cotton growers as the Choctaws and Chicasaws were, that these three tribes, principally grain and stock raisers, were more identifiable with the federal government.[1]

Kansas newspapers reported in August that "the Rebels have been tampering with the Indians and that our State is now in danger of invasion by the Savages."[2] Union spies had been sent to the Kansas tribes and those of Indian Territory. They reported that Francis "Frank" Marshall and several well-known Secessionists were moving among them, enlisting their help against the Union and Kansas. Obviously, Marshall's intent was to start an Indian war to further the plans he had outlined to Jefferson Davis. He was furnishing flour, blankets, guns, ammunition and money in return for the Indians help. Marshall and friends promised the Indians "that the entire area of Kansas, with all the towns, farms, crops and etc. should revert to the Indians, if they would side with the Secessionists and drive out the present population."[3]

Kansans, who had endured six years of border warfare, suddenly found they could be facing an Indian uprising. They were advised to organize "Committees of Safety in every village and hamlet." Anyone who refused to "take the usual oath of allegiance to the Government" would be suspect.[4]

In Missouri, the situation was worsening. Gen. Sterling Price, the former 300-pound governor, and McCulloch were advancing with an estimated force of 25,000 men upon Brig. Gen. Nathaniel Lyon near Springfield. In a battle at Boonville in June, Gov. Claiborne Jackson and his forces had been defeated by Lyon, losing control of northern Missouri to the Union. Jackson and his troops had retreated to Springfield in the southern part of the state, determined to give Missouri to the Confederacy. "I will take Missouri out of the Union, or I will take her to Hell," Jackson declared in July.[5] The Union intended to rout all rebels from that area, defeating the South's intention to make that region their stronghold.

The combined force of Rebels including Pillow, Thompson and Hardee, of approximately 50,000 men nearing strategic points in the state was all calculated to take St. Louis with its federal arsenal, and set up an invasion of the loyal states to the north. Control of the Mississippi River would enhance the invasion.

The rebels were in dire straits so early in the war. One soldier commented that their baggage trains had been left behind and their provisions expended. They were so hungry they ate green corn without any salt. "We had not a blanket, nor a tent, nor any clothes, except the few we had on our backs and four-fifths of us were barefooted." This was their condition the night before the battle.[6]

Maj. Gen. John C. Fremont of the regular army was in command of "the Western Department covering Illinois, and territories and states west of the Mississippi to the Rocky Mountains and New Mexico." Fremont had a total of 23,000 men under his command, with only 15,000 available for active duty as the rest were 90-day men whose terms would soon expire. With such an extensive area to cover, Fremont ordered the Seventh Missouri Regiment from Boonville and Col. James Montgomery's Kansas Regiment to support the beleaguered Lyon.

Then with the dawning of August 10, Lyon with 6,000 soldiers met the 15,000 men of "Old Pap" Price, McCulloch and Jackson at a creek named Wilson near Springfield. It was a bloody, disastrous battle in which the West Point graduate Lyon was killed and finally, the vanquished federals retreated north.

The Confederate victory at the battle of "Oak Hills," as they called it, was an important one. Following their victory at Bull Run in Virginia, it added zest and fervor to the speeches Pike was delivering in Indian Territory. McCulloch reasoned the victory would bring Ross into the Confederacy with Rebel control of southern Missouri now secured.[7] This engagement certainly increased the fears of the tribes—How could the federal army be the losers, they were so powerful?

It had increased the fears Ross entertained. Certainly he must have recalled the letter he had received from Henry Rector, governor of Arkansas and cousin of Elias. In January, the governor had outlined the reasons why Arkansas and the Cherokees would be "natural allies in war ... the contiguity of our territory with yours induces relations of so intimate a character as to preclude the idea of discordant or separate action. It is well established that the Indian country west of Arkansas is looked to by the incoming administration of Mr. Lincoln as fruitful fields, ripe for the harvest of abolitionism, freesoilers and Northern mountebanks."[8]

There are half-truths contained in Rector's letter. The South reiterated many times that the North would appropriate Indian Territory for another state. Yet, Pike had reported to the State Department that his successful treaty mission eventually would benefit the South, by converting the Indian lands into "the very finest state in the Confederacy."[9]

Ross called for a general meeting of the Cherokee people to be held at Tahlequah on August 21. On the 24th, he forwarded to McCulloch a copy of the proceedings in which it was agreed to form an alliance with the Confederacy. The organization of a regiment had been started with John Drew as colonel. This regiment would contain principally the Pin Indians. Drew was a friend and supporter of Ross whose long-time term as chief was tenuous.[10]

Ross was wary of Stand Watie, and had been dismayed to learn that despite his disapproval, McCulloch, covertly, had solicited the half-blood to raise a force of Cherokees on the part of the South. One of Watie's chief scouts was Clem Rogers, father of 20th Century humorist, Will Rogers.[11]

By September, McCulloch reported to Secretary of War Walker that Watie and his men were stationed on the Cherokee Neutral Lands in Kansas, and were protecting the Cherokees' northern border from any raid by the Jayhawkers.[12]

William G. Coffin, blacksmith, coke maker and potter of Indiana, was appointed superintendent of the Southern Superintendency by Lincoln in May, 1861.[13]

The Bureau of Indian Affairs was in a quandary as to this superintendency, the branch assigned to govern the Five Civilized Tribes and other Indians in the area, which extended from Indian Territory into southern Kansas. When Rector resigned, he had kept all records pertaining to his office that was located at Fort Smith. All of the Indian agents had resigned, with the exception of Leeper in charge of the Wichita Agency at Fort Cobb.

The federal government's withdrawal of troops from the territory, and the suspension of annuities to the tribes strengthened the position of the South's campaign to undermine the Indians trust in the Union. The closing of the forts had helped to seal off the entire area from the North and any communications with the chiefs and leaders were effectually discontinued.

With Rector's resignation, the money for the tribes was not sent to them because the federal government feared it would go to the Rebels. Rather an incongruous deduction as the Secretary of the Interior Caleb Smith had stressed the literal robbing of the Indians' annuities by the traders who were allowed in the area by the agents—agents who had been selected as guardians of the Indians welfare.

In his 1861 report, Smith succinctly described the atmosphere in the Indian Territory for that year. "Cut off from all intercourse with loyal citizens, surrounded by emissaries from the rebels, who represented that the government of the United States was destroyed, and who promised that the rebel government would assume the obligations of the United States and pay their annuities; assailed by threats of violence, and seeing around them no evidence of the power of the United States to protect them, it is not surprising that their loyalty was unable to resist such influences."[14]

When Coffin arrived in Kansas in June, he was carrying letters written by Dole and addressed to Ross; Cyrus Harris, Chickasaw; M. Kennard, Lower Creek; Echo Harjo, Upper Creek; George Hudson, Choctaw and to the Principal Chief of the Seminoles west of Arkansas. Dole introduced Coffin as the replacement for Rector and said that capable agents would be appointed for them. "A communication from this office has been addressed to the War Department requesting that troops and munitions of war may be furnished to your territory to protect your people against the depradations of all parties, whether claiming to be for the Union, or the avowed aiders and abettors of treason, and I have assured the President that he need have no apprehensions of trouble with your people in his endeavors to preserve the Union and the Constitution and enforce the laws, and in this assurance I have full confidence that I am not deceived." The date of the letters was May 11. Emory with his force of federal troops was on the Black Beaver road in Indian Territory heading north toward Fort Leavenworth. Also, Coffin was delayed in reaching Kansas due to personal affairs and the posting of a bond required for his position. When he arrived at Fort Leavenworth he set up temporary quarters there and began trying to reach the various tribes,[15] but was too late. Dole's letters to the chiefs could not be delivered. Indian territory was out of Coffin's reach and that of the agents he had assigned.

Senator James Lane had been appointed by Lincoln to be a brigadier general of Kansas volunteers. Although there was controversy about Lane holding his senate seat while maintaining a rank in the army, the senator left Leavenworth for Fort Scott on August 17. There he began the task of enrolling men for the Kansas Brigade.

Soon after reaching the fort, Lane determined to move north to the Little

Osage, about 12 miles, and establish Fort Lincoln. He believed Fort Scott could not be fortified and saw fit to withdraw "therefrom all trains and stores not required for immediate use. At this point we have two companies, about 100 men, engaged in erecting intrenchments and drilling."[16]

It was at Fort Lincoln that Lane dispatched messages on August 22 to the agents of the Sac and Foxes; Shawnees; Delawares; Kickapoos; Pottawatomies and Kaws. He informed the agents that "for the defence of Kansas I have determined to use the loyal Indians of the Tribes above named. To this end I have appointed Augustus Wattles, Esq. to confer with you and adopt such measures as will secure the early assembling of the Indians at this point."[17]

Wattles assured the agents that the Osages needed assistance and that Lane intended "to establish a strong Indian camp near the neutral lands as a guard to prevent forage into Kansas." Upon learning that Dole was in Kansas, Wattles notified Maj. Farnsworth on August 26. "I think it best to say nothing to the Indians till he is consulted in the matter."[18]

Lane has been criticized by historians for overstepping his authority in requesting permission to use Indians in southern Kansas. In retrospect, it was Lane who helped draw attention to the importance of Indian Territory. He saw the need to re-take it from the Confederacy and in reinforcing the region with Union troops.

Coffin, unable to perform his duties, had been assigned by Dole to do a census of the Sac and Fox in the Central Superintendency. Dole had come to Kansas to personally deliver the amendments made by the Senate at its last session to the Delaware treaty dated May 30, 1860.[19]

The commissioner was advised of Lane's plans to enlist the Kansas Indians in defending the southern border. When Dole met with the Delawares he inquired as to whether, if need be, they would furnish men for an army. The chiefs made it quite clear they did not want their men volunteering for service. However, Fall Leaf and others did report to Gen. John C. Fremont at Leavenworth for special services such as scouts and guides. Fall Leaf would attain the rank of captain.[20]

In the summer of 1861, George A. Cutler, now with the honorific rank of major, was appointed agent for the Creek Indians and reported for duty to Coffin at Leavenworth. He headed south for the Creek Agency, but on reaching southern Kansas he learned that Coffin was right. All of Indian Territory was in the possession of the Rebels. Cutler tried to communicate with the Creeks to assure them that the federal government was permanent, but he was unable to do so. He established LeRoy in Coffey County as the temporary office of the Creek Agency.[21]

Chapter 20

I Am Alive

Opothleyaholo and Ouktahnaserharjo (Sands) wrote to Lincoln on August 15, 1861:

> Now I write to the President our Great Father who removed us to our present homes, & made a treaty, and you said that in our home we should be defended from all interference from any people and that no white people in the whole world should ever molest us unless they come from the sky but the land should be ours as long as grass grew or waters run, and should we be injured by anybody you would come with your soldiers & punish them, but now the wolf has come, men who are strangers tread our soil our children are frightened & the mothers cannot sleep for fear.
>
> I was at Washington when you treated with us, and now White People are trying to take our people away to fight against us and you. I am alive. I well remember the treaty. My ears are open & my memory is good.[1]

Micco Hutki, Bob Deer and Joe Ellis, the interpreter, carried the letter to Kansas, reaching the Shawnee Agency in Johnson County the first part of September. There they met with Agent Abbott of the Shawnees. It is obvious that the intrepid message bearers did not know Coffin had been appointed.[2]

The Indians had come from the Little River settlement in the western part of the Creek Nation. It was a dangerous, yet courageous, undertaking to move through areas where Rebel scouts patrolled the northern border of Indian Territory. When they reached the Shawnee Agency they had journeyed close to 400 miles.

Abbott sent the letter on to Washington. It is unclear how E.H. Carruth, appointed by Lane as Special Commissioner, was able to read it as he was at Barnesville near Fort Scott. However, in a letter to Opothleyaholo dated September 10, Carruth wrote:[3]

"Your letter by Micco Hutka is received. You will send a delegation of your best men to meet the Commissioners of the United States Government in Kansas.

"I am authorized to inform you that the President will not forget you. Our armies will soon go south and those of your people who are true and loyal to the Government will be treated as friends."

Carruth sent a letter to the Chickasaw and Choctaws "who are loyal to the U.S. Government" in which he asked them to send a delegation to the headquarters of the Kansas Brigade. He vowed "your rights will be held sacred; you will be protected in person and property."[4]

Carruth wrote to Tusuquach, chief of the Wichitas, inviting the chief to come to Kansas with "your friends the Seminoles or send two or three of your best braves." The Keechis, Ionies, Cadoes and the Comanches were asked to meet and talk "with the commissioners of your Great Father at Washington. His soldiers are as swift as the

Micco Hutki, Creek, who braved the dangers of carrying messages and leading Indian delegates to Kansas. *Archives and Manuscripts Division of the Oklahoma Historical Society.*

antelope and brave as the mountain bear. Your friend Black Beaver will meet you here ..."[5]

Micco Hutki carried these letters to Indian Territory. Before leaving he met with Evan Jones in Lawrence and assured him that all full-bloods among the Creeks, Cherokees and Seminoles were faithful to the Union. Opothleyaholo was thoroughly loyal to the United States.

Jones was still astounded by the news of the defection of John Ross and the Cherokees and believed it had been "an unwilling surrender."[6]

On learning Hutki was returning to Humboldt in November, Jones offered him $25 if he would deliver a letter to Ross. Inserted within the letter was Dole's message that Coffin had been unable to deliver. Micco Hutki refused. Jones' speculation that the Creek was afraid of being intercepted with documents in his possession was wrong. The man was already bearing Carruth's letters to the chiefs, which, if he were captured and they were confiscated, could prove disastrous to all concerned.[7]

Jones had been disheartened by the refusal as he had tried several times to get a messenger into the Cherokee Nation. Thomas J. Livingston's band

and Col. A.M. Coffey's men along with Stand Watie and his Cherokees were zealously guarding most every path and road into portions of southwest Missouri, northwest Arkansas and Indian Territory. These men had no qualms about killing anyone loyal to the Union.[8]

Micco Hutki was successful in his mission. Carruth's rhetoric was believable. The promise of a Union army marching into Indian Territory was taken seriously by Opothleyaholo. A council was called and Micco Hutki, along with Sands, Bob Deer and Phil David of the Creeks, were delegated to return to Kansas. Representatives of the Choctaws and Seminoles accompanied them. Before these men returned to Kansas, Lane had instigated fortifications for the defense of the southern border of Kansas.

The building of Fort Row on the Verdigris River in Wilson County was started in the fall of 1861. It was constructed by order of Lane. His reason for the little stockade's existence was a direct result of a Rebel raid on Humboldt, seat of Allen County, in September 1861.[9]

Guerrillas, Osage half-bloods and dissident Cherokees, commanded by John Matthews and Thomas Livingston, looted the small German–American settlement of anything of value.

As early as August 15, Lane had informed Capt. Prince at Leavenworth that Humboldt should be fortified. It was situated on bluffs above the Neosho River and considered "the key to the Neosho Valley." The Neosho River flowed southward through Osage country and the Cherokee Neutral Lands and down into the northeastern corner of the established Indian Territory. It was an important conduit for all types of travel.[10]

Matthews was very influential in the affairs of the Osage tribe. Livingston had for a time lived in Greenwood County, Kansas. He had taken up residence at a spring noted for its salt, a stream which flowed into the Fall River. Indeed, the spring was called "Little Salt" and the Fall River "Big Salt" by the Osage. Livingston had purchased the spring from Thomas Rhodes in 1860. Actually, the spring was situated on New York Indian Lands and when in 1860 the Iroquois Confederacy and other eastern tribes did not settle there in any number, the government declared the area open for white settlement.[11]

Livingston had tested the spring water and reported the brine would yield one-half pound of salt to the gallon. When the Civil War was declared in 1861, he sold his claim to Charles Mongrain, sub-chief of the Osages. Livingston returned to southwestern Missouri, and soon organized a band of guerrillas and the name Maj. Thomas J. Livingston would be reported in Kansas newspapers and in official reports until his death in July 1863 at Stockton, Missouri.[12]

Matthews did not enjoy much fame except for the raid at Humboldt. Immediately upon the news, Lane had dispatched Col. James G. Blunt to head the patrol that included Augustus Wattles, to find Matthews "with orders to follow them to the Arkansas line or take them. I have offered a reward of $1,000 for the head of Matthews.[13]

Blunt, a former doctor in Anderson County, Kansas, left Fort Scott on September 20 in pursuit of Matthews. He recalled the chase in the 117 hand-written pages of his "Civil War Experiences" (which were found moldering and forgotten in the Kansas Historical Society basement at the turn of the century). "After hard marching for three consecutive nights, lying under cover during the daytime, we surprised their camp at daylight, and succeeded in killing their leader (Matthews)." The site of Matthews' killing was near present Chetopa, Kansas, in Labette County. Blunt would become prominent in Kansas history during the Civil War and would be the state's only major-general commissioned by Lincoln.[14]

Wattles reported to Dole that Matthews was carrying a commission from McCulloch "authorizing him to enlist the Quapaws and other Indians and operate on the Kansas frontier."[15]

In the same September 12 report of Lane's to Prince, the general wrote: "I have directed the erection of six stockades on our southern border; Captain Holt and Ford to erect one on Turkey Creek on the neutral lands immediately south of Bourbon County; Captain Miller at Humboldt; Captain Scott at LeRoy; and other competent captains, one on Verdigris, one on Fall River and one on Walnut. I have ordered a system of signals to be established by which they can arouse the country. These stockades will be completed and our southern border, I think, secure."[16]

Fort Montgomery, named in honor of Col. James Montgomery, was erected on the Fall River at Eureka in Greenwood County. The home guard was under command of Capt. L. Bemis and was manned by the volunteers during their entire term of service.[17]

The little stockade built on the Verdigris River in Wilson County was called Fort Row in honor of John R. Row who was a veteran of the Mexican War. Row was captain and Lewis C. Thompson and W.W. Brazell served as second lieutenants.

The company of mounted militia consisted of 70 to 80 men who were settlers on the Verdigris in Wilson, Woodson and Greenwood counties and they supplied their own weapons. The crude fortifications consisted of three log block houses, 16' × 24', and pickets, made of split logs eight feet and higher placed close together, surrounded it on three sides. The fourth side was the steep bank of the river. The stockade had port holes and an additional embankment had been made on the outside. All of the horses belonging to the men were kept within the stockades.[18]

Fort Row, just as was the small settlement at Belmont, 15 miles to the east in Woodson County, would be recorded in the annals of the Civil War. But no matter its importance, its name was destined to be spelled wrong. Official reports show it as "Fort Roe" and "a place called Roe's Fork."

Wilson County, the area where Opothleyaholo would lead his people, was contained within the Osage Reserve. Although it was Indian land, which in itself was never a deterrent to the white man, settlers appeared north of the Verdigris River near the present town of Coyville in the spring of 1857. During the next three years, more and more settlers pushed into the area. It was estimated that by 1860 there were more than 100 white people in the county, even though only 27 registered in the federal census for that year. The small number of registrants was the result of the 1860 drought.

Despite the white man's encroachment of their lands, the Osages were lenient with them, permitting them to stay as long as they did not desecrate any of their sacred tribal spots, destroy the timber, and did not steal their ponies.

A fine example of justice and mercy meted out by the Osages occurred in June 1857 when four horse thieves were apprehended by the Indians near the Allen–Dorn county lines. Later, Dorn County would be divided into Neosho and Labette counties. The men, with their feet tied together on the underside of ponies, were taken to Canville Trading Post and placed under guard.

Chief Little Bear of the Little Osage band arrived the next morning and in accordance with an Osage unwritten law, determined that the men would be judged by a jury of twelve men. The panel comprised six half-bloods and six full-bloods of the Osages, and it would be their task to hear the evidence and pass a sentence of guilt or innocence.

It was common knowledge that these four men were members of an outlaw organization extending from southeast Kansas into Iowa, and whose only aim was to steal Indian ponies for profit. The accused were asked to divulge the names of the members and if they did so, they would not be killed. They would be released after each one had one-half of the head shaved and one ear excised. And they must leave Kansas Territory in five days.

Only by the arrival of Chief White Hair, who took precedence over Little Bear, were the men saved their ears. He believed the punishment was too severe. The chief ruled that if they would disclose everything they knew they would suffer only one-half of their heads shorn. White Hair believed that cutting off an ear would forever brand the men as thieves, while the hair would soon grow out and give them an opportunity to become useful men again. The accused told all; ten men were served notice to quit the Osage country.[19]

In the spring of 1861, the Missourians were trying to stir up the Osages against the Union. However, Little Bear captured some of them and after warning them "they had 'talked bad talk to the Indians' he tied them with ropes to the horns of his saddles and dragged them out of the country."[20]

Prior to Wilson County's organization in 1864, it was attached to Allen County for legal matters, and Cofachique, a pro-slavery settlement, was named the permanent county seat. Cofachique was established in 1855 near present day Iola. There was much dissension between the Pro–Slavery and Free–State men in that area that later would bring about the demise of the little settlement.[21]

Wilson County historical records identify "Cofachique" as the name of an Indian princess, but of what tribe is not known. It is interesting to note that when DeSoto and his men were wandering around southeastern Georgia in 1650 they encountered a chieftainess from the town of Cofitachequi. The men were welcomed into the town by its brown-skinned people who wore clothes and shoes. DeSoto considered the inhabitants far more civilized than the Florida Indians. The explorer repaid the town's hospitality by looting the village and kidnapping the chieftainess, who later escaped.[22]

Cofitachequi was believed to be Euchee in origin, however, the Bureau of American Ethnology has established the name as Creek. Thus, it is remarkable that the county where Opothleyaholo would lead his Creeks, Euchees and others for sanctuary was already associated with a Creek name.[23]

Two rivers cross Wilson County from north to south. The Verdigris was named by French–Canadian trappers who mined its waters for beaver. Verdigris, pronounced Ver-de-gree in French, was derived from the greenish-blue banks of the river which the Osages used as a pigment for ornamentation of their faces. The river is noted in history as early as 1806 when Lt. J.B. Wilkinson, descending the Arkansas River, passed the mouth of the Verdigris and judged it to be about 100 yards wide.

The Fall River was not recorded until Kansas Territorial days. The Osages knew of its existence and followed its course on the northern side to their hunting grounds near the Arkansas River west of Wichita. The Fall River would gain notoriety when the refugees first encamped within its timber belts.

These belts varied in width from one-half mile to one and one-half miles and were covered with oak, hickory, walnut, hackberry, elm, soft maple, pecan, sycamore, ash, cherry, cottonwood and cedar. And before the advent of the white man and his axe ringing in the woods, the trees were magnificent in height and circumference.

Bluestem grass, estimated as high as a man on horseback, blanketed the undulating course of the countryside. Refugees from Missouri counties fleeing to Fort Scott during the Civil War would be drenched by the dew-laden bluestem. Along the thickly timbered streams a fescue remained green during the winter despite the elements.

Wildlife was abundant: gray and black squirrels, raccoons, opossums, and deer. Skunks and badgers were so thick their holes made it unwise to gallop a horse across the prairie. There were wild turkeys, ducks, geese, quail, prairie chickens, a few pelicans, sand hill cranes and a foraging yellow-winged blackbird that liked the settlers corn.[24]

Indian trails crossed Wilson County and eventually some were followed for freight and military travel. In addition to the Osage hunting trail along the north side of the Fall River, there was one coming from the south that had branched off of the Great Osage Trail, later Texas Road, in northeastern Indian Territory. It passed the village of Claremont, an Osage chief noted as a "builder of towns." There were three Claremonts in the Great Osage tribe. The first Claremont had died in 1828 while on a hunting trip. The Osage usually buried their dead in a seated position in a grave which had been dug to a depth of six to 12 inches, and the upper torso was brought forward to the upraised legs with the head facing the east and resting on the knees. A cairn was then erected. If an Osage was away from the village when death occurred, he or she was buried upright in the crotch of a tree, their body covered with buffalo hides and thongs securing the corpse to the trunk and limbs.[25]

In 1832, Henry Ellsworth who had been appointed to go and study the Indian country, while traveling the area, reported seeing Claremont's skeleton in a tree. Ellsworth would later be called the Father of the Department of Agriculture.[26]

The chief Claremont's name would be commemorated in the town of Claremore, Oklahoma. His trail, at least 100 feet wide, led northward through Wilson County to the ford on the Fall River southwest of Fredonia, present seat of Wilson County.

The Osages were noted for marking certain eminences along their trails as a guide for travelers. While traveling with Ellsworth, Washington Irving referred to these landmarks of the Osages. Claremont's trail was no exception and was marked in at least two places in Wilson County.

The first, coming from the south, was northeast of Elk City and the second was about three miles south of the Fall River ford. This second mound, when first seen while traveling along K–96 highway, looks as though it is a part of the hills in the background. On closer inspection, the hill stands out. It was called "Round Mound" or "Blue Mound" by the pioneers.

The Osage cairn that adorned Round Mound was of sandstone approximately ten feet high, ten feet wide, with a gradual tapering toward the apex. It was a loose stone structure built in similar fashion to the cairns that contained Osage dead.[27]

Near the base of Round Mound a branch of the trail veered northeast to another ford southeast of Fredonia. Due north from the mound and past the principal ford on the Fall River stands what has become known as West Mound with its twin South Mound about three-quarters of a mile to the southeast. These mounds were shown to be 250 feet high on the 1866 county survey map. West Mound served as a landmark not only for the Osages but for the transitory Delawares and other tribes traveling the county. During flood times, the Osage Trail passed on the north side of West Mound.

The cairn on Round Mound that directed the wayfarers along the trail disappeared during the white man's desire to progress. In their drive to build houses and barns, they carried off the sandstones to be used in foundations.[28] Today, a rural water tank has replaced the marker, just as the trail, which was deeply rutted by travois, wagons and travel of unshod hooves, disappeared under the relentless cut of the steel plow.

Chapter 21

Look to the
Beaver Road

Unable to reach Fort Smith, Coffin picked Humboldt as the place to locate his superintendent's office. Settling down to the work ahead, he reported to Dole on October 2 about the conditions in Indian Territory and why he had been unable to reach his charges due to the influence of the Rebels. "The consequence has been to render it unsafe for any person not known to be thoroughly identified with the rebellion under any pretence to visit them, or for any person at all suspected of entertaining Union sentiments to remain among them. The only tribes I have been able to reach are the Osages, Quapaws, Senecas, Shawnees, and a part of the Cherokee Nation."[1]

Apparently, Coffin had not been in Humboldt when it was raided by Matthews and Livingston in September, but he was there when it was invaded once again in the late afternoon of October 14. Humboldt's Home Guard was caught by surprise and some were captured by the Rebels and later released.[2]

On this occasion, Livingston and his men were more vicious toward the little settlement. This raid was ordered by Gen. Price in retaliation for the burning of Osceola, Missouri, in September by Gen. Lane and his Kansas Brigade. Among the brigade were men from Allen and Woodson counties.

Hearing that Price was moving northward toward Lexington, Missouri, Lane had advised Capt. Prince on September 12 that he, too, was "moving northward with a smart little army of about 1500." Despite Lane being ordered by Gen. Fremont to Kansas City to cooperate with Capt. Sturgis, he went no farther than West Point. On his return south at Papinsville, Lane's army confiscated all things of use to Price's army such as wagons, tents and supplies. Osceola, 20 miles east of Papinsville, did not fare as well on the morning of September 22.[4]

Lane reported to Fremont that Osceola "was the depot of the traitors for southwestern Missouri." It was the county seat of St. Claire County, and a town of importance located "at the head of navigation on the Osage." A distribution point for eastern goods shipped to southwest Missouri and Indian Territory, the town literally was reduced to ashes by the battery of four field pieces which shelled it. A large amount of stores destined for Price's army was destroyed.[5]

Angered, Price sent Livingston and Col. Talbott to Humboldt. Not only did they loot the town, they torched it and a large portion was burned along with Coffin's office, home, and official papers belonging to the Indian Bureau.[6]

The 300 to 400 men did not leave Humboldt until after 10 p.m. that night. Flames lighted the night sky and smoke covered the valley. One farmer was killed and one Rebel died while attempting to cut down the flag pole flying the Union flag.

The small village of Humboldt would not soon recover from the raid. Charred remains of buildings and heaps of ashes blighted the townsite. Some resourceful citizens had replaced a ruined church steeple with an inverted stool.

Soon after the raid, a militia was formed and soldiers were stationed at Humboldt. The men built log houses along the Neosho River for their quarters. On a rise, a square fortification called a "fort" by the people was erected. At one of its corners on a high post a rusty buzz saw was hung and served double duty in arousing the citizenry to invasion and calling the garrison to mess.[7]

The two raids on Humboldt confirmed Lane's beliefs that southern Kansas was vulnerable to the Rebels. And the Rebels were not through with the area. A Major Russell and his family, living about ten miles below Humboldt, escaped from the Secessionists and made their way to Leavenworth. Russell advised that Secessionists were in "Allen and Woodson counties, overrunning those counties and threatening to sweep thru' (*sic*) the whole Neosho Valley." The editor had opined: "This state has thousands of soldiers in the field, but none are left to defend our homes."[8]

Livingston became a man to be feared by the scattered settlements in southern Kansas. There were militia enrolled in certain locations, yet, their numbers were overwhelmed by the 100 to 200 men riding with Livingston.

As late as 1862, Brig. Gen. Albert Pike, then commanding the Department of Indian Territory, was critical of Livingston and Col. A.M. Coffey. Writing to Maj. Gen. Thomas Hindman who commanded the Trans–Mississippi District, Pike complained about the two men "wandering around promiscuously, all urgently inviting an invasion of the Cherokee country."[9]

As the war progressed, so did Livingston's notoriety, much like that of the infamous William Quantrill. There was an exception between the two guerrilla leaders. Livingston never killed any white soldier who was his prisoner. But he constantly harried federal troops and their supply trains moving toward Indian Territory during the campaign to return Indian refugees to their country and retake the area.

Livingston was a master in eluding the Union forces. In the spring of 1863, federal officers were recommending "Kill Livingston and there is no one else to mass and congregate these bands."[10] They were wrong. When Livingston was killed in July 1863, his men banded with Col. Coffey and they all joined under Quantrill's black flag and nearly destroyed Lawrence, Kansas, on August 21, 1863.

Coffin, having to start afresh, moved his Indian office to LeRoy, Kansas, on the Neosho River. He believed he would be safer there as it was farther away from Fort Scott which was a magnet for Rebel armies and guerrillas due to its being a supply depot.[11] The superintendent removed himself from potential danger by the Rebels, and at the same time, located himself nearer to Fort Row and Belmont.

It would not be until November when Micco Hutki returned to Kansas with the delegation requested by Carruth that Cutler would see any of his charges.

In a letter to Dole, in which Cutler enclosed statements from the Indians, he explained:

> They have travelled some 300 to 400 miles to get here, had to take an unfrequented road and were in momentary fear of their lives not because the secessionists were stronger than the Union party in their nation, but because the secessionists were on alert and were determined that there should be no communication with the Government. They underwent a great many privations in getting here, had to bear their own expenses, which, as some of them who were up here a short time ago have travelled in coming and going some 900 miles was considerable.

In the statement given by Oke–Tah-hah-shah-haw-choe (Sands), it is clear that not all of the Creeks were succumbing to Pike's oratories. "Mr. Pike makes the halfbreeds believe what he says and the halfbreeds makes some of the full blood Indians believe what he says that they [the Indians] must help the secessionists." The chief declared his disbelief in Pike and when he had refused to oppose the U.S. his life was in jeopardy. The Secessionists had offered $5,000 reward for Sands' head.

Sands went on to say:

> Never knew that Creek have an agent here until he come and see him and that is why I have come among this Union people. Have come in and saw my agent and want to go by the old Treaty. Wants to get with U.S. army so that I can get back to my people as Secessionists will not let me go. Wants the Great Father to send the Union Red people and Troops down the Black Beaver road and he will guide them to his country and then all his people

will be for the Union. That he cannot get back to his people any other way. At the time I left my union people I told them to look to the Beaver Road until I come. The way he left his country his people was in an elbow surrounded by secessions (*sic*) and his people is not strong enough against them for Union and that is the reason he has come up for help.

The statements of the Chickasaw chief, Toe–Lad–Ke, and Choo–Loo–Foe–Lop–Hah Choe, a Seminole, corroborated that of the Creek. All asked for the Great Father's help and all wanted the federal army to go with them back to Indian Territory. Naturally, the promises made by Carruth were taken seriously by the Indians, and they expected the army to return with them as witnessed in their

Black Beaver, famous Delaware guide and scout, who piloted Emory's retreat to Fort Leavenworth. Kansas State Historical Society.

statements.[12] Now began a chess game with the Indians as pawns to be moved at the direction of agents, special agent, superintendent and even the commissioner of the Indian Bureau. As always they were treated like children and as usual, presents were used to conciliate them in the interim.

When Dole received these statements, he wrote immediately to Maj. Gen. David Hunter, commanding the Western Division of the U.S. Army at St. Louis. Dole, acting on Lincoln's direction, wanted the general to assemble the chiefs at Hunter's headquarters in Fort Leavenworth. In the event Hunter could not comply, Dole instructed him to confide in Gen. Lane, "provided he can be spared from his post."[13]

"By the papers enclosed you will also see that 'a talk' has already been had with some of the chiefs who represent the Seminoles, Chickasaws, and Creeks, and that they have fully set forth the artifices by which they have been deceived...."

Uppermost in Lincoln's mind was the annuities, and Hunter was instructed "to give them the strongest assurances" that they would be paid. "You will, of course, understand the importance of having this promptly done, because, if it is not, these deluded people may be induced to join the Confederate forces and take up arms against the United States."[14]

On November 20, Hunter notified Cutler that he wanted all of the chiefs and headmen of the Creeks, Cherokees, Chickasaws, Choctaws and Seminoles, if possible, to meet him at his headquarters at Fort Leavenworth.[15] However, before Cutler had received these instructions, the agent had taken the present delegation to Fort Scott to meet with Lane. Lane had left for Washington in his capacity as senator for a session and was away when Cutler arrived. Lane had left James Montgomery in command at Fort Scott.

On November 19, Col. Montgomery reported to Lincoln about the friendly Indians' visit. "Thinking it best that they should visit Washington, I take the liberty of sending them to your excellency. Their condition is deplorable; they will tell their own story."[16]

From Fort Scott, the Indians traveled to Leavenworth accompanied by Cutler and Carruth. There they met with Gen. Hunter who agreed they should go to Washington as "they cannot at present return to their tribes." The Indians were furnished with $1,300 in clothing and $200 was given to Cutler for traveling expenses. Cutler and Carruth accompanied them on the trip.[17]

Before Carruth left for Washington, he reported to Hunter. "The wonder is not that the Indians should have seceded, but that any remained true." Carruth's opinion in regard to the Five Civilized Tribes was, "the South will not let them remain neutral." Even at that late date, Carruth maintained that if federal aid were given those who were against the Union, they would turn back to it. "And the Union Indians once thoroughly committed openly to the government, it will be a war to the death." He feared that if the government continued to ignore the problems in Indian Territory that by the spring of 1862, "Kansas will be the scene of these cruelties, northern mothers will be the victims, our children may be slaughtered, our houses burned."[18]

Hunter, in sending the delegates to Washington, told Dole: "The large number of troops assembled near Washington will no doubt impress these people more strongly than anything else could with the strength and stability of our government."[19]

For some time after the August 5 council, Opothleyaholo had been gathering his people and Seminoles, Cherokees, Euchees and others at his plantation. Indeed, the same day Montgomery wrote to Lincoln, the Creek leader already was in his first battle with Col. Cooper in Indian Territory.

For at least a week, the citizens of Burlington, Kansas, had watched bands of the Sac and Fox Indians passing through their town on the way south and west to the Walnut and Arkansas rivers in the south central part of the state where roamed those shaggy beasts called bison, commonly known as buffalo.

It was December 1861 and the newspapers in Kansas were full of articles about the Civil War that was plaguing the east and as far west as Missouri and Kansas. Perhaps in order to add local color to the issue, the editor of the

Burlington Register had composed a short item about the Indians, merely wanting to provide a brief escape from the grimness of the national news.

The Sac and Fox warriors were "gaily decked in their unique costume and sport plumes, beads, jewelry and arrows and trusty rifles and many of them have their faces painted in various colors and all have spirited ponies." They were "accompanied by their squaws, upon whom devolves all the labor of pitching, striking and packing wigwams, and overseeing their conveyances, preparing meals and doing the drudgery."

The warriors led the procession after which "came the pack-ponies laden with wigwams, neatly packed and the camp equipments, squaws and little Indians and papooses." The editor estimated that "as many as three hundred must have passed through Burlington."[20]

Among their provisions for their winter hunt was the corn they had harvested on their reservation. The women, as soon as it was "good roasting ears," had boiled it, then scraped it from the cob. The kernels were spread out on hides and blankets to dry in the sun. Stored in rawhide sacks and trunks, only what they would need to supply them for their hunt was removed. The rest was buried three or four feet in the ground where it stayed as seed until needed in the spring for a crop.[21]

Chapter 22

The Second Trail
of Tears

When Opothleyaholo had taken his stand for the Union, various Indians had begun gathering at his 2,000-acre plantation. Many, who had been threatened by the Rebel Indians, came with their ponies, cattle, hogs, chickens and their personal possessions which were either packed on the ponies or hauled in wagons.

While the grass was being depleted, the chiefs and leaders held councils to determine what they should do. When it became obvious that none of them were to live in peace with the Secessionists of their own tribes, they knew they had to leave the area and seek forage for the herds and safety for themselves. The decision having been made, some of the chiefs and leaders returned to their own people to form a caravan which, eventually, would meet up with Opothleyaholo's group.

Opothleyaholo, commencing what would become his second "Trail of Tears," moved his entourage northward toward Hitchita near the Creek Council Ground.[1] Scouts had discovered that Col. Daniel McIntosh and part of his Confederate Creek Regiment was stationed close to the council site. At North Fork Town, near the junction of the Texas and California roads, another Confederate company was in place. Earlier newspaper articles reported that Opothleyaholo had threatened to attack North Fork Town.[2]

Soon the Rebels took the warning seriously and had retreated north of the Arkansas. The McIntoshes remembered well Opothleyaholo's fierceness in war. It is possible Opothleyaholo's intention merely was a verbal feint on his part as the attack did not materialize. Whatever his reasoning, the leader instead moved his people away from the area toward the northwest making another camp at Euchee chief Long Tiger's town near present Slick, Oklahoma.[3]

Close to the Euchee town was the Dawson Military Road. This road had been the Big Osage War and Hunting Trail that moved from the east at the mounds near Claremont's village through Tulsey Town to Keystone where it proceeded south to Fort Holmes near Holdenville and the Little River area where Micco Hutki lived.[4]

Micco Hutki's caravan moved northward to camp with Opothleyaholo and for a time these loyal Indians lived in peace. It was short-lived, however, when scouts reported the Rebel forces were on the move from the east.

With guards riding point, Opothleyaholo led the caravan of thousands of men, women and children, and earthly possessions north along the military road. To the rear, Little Captain or Keptene Uchee, with fellow Euchees, Creeks, Seminoles and Kickapoo warriors wearing corn shuck badges for identification either plaited in braids or pinned to shirts, guarded the entourage. Flankers of armed horsemen protected all of the caravan.[5]

In his report, Col. Douglas Cooper stated he had tried to interview Opothleyaholo and was unsuccessful. Believing the Creek leader was seeking an alliance with the federal authorities in Kansas, Cooper resolved to "either compel submission to the authorities of the nation or drive him and his party from the country."[6]

On November 15, Cooper with 1,400 men started marching up the Deep Fork of the Canadian River toward Long Tiger's town. Finding the camp abandoned, the Confederate whites and Indians advanced northward and on the 19th captured a few prisoners. Cooper learned from them that some of Opothleyaholo's "party were near the Red Fork of the Arkansas River on their route towards Walnut Creek where a fort was being erected."[7] The Red Fork of the Arkansas is now the Cimarron River.

The Confederates pushed on, crossing the Red Fork and about 4 p.m. "camp smokes were discovered in front a short distance and the enemy's scouts were seen at various points." A Texas cavalry detachment charged upon the camp only to find it "recently deserted." When other scouts were seen beyond the camp, the Texans gave chase, and watched them disappear into the trees along a creek. Little Captain and his men had done their duty. They had brought the Rebels up to the main encampment where Haleck Tustunuggee had posted warriors behind trees and brush along the creek. The Texans soon discovered they were also outnumbered on their flanks and they retreated, exchanging shots with the pursuing Union Indians.[8]

The Rebel Choctaw and Chickasaw regiment "formed and advanced towards the enemy," but by this time the night was dark and the Rebels could not shoot until "the enemy was within 60 yards of our line." Texans and a few Creeks commanded by Lt. Col. Chilly McIntosh reinforced the line.[9]

Capt. R.A. Young of the First Choctaw and Chickasaw Regiment reported: "The prairie was on fire on my right, and as we advanced to the attack

I could see very distinctly the enemy passing the fire." Young stated the fight lasted about 15 minutes, and Cooper reported "a short but sharp conflict" after which the Union Indians ceased firing "and under cover of darkness" Opothleyaholo's forces retreated. This battle near Keystone was the first in Indian Territory and was called "Battle of Round Mountain" or "Battle of Round Mound."[10]

At the summit of Round Mountain was an Osage cairn which had directed various Indian tribes along this Osage trail. All of the tribes in Indian Territory knew of its existence. The ruins of this guidepost could be seen as late as 1939.[11]

Col. Cooper's forces did not follow Opothleyaholo. Cooper had received a message from Gen. McCulloch that Fremont and a large force were at Springfield and Cooper was to take a position near the Arkansas state line. Since the forage had been "destroyed by the enemy" in setting the fire and the command's horses weakened by the rapid marches, Cooper returned to his train which had been left at Concharty located southeast of Tulsey Town.[12] Only Cooper's forces left the area. Scouting expeditions were detailed to watch any movement of the Union Indians.

After the Battle of Round Mountain, Micco Hutki and his group had moved north across the Arkansas. The weather was changing, alternating between brief periods of sleet and snow. Hutki and his men dug caves for shelter against the elements, rounding up the dirt into mounds. Uppermost in Opothleyaholo's mind had been the protection of the children, women, and the aged from harm and they had been moved to the caves before the battle. Following the conflict, the warriors joined their people, and stayed for about three weeks.[13]

It was during this respite that white prisoners unwittingly disclosed to the Union Indians that if indeed they wanted to return home, there was nothing remaining. Their corn had been burned, their homes looted of value and burned. Enraged, the whites were soon killed for their barbarous acts.[14]

While the Union Indians were fighting for their survival, Lincoln delivered his first annual message to Congress on December 3. He discussed the problems facing the Southern Superintendency. The public press had stated "that a portion of those Indians have been organized as a military force and are attached to the army of the insurgents." The president did not discount the articles, yet, he seemed reluctant to give them credibility because "the Government has no official information on this subject." Did Lincoln mean "by official information" he had never heard from the superintendent of the Southern Superintendency? Perhaps the delegation had not met with him or they had not yet arrived. "Letters have been written to the Commissioner of Indian Affairs by several prominent chiefs giving assurance of their loyalty to the United States and expressing a wish for the presence of Federal troops to protect them."

The president did not propose any plan in the immediate future to send the troops to Indian Territory for the safety of the Native People. Rather he closed the subject by saying: "It is believed that upon the repossession of the country by the Federal forces the Indians will readily cease all hostile demonstrations and resume their foreign relations to the Government."[15]

In interviews held with Gen. Hunter on January 27, 1862; Gen. Lane on January 28, and Commissioner Dole on January 31 at the Planters House in Leavenworth, Opothleyaholo, through his interpreter, Jurant Memday, explained the events of the three battles in Indian Territory.

According to Opothleyaholo, it was John Ross who had advised them to go onto the Cherokee lands. After reaching the camping grounds designated by Ross, they were attacked that night. This would have been the Round Mountain Battle. Still believing in Ross, they had left the caves and moved to the area of the Cherokee Skiatooki's village, which was near the Verdigris River.

"While our men were greatly scattered, the main body near 'Jim McDaniel's place,' the rest in different localities, we heard the war hoop and placed ourselves in as good a position as possible to receive the attack of the rebels."[16]

Ironically, this second battle on December 9, took place at what is known as a "horseshoe bend" on Bird Creek near Turley. The "Battle of Caving Banks" or Chusto Talasah was another victory for the Union Indians.[17]

Cooper, in his report, stated that upon reaching Concharty, he received intelligence that Gen. Fremont had retreated, thus averting any attack upon McCulloch. Scouts had brought Cooper news that Opothleyaholo and his forces "had taken refuge in Cherokee country by invitation of a leading disaffected Cherokee." The Cherokee was James McDaniel, who, at that time was with Col. Drew and 500 Cherokees posted at Coody's settlement (Coody's bluff) on the Verdigris near present Nowata. Cooper knew he had to march on Opothleyaholo without delay, and finalizing preparations they moved out on November 29 toward Tulsey Town. Simultaneously, Cooper ordered Col. Sims and "all the available force of the fourth Texas Cavalry ... to move up the Verdigris in the direction of Coody's settlement."[18]

Reaching Tulsey Town, a prisoner, who had escaped from Opothleyaholo's camp, informed Cooper that 2,000 of the enemy intended to attack them. "Col. Drew was ordered to march from Coody's and form a junction somewhere on the road to James McDaniels.'"[19]

Drew misunderstood Cooper and marched to a point "six miles northeast" of Opothleyaholo, arriving 24 hours before "the main body." When Cooper reached Drew on Bird Creek on December 8, he learned Opothleyaholo had sent a message desiring to make peace. Major Pegg of the Cherokees carried Cooper's reply which assured the Union Indians that the

Confederates "did not want any shedding of blood among the Indians" and proposed a conference the next day. That evening, Pegg returned. He had been unable to reach Opothleyaholo as he was surrounded by several thousand of his painted warriors and they intended to attack the Confederates that night.[20]

When Drew's Cherokee regiment learned the news, they panicked, leaving their tents and some horses and guns.[21]

Drew's report of the dispersement of his men listed only a few names of the deserters. It is believed at least 400 Cherokees fled that night. Major Pegg, Trotting Wolf and others hurried toward Fort Gibson. Many were reported to have put on the shuck badge and were in Opothleyaholo's camp, among them Capt. James McDaniel, Lt. Skieyaltooka (Skiatooka), and lieutenants White -Catcher, Bearmeat, Wat Stop and parts of their companies. All of these men fought with the Union Indians in the Battle of Chusto–Talasah, and McDaniel followed Opothleyaholo to Kansas. Col. Drew tried to assure Cooper that reinforcements were forthcoming.[22]

The Union Indians did not attack that night, and it seems as if Opothleyaholo was practicing psychological warfare on the Confederates. He had threatened to attack North Fork Town and the Rebels had retreated across the Arkansas River. Then at Bird Creek an avowed attack had caused the Cherokees, mostly Pin Indians, to desert, weakening Cooper's forces. Cooper had formed his command at "the first alarm." Taking Opothelyaholo's threat seriously, they "remained under arms all night, quietly awaiting the enemy." They never came.[23]

As soon as it was daylight, Cooper had sent a small party to Drew's deserted camp to retrieve any equipage left at the scene. Cooper crossed Bird Creek to the east side, and with the Cherokee train, proceeded south to a new position that would put him in closer communication "with the depot at Coweta Mission and with reinforcements of Creeks, Seminoles and Choctaws who were expected at Tulsey Town." No more than five miles into the journey, the colonel received intelligence that the enemy had been found "in large force below." Soon, shots were coming from the rear, and Cooper directed "the Cherokee train to be parked on the prairie and a sufficient guard placed over it." His forces formed into three columns and at a "quick gallop" moved upon the enemy. "Along the timber skirting the main creek for over two miles, as well as a ravine extending far out into the prairie," the Union Indians could be seen.[24]

Cooper described the site of their approach was "an abrupt, precipitous bank, some 30 feet in height, at places cut into steps, reaching near the top and forming a complete parapet." The problem that had faced the Rebels was where the creek could be forded. The Union side "was densely covered with heavy timber, matted undergrowth and thickets and fortified additionally by prostrate logs." A dwelling house, small corn crib and rail fence were situated near the center of the Union line, "in a recess of the prairie, at the gorge of a bend of the creek, of horseshoe form, about 400 to 500 yards in length."[25]

The ensuing battle became a combat "at close quarters" and lasted more than four hours with the Rebels gaining the house area, thus causing the Union forces to retreat toward "the mountains."[26]

Col. Daniel McIntosh's observations of the Battle of Chusto–Talasah described the advantages that Opothleyaholo's army had had over the Rebels. "From all appearances it was a premeditated affair by them. They had placed their forces in a large creek, knowing by marching across the prairie that we would be likely to pass in reach of that place." The creek banks "were bluff and deep waters." Large timber provided fortification "on the side they occupied." On the Rebel's side "the prairie extended to the creek."[27] Haleck Tustunuggee, Billy Bowlegs and Little Captain had positioned warriors to lie in wait within the timber for the Rebel's approach.

Both sides claimed victory. Cooper declared Opothleyaholo's army "was certainly over 2,500," and based on scouts' reports, believed the enemy's loss as "500 killed and wounded." The Rebel force "actually engaged did not exceed 1,100," and their loss "was 15 killed and 37 wounded."[28] Opothleyaholo's report of the battle was "nine Union were killed; thirty rebels were found buried in holes after the battle was over."[29]

Opothleyaholo realized they needed supplies of arms and ammunition if they were to withstand another onslaught against the Rebels. Remembering past associations with the Delawares, he sent James McDaniel with a letter to their agency in Quindaro, Kansas. By the time the Delawares received it and answered, calling them "Grand Children" and assuring them they would help, it was too late.[30]

The third and last engagement northwest of Tulsey Town, now Tulsa, was in the area of Hominy or Shoal Creek near Skiatooka's settlement. Haleck Tustunuggee (Aluktustenuke) and Opothleyaholo described this battle in the interview with Lane. "We had thought the fighting was over and had no anticipation of the enemy gaining accessions. Our men were greatly scattered having gone out to kill game, hunt for food and select camping grounds. Only a few of us could fight. Opothleyaholo led us in this fight."[31]

Cooper had concluded after the second battle that "Opothleyaholo's party must be entirely destroyed." After this last battle, Cooper's supply of ammunition, which had not been adequate, was nearly exhausted when his command reached Choska, Creek Nation, on December 13. En route, he had learned that about 100 Cherokees from Fort Gibson "had put on the shuck badge," and had gone to Opothleyaholo's camp at Shoal Creek. Immediately, Cooper sent an urgent message to Col. James McIntosh at Van Buren, Ark., requesting he send "white troops into the Cherokee country" in order to dispel any further outbreaks of Cherokee involvement with Opothleyaholo.

McIntosh, who should not be confused with the half-blood McIntoshes, had been left in command of McCulloch's troops while the general was absent, having gone to Richmond.[32]

Leaving the main body of his command at Choska, Cooper, with a detachment, journeyed on to the Grand River opposite Fort Gibson, and requested a meeting with John Ross. While there, the colonel received a reply on the 14th from McIntosh that he had ordered troops to Gibson "to march against the Union Indians with certainty of success." On the 19th, Cooper crossed the Grand River to confer with the Cherokees and "greatly to my surprise found Col. James McIntosh, who announced his intention of taking the field with some 2,000 troops against Hopoeithleyaholo."[33]

The officers worked out a plan whereby Cooper's command, reinforced by Maj. Whitfield's battalion of 339 men, would move up the Arkansas River from the west and thus be in the rear of Opothleyaholo's position on Shoal Creek. McIntosh's troops with five companies of the South Kansas–Texas Regiment, one regiment and 12 companies of Texas Cavalry and the Second Arkansas Mounted Riflemen, a force of 1,380 men, would "march up the Verdigris River opposite the position held by the enemy."[34] When ready, they would have the wily Creeks cornered, or so they hoped.

McIntosh moved his command much faster than Cooper who was delayed waiting for ammunition and suffering the loss of his teamsters by desertion. He notified McIntosh that Col. Stand Watie and his Cherokees had been ordered to the Verdigris to reinforce the colonel and his command.[35]

Leaving his train and impatient to reach "the stronghold of the enemy," McIntosh and men, with four days cooked rations, headed west for Shoal Creek reaching that point at noon on the 26th. The weather was dreadful, and the sleet had built up on the guns, equipment and clothing as well as the countryside.[37]

When the advance guard had crossed the creek they were fired upon by the Union Indians lying in wait on "a high and rugged hill," the sides thick with oak trees. "The Seminoles, under the celebrated chief Halek Tustenuggee, were in front on foot, posted behind the trees and rocks, while others were in line near the summit of the hill," McIntosh reported.[38]

At the top, on horseback was Opothleyaholo and his Creek warriors. Protected by the trees, the chilly blasts of the north wind and the falling snow did not affect them as much as McIntosh's men.[39]

The attack, once begun, became more intense as the Confederate forces, slipping and falling among the ice-covered rocks, scaled the heights on foot and both armies fought hand to hand combat. The South Kansas–Texas Regiment found narrow entrances of access along the hill's side and rode toward its highest point. Others dismounted and scaled the rocks while being fired upon from above. Finally, they reached the top and "swept everything" before them. The Union Indians scattered, retreating toward the rocky gorges, only to be pursued by the Rebels.[40]

McIntosh reported "the battle lasted until 4 o'clock, when the firing gradually ceased, and we remained victors in the center of Hopoeithleyaholo's camp." The Rebels captured "160 women and children, 20 negroes, 30 wagons, 70 yoke of oxen, about 500 Indian horses, several hundred head of cattle, 100 sheep and much personal property." Among the personal property were the letters Carruth had sent by Micco Hutki. McIntosh bragged about the defeat of Opothleyaholo and his force, and that in fleeing before his troops, they were "destitute of the simplest elements of subsistence."[41]

Col. Watie with 300 Cherokees reached McIntosh as the battle was ending. Both men determined that at dawn the following day they would follow the Union Indians. Twenty-five miles into that pursuit, Capt. Coody, in charge of Watie's scouts, alerted Watie they had found the Union Indians "scattered over a large scope of country, much of it inaccessible to horses."[42]

Billy Bowlegs, King of the Seminoles, who sided with Opothleyaholo in his fight to remain true to the Union. *Archives and Manuscripts Division of the Oklahoma Historical Society.*

The ground, in Maj. E.C.Boudinot's estimation as "the roughest country I ever saw," did not deter Watie and his men. By the time McIntosh reached them, the fighting was over. More Union Indians lay dead and a number of women and children were prisoners.[43]

Col. Cooper, learning of McIntosh's victory, pushed on to Shoal Creek and on the 28th met McIntosh there. He was on his way back to winter quarters at Van Buren. The following day Cooper moved up Bird Creek and finding "footprints and other evidences that the enemy had gone up Bird Creek," camped on an Osage trail.[44] This trail originated northeast of the Caney River, a branch of Claremont's Trail coming from the south and heading north toward Kansas. Cherokees had been intercepted on the Caney trail. Seminole women and children were taken prisoner and "from them we learned that Hopoeithleyaholo had gone two days in advance."[45]

Cooper's scout of seven days had been "accomplished over an exceedingly rough and bleak country, half the time without provisions, the weather very cold (during which one man was frozen to death) was endured with great fortitude by the officers and men under my command."[46]

Cooper bitterly regretted McIntosh's precipitous attack on Opothleyaholo. If only McIntosh had waited for Watie, the original plan to trap the Creek leader "would have been attained and the machinations of the arch old traitor forever ended."[47]

Perhaps McIntosh's reasons for his impetuosity is contained in a December 15 letter to S. Cooper, adjutant-general at Richmond. The colonel asked to be "removed from this section of country" and relieved of his command. "I do not think any battle of importance will be fought during the next year west of the Mississippi River. Probably none other than a guerilla war will be kept up."[48] McIntosh had fought in the Battle of Wilson Creek, and since that time the situation in the area had been relatively quiet for the West Point graduate. There had been skirmishes but nothing like the battle near Springfield.

It is clear in this letter that the 34-year-old man wanted to serve back east and sought a chance to rise in the ranks. On the 16th, McIntosh informed the adjutant-general that learning more about the "disaffection of the Cherokees" and the "increasing force of Hopoeithleyahola" he had decided to send additional men to help Cooper and he, personally, would take command. "I hope to soon settle matters in the nation."[49] McIntosh's obvious ennui had abated. For the present he had found a war. Although he stayed in the west, before the Battle of Pea Ridge, Arkansas, in 1862, McIntosh became a brigadier general and he, along with McCulloch would be killed in that conflict.

Following the Battle of Chustenahlah on Shoal Creek, reports indicated that Opothleyaholo, with 200 to 400 warriors, all on horseback, had headed north toward Kansas.[50] Past historians believe in all the confusion and fear that he had led his people toward the west, backtracking for many miles, toward the Arkansas River. Certainly hundreds must have fled for the Black Beaver road in that area. There is evidence that many of the people, scattered in the two previous battles, had fled to the upper Arkansas River and north to the Kansas line.

In this last engagement, however, with an Osage trail crossing Shoal and Bird Creek east to the Caney River and Claremont's Trail, it seems logical that Opothleyaholo would have headed for that thoroughfare.

It was now near the end of December. When Micco Hutki had returned from escorting the delegation to Kansas, he had informed them that those people were to meet with Gen. Lane. With the assurance that federal troops would be sent to help them, the Union Creek leader had decided to move nearer the Kansas line. But that had been in November and Sands and the delegation had never returned.

Carruth had written to them from near Fort Scott. Having lived almost 25 years in Indian Territory, Opothleyaholo had known of the two federal forts, Scott and Leavenworth, in Kansas. He had, also, used many of the Osage trails crisscrossing the area. Having demonstrated his prowess as a tactician to move his followers away from the Confederates, it appears totally uncharacteristic for him to have headed west instead of east.

Opothelyaholo and Haleck Tustunuggee had had to face reality—no federal troops were coming to aid them. Therefore, with their caravan, which had stretched for miles, now in ruins, and routed in all directions, they knew they must head for southeastern Kansas to find their chief and any federal help. They could never return to their homes until this was accomplished. Claremont's Trail would bring them into the proximity of LeRoy and Fort Scott. The density of the timber belts along the Verdigris, would only impede their progress on horseback. It would, of necessity, be a slow, arduous trek toward Kansas due to many of the women, children and aged that had to walk. Many of them would seek travel through the timber, but Opothleyaholo and his men would move out in the open.

Opothleyaholo led these people northward into Wilson County and although snow and sleet were falling, silhouettes of the two cairns, shrouded in white, would be dimly visible.

They forded the Fall River and headed north and northwest following the Osage Hunting Trail until it turned west at another ford above later New Albany. Here Opothleyaholo stopped among the thick timber. Runners were dispatched to Leavenworth and Fort Scott.

On January 16, 1862, the Leavenworth Daily Conservative reported the news. The Union Indians "are now in this state," driven to the Kansas southern border.

Chapter 23

A Place Called
Roe's Fork

When Cutler had returned with the delegation from Washington on Friday night December 27, he felt gratified, believing the Indians' confidence had been strengthened in the power and stability of the federal government. The agent gave the news to the paper that the government would soon reclaim Indian Territory and the massive undertaking would be commanded by Gen. Lane with a force of at least 10,000 men.[1]

Dole's suggestions to send troops into Indian Territory were finally considered by the War Department. The department had decided to organize and send a force composed in part of 4,000 volunteers "to be raised amongst the loyal Indians of the Central Superintendency."[2]

On their return to Kansas, Sands and the delegation were interviewed by Coffin who found them "to be in fine Spirits." Bearing presents of pipes, tobacco and sugar, they traveled on to Fort Scott to wait for reinforcements before returning to Indian Territory. Their livelihood, while in Kansas, was in question. Their annuities still were being withheld.[3]

Cutler returned home to LeRoy, and awaited the arrival of Dole who was expected at Fort Leavenworth. Learning of the battles in Indian Territory, the agent wired Dole: "Heopothleyoholo with 4,000 warriors is in the field and needs help badly. Secession Creeks are deserting him. Hurry up Lane."[4]

Two weeks later, Cutler was chagrined to learn "that a large body of Creek Indians had been driven from their homes and were then on their way to Kansas."[5] Before leaving for Leavenworth to consult with Coffin and Gen. Hunter, Cutler was apparently in contact with someone who had seen the refugees on the Fall River.

An article in the *Leavenworth Daily Conservative* on January 17 cites information about the Indians given to them by Cutler. "There are now 400

George McIntosh Troup, Georgia governor, who was determined that all Creek land within the state be ceded to Georgia. *Georgia Historical Society, Savannah, Georgia.*

Indians at Fall River and in a deplorable condition. They have no provisions and hundreds more are daily expected there." The Indians attributed their defeat to the fact "the enemy had artillery and we had none." The settlers, which were few, were trying to give them enough "food to keep them alive. They were fourteen days coming up from the Nation."

Without funds for this emergency, Coffin applied to Hunter for his assistance. Hunter complied by ordering food to be sent to the camps. He advised Coffin that the army could not supply clothing and blankets. Coffin would have to do that. Hunter, also, ordered A.B. Campbell, surgeon of the U.S. Army, to visit the refugees and report their condition. Thus, it would be the army and not the Indian Bureau who first saw the Union Indians. Coffin, who must have been perplexed by this turn of events, and Cutler agreed to remain in Leavenworth until Dole arrived.[6]

When Campbell reached Burlington he was told "that the principal part of the friendly Indians were congregated and encamped on the Verdigris River, near a place called Roe's Fork, from 12 to 15 miles south of the town of Belmont. I proceeded there without delay." Campbell was appalled by the scene.

He was not alone. The little garrison at Fort Row had drilled and practiced warfare on the south bank of the Verdigris immediately opposite the mouth of Big Sandy Creek. Then the weather had turned cold with sleet and snow and the men went into winter quarters. The volunteers with names such as Row, Brazell, Thompson, Walkup, Craig, Penturf, McFarland, Hase, Michaels, Shaffer and Williams and others had never visualized the horror that was unfolding around them.[7]

In the years following, when they had become elderly, and the grandchildren gathered around them on a Sunday afternoon for tales of the past, these men told about the suffering they had witnessed during the winter of 1861–62 at a place called Roe's Fork. Although most of these men went on to fight in the Civil War, they would never see again the incredible anguish of a

Col. A.B. Campbell, Army Surgeon, Fort Leavenworth, the first authority to see the hapless refugees at Fort Row, Wilson County, Kansas. *Kansas State Historical Society.*

people like the refugees that winter. The men had never had to embroider the facts in an effort to interest the children; the facts spoke for themselves.

Just who had conducted a census of the people at and around the fort is unknown, but according to Campbell it had been done a few days before he arrived. The count had been approximately 4,500 souls and others were arriving daily. Campbell was advised by a few chiefs that more than their number was "scattered over the country at distances varying from 25 to 150 miles, and unable, for want of food and ponies, to come in." Many were collected on the Cottonwood, Fall and Walnut rivers.

It was difficult for Campbell to describe "the wretchedness of their condition. Their only protection from the snow upon which they lie is prairie grass, and from the wind and weather scraps and rags stretched upon switches; some of them had personal clothing; most had but shreds and rags, which did not conceal their nakedness, and I saw several ranging in age from three to fifteen years, without one thread upon their bodies." He told of Hogobofohyah, second chief of the Creeks, who was sick with a fever, and had hardly anything to keep him warm. "His tent (to give it a name) was no larger than a small blanket stretched over a switch ridge pole, two feet from the ground, and did not reach it by a foot on either side of him." Most lodges were worse than this man's.

The Chicago commission, Campbell reported, had sent boxes which contained "thirty-five comfortables or quilts, many of them only two feet and two feet six inches wide, forty pairs of socks, three pairs of pantaloons, seven undershirts, and four pairs of drawers, a few shirts, pillows, and pillowcases." Unpacking these few items, and putting them into a wagon, Campbell had the wagon "driven round the margin of the woods." He walked through the woods, and selecting "the nakedest of the naked," he doled out the articles. "When all was gone, I found myself surrounded by hundreds of anxious faces, disappointed to find that nothing remained for them.

"They greatly need medical assistance," the doctor said. "Many have their toes frozen off, others have feet wounded by sharp ice, or branches of trees lying on the snow; but few have shoes or moccasins." The Indians were suffering "with inflammatory diseases of the chest, throat and eyes." The ones who were coming into the camps would get sick as soon as they ate, having been denied food for quite some time. Campbell was also concerned about the horses "which lie dead in every direction, through the camp and on the side of the river." He knew they had to be removed and burned, "lest the first few warm days breed a pestilence among them. Why the officers of the Indian Department are not doing something for them I cannot understand; common humanity demands that more should be done and done at once, to save them from total destruction."[8]

While Campbell was wondering about the Indian Bureau, Cutler and Coffin remained in Leavenworth during January and, finally, on the 30th, Dole arrived. One can only speculate how long they would have remained there waiting for the commissioner. When Lane interviewed the Indian leaders, the agent and superintendent were present along with Maj. Fielding Johnson, Delaware agent; Maj. John Burbank, agent of the Iowas in Nebraska and Maj. W.F.M. Arny, then agent of the Apaches in New Mexico.[9]

Unfortunately, during their prolonged wait for Dole, many, many of the refugees on the Fall River and at Delaware Springs in Wilson County were literally freezing and starving to death. In the first month after their arrival, at least 240 Creeks had died, which is horrifying; still, it was amazing that not more of them had perished.[10]

"They are now living in the timber, with only bits of tents to protect them from the cold," Opothleyaholo told the authorities in Leavenworth. When they had left the Indian country "there was a great abundance of corn," and they feared most of it had been burned or carried off by the Rebel army.[11]

Opothleyaholo firmly believed John Ross was a Union man.[12] This statement contradicts an earlier one attributed to Opothleyaholo. That one had Opothleyaholo convinced that Ross had betrayed them.[13] "He has managed his affairs so adroitly that the Cherokees have not been molested by either side," Opothleyaholo said. All of the Creek men were wanting to fight, but they had to be assured their women and children would be provisioned and protected while in Kansas.[14]

Before leaving Leavenworth to return to their people, Opothleyaholo and Haleck Tustunuggee wrote a letter to Lincoln affirming their conviction that Lane was the only warrior who could place them in their country again. "Our people have heard of Gen. Lane many seasons ago. They have heard how with but a handful of warriors he beat back the enemy when they were as numerous as the leaves of the forest and restored peace and quiet to Kansas."

As to the condition of the refugees, they told their Great Father: "Our people have suffered a great deal. They have been driven from their homes in the dead of winter when the earth was clothed with white. Many of them have frozen to death. All of them have lost all they possessed. There are now 6,000 women and children in Southern Kansas without tents, but scantily clothed, and exposed to all the horrors of a severe winter." The men and their people wanted Lane to lead them back home. Such courage is unfathomable. Here was a people who despite their suffering, were willing to fight to reclaim their land. And Lane was the one they felt who could do it. The refugees were willing to follow him wherever he would direct. And all of them together would "sweep the rebels before them like a terrible fire on the dry prairie."[15]

The letter did reach Lincoln as there is an endorsement from John Hay, his private secretary, to Maj. Gen. McClellan, dated February 4: "My Dear Sir: The President directs me to send you the inclosed, with his respectful salutations."

While in Leavenworth, Dole had asked John W. Turner, captain, and Office Chief Commissary of the Department of Kansas, to offer suggestions that he might entertain after having visited and supplied food for the refugees at Fort Row. Turner, from his Leavenworth office, reported his findings. The captain felt they were in a good locality "to sojourn" until definite arrangements could be made. "It is on Indian land and sufficiently removed from settlers to obviate the difficulties and disputes which would certainly arise if brought in close contact." Since the settlers were the interlopers, "they can raise no objection to these Indians being here or the free use of timber."

For the sake of supplying the refugees, and attendant transportation costs, Turner mentioned the Neosho River valley as "the only other favorable locality for them." However, this area would be objected to by the settlers who "mostly owned and occupied it." They had husbanded the timber and "the Indians never regard these things. Ten thousand Indians would stretch along the river bank for several miles in their encampment." Turner's consensus was it would be cheaper to transport the supplies from the Neosho to the Verdigris than to pay for any damages the settlers would certainly require on the Neosho.

The captain was very thorough in his proposal about clothing, shelter and food for the refugees. "It will be necessary, considering the extent of their encampment and the number of Indians, to have three or four log houses erected at suitable points within its limits, for issuing depots, with a person in charge of one or two."[16]

It would be this last suggestion of making a permanent point for supplies that would result in the hamlet of Belmont, in the neighboring Woodson County, becoming the agency for not only the refugees, but the Osage Indians as well. A small fort came into existence at the same time and although Fort Belmont, like Fort Row, is not listed with the National Archives, the War

Department or the Fort Leavenworth Museum, there are a number of reports in the War of the Rebellion and the reports of the Commissioner of Indian Affairs substantiating their importance during this time.

On February 10, Dole contacted Dr. William Kile who had been appointed by Lincoln to Lane's staff. Lane had made him brigade quartermaster. Dole wanted his former business partner to act temporarily as a special agent "for the purpose of purchasing and delivering to William G. Coffin such quantities of clothing and provisions as, in your judgment, may be required to prevent suffering amongst said Indians." Dole wanted Kile to consult with Coffin, but before doing that, Gen. Hunter was ready to turn over to Kile "a considerable quantity of bacon belonging to the army stores at Leavenworth, which will reduce very much the amount of meat needed." The quality, not the quantity, of bacon would be discussed by the Indians and whites within a few months.[17]

Also on the tenth, Dole wired C.B. Smith: "Six thousand Indians driven out of Indian Territory, naked and starving. Gen. Hunter will only feed until 15th. Shall I take care of them on the faith of an appropriation?" Smith replied: "Go on and supply the destitute Indians, Congress will supply means. War Department will not organize them."[18]

Originally, only the Indians of the Central Superintendency were to be mustered. When Dole arrived and met with Opothleyaholo and Haleck Tustunuggee, he soon discovered that the refugees were willing to enlist and, along with the army, fight to recover their homes. He had instructed Coffin to begin enrolling them at Fort Row.[19]

While Dole was traveling to Kansas, Edwin M. Stanton had replaced Simon Cameron as secretary of war. Cameron had resigned due to his alleged involvement in fraud. Stanton did not want any Indians in the army, and countermanded the orders for Lane's Expedition.

And on this same date, Dole, who from all the correspondence sent from him to various men seemed to have been quite involved with the Indian situation, notified Baptiste Peoria that he had appointed him as U.S. agent to visit tribes that could be safely reached in Indian Territory.[20] Peoria was well-known in the Indian Bureau having been employed by the Indian agencies in Kansas as early as 1832. In 1833, he had witnessed, as an interpreter, the signatures affixed to the treaty at the Indian Peace Council called by Commissioner Henry Ellsworth at Leavenworth in November.[21]

Baptiste Peoria, pronounced Bateese Paola, knew many of the people involved in the Civil War. He had been the interpreter while Asbury M. Coffey was agent for the Miamis and the Wea, Piankeshaws, Peorias and Kaskaskias, known as the Confederated Tribes, at the Osage River Agency. Now in 1862, the former agent was Col. Coffey who, along with Livingston and Stand Watie, was creating havoc in the Cherokee Neutral Lands and Indian Territory.[22]

William Dole, Commissioner of Indian Affairs, who met with Opothleyaholo at Leavenworth in January, 1862. *Kansas State Historical Society.*

Peoria, reputed to have been born in 1793 at Kaskaskia, Illinois, had visited Washington in May and June 1854 in regard to treaties with the Miamis and the Confederated Tribes.[23] In 1855, he, A.M. Coffey and two other men were corporators of the Paola Town Company which had been named in his honor.[24] Peoria engaged in the mercantile business, farmed and dealt in livestock. He was considered "a man of rare ability, much attached to the Indians in the agency and, as their managing agent in the transaction of business, is of incalculable advantage to the tribes."[25]

Peoria was instructed by Dole to assure the Indians in Indian Territory of "the friendly disposition towards them of the people and the government of the United States." The commissioner, in ending his letter, stated: "You may also assure these people that should they adopt the course you advise, their Great Father will send his army to protect them from his enemies."[26]

After consulting with Dole, Coffin had alerted the other agents to meet him at Fort Row. Upon his arrival, about February 10, the superintendent could not believe what he saw. He estimated that "12 to 15 hundred dead Ponies are laying around in the camps and in the river." The five wagon loads of blankets, clothing, shoes, boots and socks had been distributed, with a small amount retained for those who were still coming into the camp. This report with a dateline of February 13, Fort Roe, informs Dole that Coffin had sent men and three wagons back to the Neosho River for supplies of beef, pork, corn and meal. Citing army regulations allowing 30 cents per day for subsistence, Coffin had reached an estimate of 15 cents per day for each Indian. "I feel confident that leaving off Sugar and Coffee, it can be done for that, transportation included."[27]

Dole notified Coffin on February 11 that Stanton was opposed to having Indians in the army. Coffin was to advise the chiefs that Washington had not authorized it. Yet, Dole encouraged Coffin to ascertain the numbers willing to enlist. The commissioner had not given up hope that the Indians would be used in the future. In the meantime, it was a dire necessity to return them to Indian Territory in time to plant their crops. Money and provisions for the destitute souls was meager and Dole knew any delay surely would increase their sufferings and even death.[28]

The Emporia News reported refugees were located about "five miles below town on the Cottonwood." These Indians, about 200 in number, were living on hominy. Their clothing was in disrepair and their shelters were old wagon covers for tents, buffalo robes strung over pole and dilapidated quilts rigged to protect them from the cold. They were more fortunate than those on the Fall and Verdigris rivers. Many Emporians had furnished them with "old quilts, coats, pants, vests, boots, shoes, etc., which added greatly to their comfort, and seemed to please them 'muchly.'"[29]

On February 13, Coffin reported that Agent George C. Snow of the Seminoles was at Fort Row. "Dr. Cutler has not yet arrived."[30] Cutler did not disclose in his annual report of 1862 when he finally left Leavenworth, but it was after receiving full instructions from Dole.

"I started for the camps of the southern refugee Indians which were at that time located on the Verdigris; and on reaching them, I found the terrible tale which had been told me most too true, but only a shadow of what really existed."[31]

Chapter 24

Wretchedness Most Complete

"If we were to say they were well clothed, there would be ten thousand square feet of nakedness gaping forth its contradictions," Coffin told Dole on March 3. The refugees had been in southern Kansas since the middle of January and efforts to feed and clothe them had been a disaster itself.[1]

By the time Opothleyaholo and Haleck Tustunuggee had returned to the so-called "holding camp" on the Verdigris, the population had grown dramatically. The sight of the thin bodies, the tattered remnants of clothing, the bare feet, naked bodies, and the pleas by the refugees for food and shelter had devastated both men. Ponies lay dead within and without the camp. The little children, who at home had been happy and carefree, now clung to the ragged gowns of their mothers, plaintively begging for food.

Amidst all of this agony, Billy Bowlegs and Little Captain arrived. The people had feared Little Captain was dead as they had not seen him and many, many others since the last battle. Bowlegs and his men had covered the rear of the retreating Union Indians and had fought valiantly against Stand Watie and the others. Coffin saw Bowlegs and Little Captain as officer material for the Indian regiments and suggested it to Dole in one of his reports.[2]

Dr. Kile had visited the camp and assessed the needs of the Indians. Despite the attempts to provision them, relief was slow in coming. *The Leavenworth Daily Conservative* in its local items called attention to the destitution and sought help from the charitable in the state.

And then the news came that the enlistments of the refugees must stop. Coffin and the agents struggled to explain, unsuccessfully, the political involvement in the decision. Certainly, they would never have told them that the War Department hesitated to have "savages" fighting "southern gentlemen."[3] The chiefs and leaders took this latest disappointment into their own care and

Artist's conception of the little Fort Row on the Verdigris River in Wilson County, Kansas. Courtesy Isabelle Cook.

quickly called a council at Fort Row the last week in February. Their supply of arms and ammunition was deficient, yet, they were willing to use what they had for their ablest men and "go down with the army on their own hook and aid in driving out the Rebels from their homes in time to plant a crop for this season." The pitiful allotment of corn would have to be rationed further in order to strengthen their best ponies for the journey.[4]

Even the army going into Indian Territory was in question. Lane, who had expected to command the Indian Expedition, had convinced Lincoln that he and Gen. Hunter were in accord with the proposed plans. The senator, who had ingratiated himself with Lincoln since the earliest days of his presidency, returned to Leavenworth and learned that Hunter intended to command the expedition. Lane approached Opothleyaholo and Haleck Tustunuggee with the news and they subsequently appealed to Lincoln on Lane's behalf. By the end of January, Lincoln resolved the controversy between the two men, instructing Lane that he was "under the command of Gen. Hunter."[5]

Lane despaired, and by the end of February, he had decided to return to the Senate. If he could not lead the noble red man back to his home, then he would have nothing to do with the expedition. Still, the man could not relinquish his plans so easily. On returning to Washington, he learned that the Department of Mississippi, which included Kansas, was then under Gen. Henry Halleck's command. And Halleck had appointed Brig. Gen. James W. Denver to head the new District of Kansas, replacing Hunter. Lane did not like Denver, the ex-territorial governor of Kansas, and protested to Lincoln who subsequently asked Halleck to rescind the order. Halleck then placed Brig. Gen. Samuel D. Sturgis in command. Sturgis, a colonel at the time, it will be remembered, had evacuated the Union troops from Fort Smith when Averell had arrived there in April 1861 on his secret mission.[6]

Coffin and the agents were inept at handling the predicament of the refugees. Although their reports do not reflect any apathy toward their charges, the refugees receiving meager rations or none at all, claimed the representatives of the Indian Bureau treated them "as though they were slaves and possessed no rights worthy of respect."[7] Dr. Kile had ordered shoes as had Coffin, but as of March 3, neither of the orders had arrived.

Instead, with snow and sleet on the ground, the superintendent had decided to move the refugees to the Neosho River in the vicinity of LeRoy. As discussed by Turner earlier, the site would be fine, but the trouble with the settler-owners of land was foreseeable, and not conducive to the move. Coffin, riding his mule about the area, had convinced the white people to allow the Indians to stay there temporarily. He fully intended to move them much farther north.

With this in mind, he and Dr. Kile traveled to Fort Row to impart the news to the Union Indians. His report stated that by the time they had arrived, at least 1,500 Indians had already left for LeRoy. Coffin, so often rambling in his reports, did not explain how these Indians had learned they were to be moved. Of those who had started on their way, many were barefooted; many more were naked. The temperature had dipped to the "lowest of the season," but that did not deter Coffin. Dr. Kile remained at Fort Row "to settle and close up business," while Coffin sought teams and wagons to transport those unable to walk. Coffin persevered in his quest, figuring it would require three teams to 100 persons. Destitute of money, he admitted the transactions would have to be handled by government vouchers, something the settlers did not like. Coffin proposed $2.50 per day per team and wagon.[8] How many of the conveyances he managed to secure is unknown, but one of the suppliers was a J.P. Hamilton, Sr., of LeRoy.

Hamilton, telling of his experiences in the *LeRoy Reporter*, August 14, 1931, related that most of the Indians were encamped in what had been a heavily timbered bend of the Verdigris. All that remained of the trees was the stumps, and the area looked as bare as the prairies. As to the physical and mental condition of the refugees, he said: "This was wretchedness most complete."[9]

On March 3, Congress passed an act allowing the annuities of the hostile Five Civilized Tribes and the Wichitas to be used for relief of the "Loyal Indian Refugees." No one but the Indian Territory tribes would have this money.[10]

Opothleyaholo, understandably disillusioned by all that had transpired, refused to move the 30 miles to LeRoy. It would take the refugees farther away from their homes. The matter of hygiene was becoming serious. The Verdigris water had become polluted with the carcasses of hundreds of ponies and was unfit for human consumption. And having to transport supplies from Humboldt to Belmont had been expensive. LeRoy would position them closer to that supply depot. Earlier, when Turner had left Fort Row, the settlers had provided a few supplies, not out of charity but with an eye to monies they believed the government would allow the Indians. These transactions were done with inflated prices. The Indians were in debt to them and the government sought to move them farther away from the problem.[11]

In the neighboring state of Missouri, the federals had reclaimed the Springfield area only to withdraw once again to Rolla and eventually St. Louis. Gen. Fremont had been replaced by Hunter and the Confederates had retaken Springfield for the second time.

While the Union Indians were retreating to southern Kansas, the campaign to keep Missouri in the Union, starting in September 1861 and aborted in November with Fremont's dismissal, had to be reopened the following January. And on March 7, the opposing armies met near a series of hills near Leetown in northwestern Arkansas named Pea Ridge by the natives. In the area was Pratt's Store and the Elkhorn Tavern run by a man named Cox who, with his wife and mother, hid in the cellar during the battle.

Gen. Samuel R. Curtis was in command of the Union troops numbering 10,500 and Earl Van Dorn, Price and McCulloch commanded the 16,202 Confederates. Brig. Generals Pike and Watie were on hand with their Indian Brigade.

McCulloch, the old Texas Ranger (some say he wore his dove gray velvet uniform, others his buckskins), died on the first day of battle while leading a charge of the 16th Arkansas Regiment. And the young West Pointer, James McIntosh, who had fought Opothleyaholo in the third battle, was also killed the same day.

Van Dorn, the small, handsome soldier who had campaigned to march against St. Louis and into Illinois instead, was defeated on March 8 by the Union forces. The Army of the Southwest at the Battle of Pea Ridge gained peace for the Missourians and settled for the time being any Rebel infiltration into the state from Arkansas.

But Pike would come under fire when it was reported that some dead soldiers had been scalped. The Indians were blamed for the atrocities, yet, solid proof was not evident. According to Pike's reports for that period, it appears that in 1862 there was a plot to undermine him in the Indian Territory.[12]

Word already had been received that Stanton had ordered Gen. Halleck to "detail two regiments to act in Indian Country. Five thousand friendly Indians will also be armed to aid in their own protection (the refugees) and you will please furnish them with necessary subsistence."[13] Coffin and Cutler undoubtedly conveyed this news to the chiefs and leaders. But they were not so easily convinced.

On March 26, Opothleyaholo, Micco Hutki, Haleck Tustunuggee, James McDaniel, Long Tiger and others drafted a letter of protest to Lincoln. The men detailed their fighting in Indian Territory and their subsequent flight to southern Kansas, where "we felt that we sojourned among friends. Our people when compelled to leave their homes, were in a prosperous condition—possessed well improved farms, and were living in houses far better than those we see in southern Kansas." They were neglected by their agents and superintendent. "We ask our agents for greater supplies that our wives and children may not starve, and they answer: 'We must obey orders,' and our people continue to starve."

They informed Lincoln that ordered to move the camp to LeRoy, they had been refused transportation for their sick. "Only four two-horse waggons have been detached" to move several hundred "Creeks on the Verdegree" and 60 were "dangerously sick." The refugees told about their supplies being withheld, and "our agent tells us one Thing today and something different tomorrow, and our Supt. serves us in the same manner. They order us further North—we refused to go—they tell us we must go—but we are determined to die where we are, or return to our homes." They requested an expected payment to be withheld from them until their agents, Cutler and Coffin, were removed.

Opothleyaholo alleged that Coffin was the one ordering them to eventually be moved to the Sac and Fox Agency "seventy miles North of this point. We cannot go—our horses are dying, and one of our camps are surrounded by twelve hundred of their putrid carcasses—no corn being allowed us to save Their lives. Not only our horses, but our people are dying daily—our camps on the Verdegree and Neosho are lined with graves."

The Creek leader who, according to Thomas Yahola, carried treaties with him at all times, stated: "We came here not to live at the expense of the government, but were compelled to flee before a superior force of its enemies, and expected to find here the protection that your government was unable to extend to us in our own Country; as her treaties provided. We desire not to be moved further North even to be fed—we now buy many of our supplies with our own individual means. It is not for the protection of our rights in the Country of the Sacks and Foxes that our treaties provide, but in our own. Send to us ammunition and transportation as early as possible—we ask no more—Will our Great Father grant this just request and petition of his Loyal Children?" Lieutenants C.M. Meck and A.C. Smith and Capt. Charles F. Coleman duly witnessed the signatures and attested "we believe it truly represents the views and wishes of the Loyal Indians in Kansas."[14]

A separate letter was enclosed to Dole, requesting him to give the letter to Lincoln. The Creeks asked that Edwin H. Carruth be appointed as their agent. "He is intimately acquainted with our people, and well understands the causes that divide our councils, and could, we think, better harmonize the conflicting political elements in our Country than any other man." Carruth had recently been appointed agent for the Wichitas, a position that had been held by Leeper until he joined the Confederacy. Carruth, to be maligned by Coffin in the future, had declined the Creeks' offer to be their agent.[15]

A correspondent for the *Leavenworth Daily Conservative*, signing an article titled "Condition of the Loyal Indians" with an "E," extolled about the situation in Indian Territory leading to their retreat to Kansas. "The stand they took saved us from invasion last fall. The secesh Creeks, Cherokees and white miscreants among them, had too much to do to keep down Union feeling at home to allow of their making an inroad into Kansas ... I wish every loyal man could hear them tell, as I have, all they have suffered—it would be a long tale, full of horrors, but no man would get up from the recital, without feeling that were it possible to get such a regiment of tigers, it would be fair to use them in the war our enemies have inaugurated in the Southwest."[16]

"Not fit for a dog to eat" was the critique of the chiefs and leaders with regard to the bacon they had received from Fort Leavenworth. In the latter part of March, George Collamore, quartermaster general of Kansas, together with Rev. Evan Jones, had visited the encampment which extended approximately seven miles in the timber along "the Neosho river bottom." At Dole's request, Collamore had issued a report to the Indian Bureau concerning his inspection.

Collamore had come to Kansas in the winter of 1860 as a representative of the New England Relief Society in conjunction with the severe drought that had gripped the region. He remained in the state and became associated with Lane. He was appointed quartermaster general on May 4, 1861, as a member of Gov. Charles Robinson's military staff. His past experiences dealing with the drought victims had not prepared him for what he saw near LeRoy.

Collamore did not find any "comfortable tents" among the 7,100 persons in the encampment. Rather he depicted the shelters as being rudely made "of pieces of cloth, old quilts, handkerchiefs, aprons, etc. stretched upon sticks." Many of them were "scarcely sufficient to cover the emaciated and dying forms beneath them." The man found Opothleyaholo's daughter under such a shelter. She was "in the last stages of consumption." Although Opothleyaholo was considered one of the wealthiest and more powerful Indians in the Indian Territory, in Kansas he was like the other refugees, impotent to provide the needed care for his daughter and the rest of his family.

Many of the refugees were incurable, "their disease being consumption and pneumonia brought on from exposure and privations of the common necessaries of life." Added to the diseases were the 100 amputations of frosted limbs. "Among them I saw a little Creek boy about 8 years old with both feet taken off near the ankle."

At least 240 Creeks had died. "Those of other tribes sufficient in like degree," Collamore wrote. Visiting in "almost every lodge of several of the large tribes," Collamore's assessment was all of the tribes had "the same destitution and suffering among them."

On his last day a cold, drenching rain fell "and for eight hours I went from lodge to lodge, and tribe to tribe, and the suffering of the well to say nothing of the sick is beyond description."

The chiefs informed him the "Rebel emissaries" had predicted that food, clothing and shelter would not be obtained "from their Union friends." Having now come to the realization that the Confederates had been right, the refugees were filled "with suspicion and discontent."

"Thus this large number of people have been deprived of shelter for some four months and they have been supplied with clothing wholly inadequate to their actual wants. Some whom I saw had not a single garment on their bodies."

Collamore cited the insufficiency of food in quantity and quality. Only the sick, and then only when requisitioned by a doctor, had received coffee, sugar, vinegar and pepper. Flour had been allotted at one pound per person per week, and "a scanty supply of salt." This flour later would be reported as condemned at Fort Leavenworth.

When Collamore talked to the agents about the bacon, he learned that it, too, had been condemned by the army at Fort Leavenworth. Many of the Indians had become ill after trying to eat it. However, what had been considered poisonous to the troops had been adjudged all right for the refugees consumption. "A reliable person who saw the bacon before it was sent to them, who is a judge of the article, pronounced it suitable only for soap grease," Collamore explained.

Opothleyaholo had assured Collamore that "his people were willing on being properly armed to fight their own way back." Hearing there were nearly 6,000 Rebel Indians and whites in Indian Territory, the Creek leader knew he would have to have "assistance from our troops" in order to return to their homes.

"Notwithstanding all their hardships and disappointments, these people, who have exhibited a courage and endurance beyond any in the United States breathe but one spirit of fidelity to the Union.... They ardently desire to return to their farms…. We cannot shut our eyes to the demoralizing effect upon them should they remain in their present condition."[17]

Opothleyaholo's information concerning the number of Rebels in his country had come from Baptiste Peoria's intelligence of the area. Peoria, reporting to Dole through G.A. Colton, U.S. Indian agent, had visited that country soon after being appointed to do so. Calling his mission "somewhat difficult," he had cautiously entered the region, evading the spies who watched during the daytime "and hired assassins during the night" who killed those "whom neither money could buy or threats silence."

The detailed report not only explained the conditions of the Indian Territory as Peoria found it, but the history of the Confederates' active involvement in seeking the Five Civilized Tribes to align with them.

"I found the whole country, as might have been expected, in a very troublous, disturbed condition—in fact a reign of lawlessness, violence, and terror existing—Influenced by considerations mainly of those enumerated, a large majority of the various tribes living in the Indian Territory are avowed secessionists."

Peoria referred to Opothleyaholo's gallant stand against Pike. The leader had reminded his people, "that a long time ago they had made peace with their Great Father and agreed not to fight anymore, and warned them over and over again that bad white men were getting them into trouble, that they had agreed to remain neutral but they had taken the hatchet and gone over to the other side, and for his part he was not in."

The status quo in Indian Territory at the time of Peoria's reconnaissance centered on Stand Watie and Col. Coffey, whom Peoria had known for many years. "Stanwaite and Coffee are now watching the line between Kansas and the Cherokee country. Whenever a force moves down into that country they retreat to Fort Gibson, where they claim to have large forces, some five or six thousand, composed in part of Texans and Arkansans. The country between the Neosho, Grand River, and the Verdigris is excellent for pasturing, has plenty of wood and water, and is the only desirable route over which the expedition can move to reach Fort Gibson."

The scout's consensus was that the Rebel Indians who had been deceived would, with communication and the presence of federal troops in the territory, "throw down their arms and return to their allegiance. There are a good many left behind who are loyal, who will go over to the north as soon as the Union army gets there." Peoria cautioned, however, provided "that the soldiers composing the expedition are careful to avoid jayhawking of every kind." The man's foresight would be borne out in the months and years ahead. Indian Territory was looted by both the Union defenders and Rebel adversaries."[18]

With accusations of "a sneaking conspiracy" and Carruth "deep in the plot" and his coming "to LeRoy Stealthily in the night," Coffin took time to

write to Dole from Humboldt on April 2. He was on the way to the Osage
Catholic Mission in southern Kansas "to help Major Elder try to make a treaty
with the Osages." Despite suffering "a very bad head ach tonight," presumably
brought on by having had to swim "the Neosho twice today with my mule,"
Coffin extolled about the plot of those encouraging the Indians to have him
and the agents removed. Carruth had escorted "two or three chiefs to go with
him to Iola and Sign the Paper." This was in reference to the memorial sent
to Lincoln by Opothleyaholo and others on March 29, and Coffin charged that
most of the names had been forged by Carruth.

"Mr. Smith Correspondent of the *Cincinnati Gazett* was their grand
Scribe," the superintendent alleged. He was certain that Carruth, Smith and
"their minions" had stirred up the Indians' demands for flour, sugar and coffee.
Obviously, he did not believe his charges could have used their own initiative
in making the demands. "That the government forwards the money to us out
of their annuities to do So and we put the money in our pockets," letting "them
eat corn meal Poor Beef and Bacon."

And Carruth was blamed for the "Creeks on the Verdigris" not wanting
to move nearer LeRoy. Coffin fully intended to hold an investigation in the
matter when he returned to LeRoy.[19]

By April 8, Coffin was to face another problem. When the second order
to enlist the refugees came, the Indians were at first skeptical. The second
order had come as a result of Dole notifying Interior Secretary Smith of the
advisability of recruiting them to get the refugees back home. Dole, also,
"obtained an order upon the commandant at Fort Leavenworth for two thousand rifles, and suitable ammunition to arm the two thousand Indian home
guards."[20]

Whether Coffin used the promise of guns and ammunition as an incentive
for enlistment is not known. He did, however, visit with Opothleyaholo about
the items. He told the Creek that for each gun given to an Indian, that Indian
had to accompany it on the expedition. He assured Dole "but I know enough
of the Indian character to know that it will be next thing to impossibility to
get a gun away from one when he once gets it." Clearly, if Coffin didn't have
a problem at the time, he worked to conjure up one. What a shame that a starving Indian might be supplied with equipment to hunt game to feed the people. Coffin even entertained withholding the guns until the enlistees were on
the road for a day or two before distributing them. "But that would make them
mad and they would not go at all … they all seem anxious to go."

He remarked that "the mortality amongst them is great more since warm
weather has set in than during the cold weather. They foolishly physic themselves nearly to death, dance all night and then jump into the river just at daylight to make themselves bulletproof." He believed such antics had caused
many deaths. "Long Tiger, the Uchee Chief and one of the best amongst them

died today—yesterday we had seven deaths and there will be not the less today."[21]

Coffin had not wanted to admit that the deficiency in food which left the refugees deprived of life-giving nutrients, more than their religious and ceremonial customs, had contributed to the continued deaths among them. Surely he lacked knowledge about their ceremonials that had been ingrained in them since birth. Even today, the descendants claim it was such observances that sustained their ancestors at that horrific period. Though the good superintendent boasted about knowing their character, he, like so many others, didn't have an inkling of what it meant to be a native person.

Chapter 25

The Indian
Home Guards

As the person in charge of 8,000 indigent Native People, Coffin had acquired a particular fame for himself. When Congress approved appropriations for the refugees, taken from their annuities, it was a requirement that Coffin advertise in the leading Kansas newspapers, inviting bids by contractors of provisions. Perhaps the advertising in the *Leavenworth Daily Conservative* had prompted that one member of the Fourth Estate to allow some publicity about the Loyal Indians. Appearing in the April 16 issue was a lengthy article titled "The Southern Indians" written by Coffin with a dateline April 12, LeRoy.

The superintendent's lead read: "There is not much transpiring here that would be likely to interest your readers." This pessimistic statement alone would discourage them. Following a long accounting of a steam boiler explosion, Coffin enlightened the reader about the Creek and Seminole black drink ceremony, the concomitant vomiting, and dancing followed by the immersion in the Neosho. "During their exercises they have their enchanters around at different points to invoke the good spirits in their orgies." Not one to leave the proverbial stone unturned, in order to put the blame on the Indians' rituals rather than where it should have been placed, lack of proper care by the Indian Bureau, Coffin, once again, assessed their acts as a "ridiculous absurdity." He believed the medical men would "fail to see anything well calculated to promote health."

The superintendent obviously approved the game of ball by the refugee men. He found it very exciting to see "one hundred men stripped stark naked except a breech clout, the most athletic, muscular and powerful men, too, that I ever looked upon all exerting themselves to the utmost stretch of human exertion, with the wildest and most exciting shouts of triumph, defiance and determination, such as no pen can describe."

Coffin closed the article with an invitation for good Kansans to come see the game. "We will get up one for your especial benefit; so come down, and we will give you items enough to keep you all summer." Just what the "items" were is left to conjecture.

Unquestionably, had he truly been concerned about the refugees' welfare he would have appealed to the Kansans for flour and bacon that had not been condemned, and clothing and shelter. But Coffin was a cautious man and a show of altruism at this time would have led to speculation about his efficacy as superintendent. The man chose instead to exploit the Indians and their customary ball game as if both were a bizarre sideshow for the amusement of the whites.[1]

Coffin's invitation worked. People came from far away and the immediate area to witness the games. Officers would bring their wives from Leavenworth to watch the sport.[2] Now, more than 130 years later, the Native People's ball game still is being observed by them in Oklahoma. Despite the refugees' continued existence in those horrendous conditions, they were able to carry on with their rituals and customs. What may have appeared as inane to ones like Coffin, was a spiritual uplifting to a people who refused to be defeated.[3]

When the guns arrived at LeRoy on April 16, the refugees' hopes of returning home was no longer an abject longing but a reality. Unfortunately, many of the enlistees would learn later that the weapons they had received would not even shoot.[4]

Fifteen hundred volunteer refugee Indians, together with a number of Delawares and Osages would eventually provide two regiments. And just when it seemed that the start south toward home was imminent, Gen. Sturgis issued an order prohibiting the organization of Indians for military service. Anyone who violated his order would be arrested.

Major Minor, along with soldiers to enforce the injunction, came to LeRoy to deliver the order to Coffin. It was not stated in the orders, yet, Sturgis was of the same opinion as the War Department. "It was not the policy of our government to fight high-toned southern gentlemen with Indians."[5]

On the 29th, Coffin replied to the general, stating, "I am acting under the control and direction of the Interior and not of the War Department." He added that Minor was "strapped, that no funds were given him to pay his expenses; that he had to beg his way down here." Coffin generously paid Minor's bill at LeRoy and gave him five dollars for the return trip to Leavenworth.[6]

Mustering continued and Sturgis' injunction was investigated and touted as "Illegal Order No. 8."[7] Sturgis and other officers were ordered arrested. The general was replaced by Brig. Gen. James G. Blunt. Militarily, Kansas was reorganized into the Department of Kansas. All of this was done quickly and Dole was led to say: "The changes in the command of the Kansas military department were so rapid that I have been unable to keep pace with the proceedings."[8]

The continual bickering between the War Department and the Indian Bureau had its start when in 1849 the bureau was transferred to the Interior Department. Only bureaucracy has the ability to confuse; although the Indians were under the control of the Interior, yet only the Secretary of War had jurisdiction over the awarding of Indian post-traderships. The post trader, dealing with the Indian, was at liberty to commit frauds upon the Native People, and the Interior Department was helpless to solve the problem unless the War Department intervened. Most of the time, the War Department was too busy annihilating the Indians to care about any frauds perpetrated upon them.

This problem would manifest itself in 1876 when William W. Belknap, secretary of war, Grant Administration, would resign his position because the House of Representatives had passed a resolution asking for his impeachment. Allegedly he had had profited from trading-post sales, gleaning from one post as much as $6,000 in one year. Impeachment hearings were held but with Belknap's resignation no sentence was passed. Army men, including Custer, had contended that the Indians would fare better under military supervision as in the old days. The reality is that the Native People never fared well under either department. They were viewed as a pestilence to be removed from the American's country.

Having won the hassle with Sturgis, Coffin proceeded forward with the formation of the Indian Home Guards. He journeyed to Leavenworth to complete the plans for the organization of the Second Regiment.

On the day of Coffin's departure, the refugee tribes met with the Osages at LeRoy. Those indigenous people were willing "to take up arms and go with the Expedition to Indian Territory. Fall Leaf is raising a company of Delawares and part of them have already arrived at LeRoy."[9]

The two Indian Home Guard Regiments soon became a subject of ridicule by the press and the white soldiers. When Coffin was preparing to leave for Leavenworth, Opothleyaholo had requested "you must bring us down some wagons that shoot."[10] Unschooled in military vernacular, the Creek leader's statement was printed in the newspapers, reported by Coffin. Obviously, Opothleyaholo had not known they were batteries, but he had remembered their awesome power at Horseshoe Bend and during the recent battles in Indian Territory. His request was a sensible one and should have been reported privately to the authorities in charge at Leavenworth, not given to the local daily rag for the reader's amusement. Such leaks to the newspaper, while building Coffin's esteem, simultaneously underscored his contemptuous nature.

The public derision of the Indian soldiers did not stop. In an article, "From Fort Scott," appearing in the *Leavenworth Daily Conservative* on June 17, the correspondent depicted the Indians as stalling their departure for home until they received "clothing, camp and garrison equipage, because those things were promised them." The Indians had been "amply provided with arms, ammunition and stores," the writer assured, "but they will not move a peg until they see the wagon-shooting apparatus arrive at Iola. The medicine man wants a week's time to prepare his charms, roots and yaabs!"

The "Big Ingins–the chiefs" advised that their soldiers could not march until the promised shoes arrived. The writer suggested that the shoes "be constructed with heels on both ends, and then their foot-prints will completely disguise which route they are taking." Such worthy advice was followed by the mention of the next meeting of the pious social at which time "expected prayers will be offered up for the success and preservation from harm, and a speedy return to their wigwams, of these two regiments of fascinating 'children of the forest.'"[11]

On June 25, Coffin reported to Dole that he had just returned from Humboldt where he had seen the Union Army and the two Indian Regiments, under the command of Col. William Weer, leave for Indian Territory.

"The Indians with their new uniforms and small military caps on the Hugh Heads of Hair made rather a Comecal Ludecrous appearance. They marched off in Columns of 4 a breast singing the War song all joining in the chorouse and a more animated seen [*sic*] is not often witnessed."[12]

Billy Bowlegs, King of the Seminoles, became the captain of Company A, First Regiment, Indian Home Guards. Micco Hutki was captain of Company F. Little Captain led his Euchees in Co. K, Second Indian Regiment with a rank that befitted his name. The Indian Home Guards were formed as infantry, but those who had ponies used them. In all, whites and Indians, the expeditionary forces consisted of 6,000 men commanded by Col. Weer.[13]

By June 26, they had marched as far as Baxter Springs in the Cherokee Neutral Lands. There they joined Col. Charles Doubleday and Col. Frederick Salomon who had been fighting Watie at Cowskin Prairie southwest of Neosho, Missouri. It was at this point that Lt. James A. Phillips, acting assistant adjutant general, dispatched a letter to John Ross. He assured the chief that the Union knew he and his people were loyal. "My purpose is to afford you protection and to relieve you and your country from your present embarrassment."[14]

Dole had suggested to Coffin that Carruth should accompany the troops. Following that subtle order, Coffin appointed Carruth and H.W. Martin as special Indian agents. The men were to assure "all loyal Indians in the Indian Territory" that the U.S. Government would protect them and "not shrink from any of its Treaty obligations with all such of the Indian Tribes." Indians "whose loyalty is beyond doubt" should be assisted in their suffering after consultation with white officers. The country through which they passed was to be surveyed as to condition, crops and livestock. All of this reconnaissance was important in determining when the Loyal Indians could be returned home. Rev. Evan Jones, who had been in exile for a year, traveled with them carrying a message for Ross.[15]

Brig. Gen. Pike had been expecting this invasion of Indian Territory since the Battle of Pea Ridge. He had released general orders on June 23, assigning Col. Cooper to command the "Confederate and allied troops" north of the Canadian to the Kansas and Missouri lines. Cherokees and Creeks were to position themselves north of the Arkansas. Pike believed the Verdigris would be a good place for them "to observe the approach of any hostile Indian force."[16]

James J. Clarkson had raised 400 volunteers in Arkansas, and, with Pike's consent, had entered the Cherokee Nation to reinforce troops there. Pike was appalled to learn that Clarkson had been placed "in command of three Indian Regiments in the Creek country," blaming the colonel's appointment on Gen. Hindman or Col. Charles A. Carroll, commanding at Fort Smith. Carroll insisted that Watie and Drew had requested Clarkson to command, but only until Pike arrived.[17]

Pike had no intention of moving any farther northward than the Canadian. He had established his headquarters at Fort Ben McCulloch on the Blue River, built by the troops and named in honor of the fallen leader. As he could not get supplies at Fort Gibson, and not wanting the roads from Fort Smith to Washita and Texas left open behind him at Gibson, Pike had moved to this area, 30 miles north of the Red River, where he felt he could guard those roads. Should Opothleyaholo come down "his aim would be country he lived in, west of the North Fork."[18]

The general had been hampered by the appropriation of guns, ammunition and other necessities for the Indian troops by Gen. Earl Van Dorn for his army. Positioned as he was, he was sure supplies would be more forthcoming from Sherman, Bonham and Preston, Texas, and out of the reach of Van Dorn. Pike's Indians were rendered ineffective by the lack of equipment.[19]

Pike had tried to convince Hindman that Van Dorn's confiscation of his supplies had "been actuated by personal hatred of me." This hatred, Pike knew, dated back to the fall of 1858 and Van Dorn's slaughter of the peaceful Comanche men, women and children near Fort Cobb. Van Dorn, supposedly, had been unaware that they had been promised protection by the commandant at Fort Arbuckle. Pike had sent many reports to the government detailing the atrocity and, obviously, he had been singling out Van Dorn as the villain.[20]

The Creek Nation was panicking with news of the invasion. They feared Opothleyaholo would come down west of the Verdigris toward North Fork and they would be driven out or murdered. Pike ordered a Choctaw regiment and Stevens' regiment to the area. He wanted to give assurance that they would not be left alone to face Opothleyaholo's "tender mercies."[21]

Col. Weer ordered the First Indian Regiment, consisting of Creeks and Seminoles, to scout in advance of detachments of the "6th, 9th and 10th" on the Grand River. Weer had learned that Clarkson and his men were somewhere in the area. Col. Ritchie's regiment was in advance near Cowskin Prairie. Ritchie was determined to drive Watie, Raines and their 1,400 men from that position. They were unsuccessful, Watie leaving his prepared breakfast for the enjoyment of Ritchie's men in the Second Indian Regiment.

The scouting party discovered Clarkson and his "Arkansawyers" encamped at Locust Grove in the Cherokee Nation. A forced march on a dark night, over a trail leading through stretches of prairie and dense woods,[22] brought them to his headquarters. At dawn on July 3, the First Indian Regiment led by Lt. Col. Wattles and Maj. Ellithorpe, "were the first in the fight." Carruth and Martin, writing to Coffin, had not heard of any white man firing a gun "unless it was to kill the surgeon of the 1st Regiment."[23] One hundred Rebels were killed. Clarkson, his supplies, and 100 men were captured. The rest of the men fled in panic to Tahlequah where they alerted the Cherokee Secessionists of the Federal advance.[24]

N.B. Pearce, acting quartermaster at Fort Smith, reported the engagement to Hindman on July 5. "For the last 24 hours men have been coming in from Clarkson's headquarters, 30 miles north of Tahlequah." Their horses were broken down, they lacked arms and many of them were "minus their hats." He confirmed the capture of Clarkson. The camp had been "taken by surprise and we not firing a gun." The enemy was there "before they had any intimation of their approach." Pearce deplored the loss of 50 wagons and "some 50 to 100 kegs of powder that Clarkson had taken from Fort Smith." The Confederacy would have been better off if only Clarkson had been lost, and not "that of the train and powder."

Pearce concluded his report, regretting that thousands of arms and ammunition were in the hands of "these no-account Indian commands." Stand Watie, in his opinion, was "the only one worth a cent" as he was mostly white. "I tell you, general this dog-on Indian business is enough to break up any government in the world."[25]

While Pearce was lamenting the Confederacy's support of the Indians, the Battle of Locust Grove was considered a triumph for the Union Indians. Carruth and Martin believed it was an injustice "to claim the victory for the whites."[26]

Hindman ordered Pike to Fort Smith to take command of the forces in Indian Territory. He wanted Pike nearer to the field of operations due to the troops in Indian Territory and northwest Arkansas being disorganized. Pike sent the mounted Texans, whom he considered worthless against infantry and artillery, to the north. As for himself, he was still rankling over the use of his Indians at Pea Ridge and determined he would stay in Indian Territory where his command was located. He planned to go to the Canadian to be near Cooper. "The Arkansas River is not defensible," he told Hindman. The federals might be stopped on the south side of the Canadian, provided they would come that far.

His intelligence of the invasion showed the Indians under Weer and Doubleday to be moving down the Verdigris with Blunt bringing up the rear. He projected their strength to be 14,000–15,000 men. Of course, Blunt was not in the expedition. He was at Leavenworth. "The simple truth is, general, that if the Federalists want to take the Indian country there is nothing to oppose them." His Indian troops had been plundered of supplies, were "unpaid, half naked, unshod," yet, they were still impressed by the Confederacy's wealth. But Pike knew it was going to take more than their high spirits to battle against the Union. They needed white troops to help fight.[27]

Pike's only hope of the Union aborting its advancement lay in the drought that extended from southern Kansas into Indian Territory. The corn and grass had been destroyed and water was scarce. It would be impossible for a large force of federals to march "any distance into this country."[28]

On July 14, Capt. H.M. Greeno with one company of whites and 50 Cherokees, was ordered by Col. Weer to Park Hill, John Ross's residence. Carruth, Martin and Jones accompanied the detachment. Upon their arrival, Ross, William Ross, a lieutenant colonel in Drew's regiment, and Maj. Key were arrested by Greeno. John Ross was then released on parole.

Col. Cooper, at Fort Davis, three miles below Fort Gibson on the Arkansas, had requested Ross to issue a proclamation to recruit Cherokees to assist him in resisting the Union forces that were penetrating the Cherokee country. With Greeno at Park Hill, Cooper's plea for help came to an end.

When the Union detachment reached Tahlequah, they found that the Secessionists had departed and the women pled for mercy for their friends and family should they fall prey to the Union army.[29] The expedition pushed on towards Fort Gibson where they halted while scouts were sent to Fort Davis. They brought back news that the Rebels were massing in great force there.[30]

Gen. Blunt's goal for the expedition was to rout the Rebels, maintain the country they had taken, return the refugees to their homes, and hold a position to cover Kansas and southwestern Missouri until additional troops were available. He intended to "take the field and operate against Hindman in western Arkansas." He had not foreseen the problems that would arise among the white officers.[31]

From the camp on Grand River on July 18, Col. F. Salomon of the Ninth Wisconsin Volunteers issued a statement to all corps commands that he had arrested Col. Weer and assumed command. Salomon felt Weer was a detriment to the forces. They were 160 miles from Fort Scott, the base of operations, and no communications "left open" behind them. A council of war convened the day before had decided that safety for the troops "lay in falling back to some point from which we could reopen communication with our commissary depot." Weer had annulled the decision and decided to remain where they were. With only three days rations left, he ordered the command on half rations. "Reliable information has been received that large bodies of the enemy were moving to our rear, and yet we lay here idle," Salomon reported. He knew he was justified in removing Weer of his command.[32]

It is remarkable that on the 19th, Blunt sent a dispatch to Weer, which in essence corroborated the viewpoints of both men. "You will endeavor to hold all the ground that you have obtained occupancy of," Blunt wrote, and he cautioned Weer to be vigilant that "your communication with Fort Scott is not cut off."[33]

On the 20th, Salomon, then encamped on Wolf Creek in the Cherokee Nation, notified Blunt of his actions. Salomon depicted Weer as an abusive, violent man, and was either insane "or perhaps that his grossly intemperate habits long continued had produced idiocy or monomania."

The new commander had stationed the First and Second Indian Regiments to observe along the Grand and Verdigris rivers. Captains Fall Leaf, Jim Ned and other Indian officers scouted near Fort Gibson along the Arkansas. With the assurance that he intended "to hold the country we are now in," Salomon sent Maj. Burnett with a small escort to deliver the message to Blunt at Fort Leavenworth.[34]

On the same day, Blunt, unaware of what was transpiring, wrote to Stanton. "The Indian Expedition has so far done excellent service and accomplished the work laid out for it." He was concerned that Price with the united forces of McBride, Rains and Stand Watie, a total of at least 30,000–40,000 men might attack the Indian Expedition. Gen. Curtis and his Union army had left the borders of Kansas, the Cherokee Nation and Arkansas on a march to the Mississippi. There they stationed themselves at Helena, south of Memphis, Arkansas. Blunt's intent was to oppose the Rebel army "and to protect the extended boundary from here to Fort Gibson alone, upward of 300 miles, I have only about 5,000 men, including Indians raised by your order." He asked Stanton to send him infantry and a supply of good arms.[35]

When Blunt received the news of Weer's arrest, followed by the intelligence that Salomon with all of the white troops was retreating to Fort Scott, he sent an order to Salomon to halt the retreat at the point he received the order. Blunt commanded him to send white reinforcements to the Indian Regiments still in Indian country. The general hastened to Fort Scott and was surprised to find the entire command there. Salomon, it was learned, had been at Baxter Springs when Blunt's message arrived.[36]

John Ross and his family with other Cherokee officials had seized the opportunity to flee their country and accompanied the retreating troops. The chief had brought the nation's treasures with him. Cherokee people, mostly women, the aged and children had moved with the army, afraid of Stand Watie and the others.[37]

Drew's regiment of Cherokees had surrendered and came within the

Union lines. Blunt accepted their offer to fight for the Union. He organized and mustered them into the Third Indian Regiment with a complement of 1,200 men. He appointed a white lieutenant for each company and Maj. William Phillips of the First Indian Regiment was to be in immediate command.[38]

Blunt convened a general court martial in regard to Weer's arrest. When he found that most of the officers were involved, pro and con, the time that would be used to investigate the affair would be too long. Anxious to get his command back to Indian Territory, he terminated the proceedings and "restored such officers as had been placed under arrest."[39]

Carruth and Martin, who had remained with the Indian Regiments, reported to Blunt about the unexpected retreat of the army. They deplored the fact that "the families of the warriors, retreating with us in obedience of orders," would be vulnerable to Watie and enemies "who know no principle but revenge, and boasts that he will make the country a desert."

The men charged the retreat as "shameful," and begged Blunt "in behalf of the Cherokee nation, especially that portion of it, whites and Indians, who have for months slept in thickets and canes, to do something speedily to arrest the desolation that will follow …"[40]

Col. R.W. Furnas and other commanders, who were left behind with the Indians, held a council and decided "that the safety and preservation of the commands depends upon consolidation." Accordingly, the Indian Regiments and one section of Capt. Allen's battery became the Indian Brigade commanded by Furnas. The force was removed to the Verdigris. On the 23rd, Furnas was ordered by the retreating Salomon to bring the command to Horse Creek near the Kansas border. He obeyed, "my command being without one day's rations and not one ounce of medical stores on hand." Salomon called the Indian Brigade his advance, but in truth, he placed them so as to protect his retrograde march.[41]

Carruth and Martin notified Coffin and suggested "one regiment of whites with the Indians would be of great service." They concluded, however, that the plundering had lessened since the departure of the white troops. "Everything was then laid to the Indians. Nearly everything in the shape of subsistence is used or destroyed in the progress of our army. The 'protection' we are now giving would ruin any country on earth."[42]

There had been near mutiny among the Indian soldiers following the army's retreat. They believed "that the government was to reinstate them in possession of their lands." After they were back in their own country, then they would have been left as "home-guards to defend the country." Now, the white men had left them depleted in strength, equipment and food to face their Indian enemies.[43]

Pike was relieved of his command by Hindman. He sent a letter of resignation to President Davis, detailing his reasons for such action. He depicted himself as "a mere automaton," required "to obey orders sent from a distance." The man was tired, "disheartened, disgusted" seeing all of his efforts to outfit the Indian regiments come to naught.

He postscripted the letter with the information that Seminoles were deserting their country. They had heard Opothleyaholo was coming. Jumper, the chief, had been left with only 100 men, and he had asked for help from the Chickasaws. "Thus these poor Indians are made to fight each other because there is no white force in the country. The Cherokee and Creek countries are irreparably lost."[44]

The first Indian Expedition had ended as a failure. The white troops disregarded the Indians and plundered at will, and in many cases completely gutted homes they were there to defend. With their booty they had deserted, leaving the Indians helpless to hold the positions they had attained. Facing superior numbers, the Indians had fought to stay where they were, but with their train in peril, they had had to retreat themselves. In August they were back at Baxter Springs. Still the Confederacy controlled Indian Territory.[45]

The unconscionable act by the whites resulted in the destitute refugees having to face another winter in Kansas, their population increased by the refugee Cherokees at Fort Scott.

Chapter 26

Removal to Sac and Fox Land

By September 1862, another Indian Expedition was underway, this time with Blunt in the field. Most of the fighting in this campaign to repossess Indian Territory would not take place there but in western Arkansas and southwestern Missouri. Blunt's plans centered on his premise that once the region bordering the territory was cleared of the Rebels, the Confederate forces in the Indian country would be weakened dramatically by such a loss.

Back in the refugee camps, it was inevitable that the two cultures, whites and Indians, would clash. As Turner had predicted, the settlers would not tolerate their timber being used. Cutler and the other agents labored to make the Indians understand they were destroying valuable trees owned by the whites. Ultimately, like everything else that had transpired in their lives, they gave in to the demands of the superior race. Cooking fires had to be maintained and surreptitiously, they supplied themselves with wood.[1]

When the Indian soldiers returned to the encampments they were angry to find their families and friends still in need of food, shelter and clothing. Even the Osages, who had joined the regiments principally as scouts, were dismayed to find many of their own starving at LeRoy. Their agent, P.P. Elder had failed to keep them provisioned. The Indian soldiers had been assured that their people would receive improved care by the government. Not only were the refugee soldiers fighting to recover their home land, but they, as Union soldiers, were aiding the North in their fight against the South. They were led to believe such duty would result in better conditions for their families and friends on the Verdigris and Neosho rivers. In their endeavors to fulfill the two-fold responsibility, they had overlooked the truth that the federal government had failed to keep a treaty or a promise thus far. Basically, nothing had changed; their families were still in desperate need. Once more the Indian Bureau had failed.

Coffin, the nepotist, had hired his son, E.E., for commissary duty "to attend to the receipt and delivery of the provisions," subject to Dole's approval. Coffin's brother, S.D. had been appointed by a Dr. Carter as physician for the refugees and Dr. A.V. Coffin was directing physician for them. The supply of medicine for the Indians always had been "short" and Coffin repeatedly asked Dole for help.[2] Complicating the refugees' health was an outbreak of Caucasian diseases: measles and smallpox. As instructed by Dole, S.D. Coffin and Dr. H.C. Ketcham had vaccinated hundreds at LeRoy after skillfully overcoming the Indians' natural superstitions.[3]

The Seminoles at Neosho Falls were being attended by Dr. Alexander McCartney.[4] Soon after the Civil War, McCartney would help establish Neodesha in Wilson County, located at the confluence of the Verdigris and Fall rivers. This site had been a favorite camping spot of the Osages as they had traveled west to buffalo country. It was at this place in February 1863 that the Osages were encamped during a heavy snowfall, arrayed for battle against Jim Neel's band of Delawares. The Delawares had been to Indian Territory to steal ponies, and returning through Osage land added some Osage ponies to the string. They were pursued, the Osages killing two Delawares. Back at their camp on the Verdigris, Neel and the others "swore vengeance against the Osages."[5] Coffin, on learning the facts, dissuaded the Delawares from immediate action until he could council with the Osages. "Bad weather, impassable roads and high waters" precluded any meeting and with the passage of time, tempers cooled.[6] The problem of Delawares and Kickapoos "jayhawking" in the Indian Territory had occurred repeatedly during the entire stay of the loyal Indians in southern Kansas.

Charges against the refugees of theft and murder became common and most of the crimes could be blamed on the white whiskey peddlers. Soon, Coffin's "bacon department" building was consigned as a jail, with the prisoner always being an Indian.

The rustling of the Union Indians' cattle and horses was moving forward at a rapid pace. Unscrupulous whites, among them army officers, and Indians had made trips to Indian Territory to drive thousands of cattle and ponies north into Kansas. Many of the refugees recognized their brands or marks on the stock and claimed them, if they were fortunate enough to be close to the droves. Army officers, represented by white citizens, then sold the livestock to the contractors, the proceeds shared by those in charge and their minions. The Indian Bureau re-purchased the beef at exorbitant prices to feed the refugees. Their annuities were being used and wasted to buy the beef that was their own property originally. The rustling would continue unabated and in 1865 the Southern Superintendency had estimated that the Indians lost as many as 300,000 cattle and $4.5 million in monies. Ponies and horses had been sold to whites who were indignant when the refugees claimed them as their own.

Hostilities erupted and it was reported that Indians were killing whites and that "whites so enraged at conduct of Indians that they leave the dead ones to rot on the prairie."[7]

In order to prevent the antagonism between the whites and Indians from developing into a war, Coffin knew the refugees must be moved elsewhere and quickly. Despite the deprivations of the Osages, Chief White Hair and sub-chief Charles Mongrain had invited the refugees to move to their land until they could be returned home. Opothleyaholo and the other leaders declined the offer.[8]

Dr. Kile had found that provisions could be purchased "on better terms" at the Sac and Fox Agency. Perry Fuller, former Indian agent at the agency, was the contractor there, and Robert Stevens was still operating on the reservation with additional stone houses being constructed. "The supply of Timber is better there from the Timber cut down for lumber to build the houses for the Indians," Coffin explained to Dole.[9] With the deterioration of relations at LeRoy, the drought that had ruined the corn crop in southern Kansas and the failure of the Indian Expedition to make significant inroads into Indian Territory, Coffin began in earnest to seek the refugees' removal to the Sac and Fox Reservation.

In March, three Sac and Fox chiefs had visited Opothleyaholo and other leaders at LeRoy. Moses Keokuk, son of the famous chief Keokuk, and his successor, was one of the men who offered their reservation as a haven for the refugees. As seen in the memorial to Lincoln, Opothleyaholo was adamant about moving north instead of south toward home. After four days of counciling, and being refused, the Sac and Fox men took their departure north.[10]

Coffin told Dole of his annoyance with the whites "Selling their Spirits" to the Indians. Because they were now on "Individual Lands" it was impossible to control many problems such as timber and whiskey sales. Coffin was convinced that the sale of liquor could be controlled if they were with the Sac and Fox. Their reservation was considered common land, and the Indian Bureau representatives would be able to sanction such transgressions by the whites in their efforts to seduce and dupe the Indians. The theory was admirable, but in reality, impossible.[11]

The offer by the Sac and Fox chiefs appeared benevolent, but as time would prove they had developed a sort of "white man's" skill in changing disaster into an asset. Their reservation was dotted with derelict houses and as Stevens was erecting more, which they didn't want, it was deemed advisable to utilize all of this property. They knew the southern Indians were used to living in houses and, despite their vandalized condition, surely the refugees would be eager to move into their houses on the reservation. The only thing the refugees had been eager to do was return home to Indian Territory.

In September, Cutler reported there had been nearly 400 Creek deaths since coming to Kansas. "Their wants are many yet, and will continue so until they can be restored to their own country."[12] With the failure of the Indian Expedition, there now loomed the specter of another winter in southern Kansas, and with the settlers wanting the refugees anywhere but near them, the Sac and Fox invitation could no longer be ignored. There were no alternatives, except for the Osage country and there they would be exposed to the winter weather. The prospect of living in a house with a roof overhead surely helped convince Opothleyaholo to make the move. But was he aware that the 150 houses had no doors, windows or floors? And would it have mattered had he been apprised of their condition? The man could no longer endure the suffering of his family and his people.

It was a repeated process in moving thousands of Indians to the north. All of the tribes complied except for the Seminoles who refused to leave the Neosho Falls location, and the Cherokees who had come to Fort Scott, then to Neosho, Missouri, and finally to their own neutral lands. With the Cherokees, it was a different situation as Blunt intended to return them to their country during the second Indian Expedition. By the latter part of October 1862, Opothleyaholo and all of the refugees were on Sac and Fox land.[13]

Coffin was exceedingly occupied in the moving venture, but he had taken time to study the fate of the southern Indians when they returned home. He was in constant communication with the Indian Bureau and while he was in Washington in September, he wrote to Charles Mix, acting commissioner of Indian Affairs. Dole had come west to survey the conditions for himself and do a little treating with Kansas Indians.

Coffin foresaw new treaties with the tribes and felt his suggestions would result "in great good" for all concerned; "the Indians, the government and the country generally." The treaties should "provide that the Indians shall take their lands in severalty." The policy of holding their lands in common "does not work well with white men." Why the white man should be concerned about the "common lands" when the Indians were to have their country in perpetuity, can only stamp Coffin as one who was scheming with the many of his ilk to appropriate the lands for himself. The habit of letting the Indians have common lands did not work well for those "whose habits of indolence and idleness are well known," Coffin wrote. Their "indolence" and "idleness" had produced through the short period of time west of the Mississippi, thousands of livestock, hogs, horses, corn and cotton crops and many successful markets with the outside world. Had they not been so lazy, one can only imagine what might have been produced by the Five Civilized Tribes.

Coffin wanted the treaties to provide surveys of all the reservations "valuable for agricultural purposes and after the Indians make their selections, open up the balance to sale and settlement by the whites."

He did not believe that Indians in the north should be moved to Indian

Territory. In his "humble opinion" it would require a military presence to keep peace. There would be depredations committed by the Indians against each other, "cattle, mules, ponies and horses" being the target. The dangerous consequences he envisioned should the northern Indians be moved south would be "almost unavoidable amongst a savage people who are living in close contact and leading the roving, vagabond life as they do." Coffin did not designate "the savage people" who were vagabonds, but if he meant to include the Five Civilized Tribes, his ignorance was showing once again. These tribes, Creek, Cherokee, Seminole, Choctaw and Chickasaw, had never been a roving people after they settled in the southeastern part of the U.S., and certainly had not moved back and forth since their relocation west of the Mississippi.

The superintendent had a solution to the whole sordid situation. "If much the largest portion of the Indian Territory was settled up by an enterprising and industrious white population" the Indian would see the advantages of being like the white man and become more civilized. With the white man's presence, there would be no need for "a military force" among them.

Should the Five Civilized Tribes be allowed to continue as they had in the past "their early extinction cannot be so very deeply regretted by either the philanthropist or the statesman, as their present mode of life makes them of no use to society, the government, or themselves; their lives are aimless, worthless and useless to themselves or anybody else." The superintendent knew that unless his recommendations were put to work there was no future for the Indians except a lingering in "a miserable existence." Any "miserable existence" experienced by the Native People had been the result of avaricious, meddling Americans.

"The Indian country is too good a country to be entirely dedicated to so worthless a purpose." Coffin suggested that if his course "should be adopted" the Indians lives and characters would change "for the better" and they could be "rescued from utter extinction and oblivion."

But the ultimate goal of Coffin's plan was no different than those who had passed before him. "The Indian Territory would soon become one of the most prosperous and powerful States in the Union."[14]

In November 1862, Gen. Thomas Hindman ordered the arrest of Pike.[15] A tireless communicator, Pike issued a statement to the Five Civilized Tribes. He explained that the primary reason for his resignation was Hindman's order directing him to leave Indian country for Fort Smith where he was to organize troops to defend northwestern Arkansas. His area of operations was Indian Territory and there he had intended to stay. His open defiance had brought about his downfall. He warned the Rebel Indians that the North would never forgive them for joining the Confederacy. Their lands would be forfeited and divided among the Union soldiers. Their monies would also be forfeited. Any debts owed by the federal government would be confiscated and they would "put an end to your national existence."[16]

While President Jefferson Davis considered the resignation, Pike requested a leave of absence to visit his family in Little Rock. Hindman ordered him to Little Rock, but it would not be until November that he saw his relatives. After the visit, instead of returning to headquarters, he traveled to Grayson County, Texas, and subsequently entered Indian Territory again.[17]

Immediately, orders for his arrest were issued and by November 19 he was a prisoner of "a captain and forty-eight men of Shelby's Missouri Brigade" in Warren, Texas. While there he notified Davis of his whereabouts, explaining he was seized near Tishomingo in the Chickasaw country after returning to Fort Washita from Fort Arbuckle. He had intended to march to the Wichita Agency at Fort Cobb "to repel any invasion of hostile Indians." He readily admitted he had reassumed his old command. "The course pursued by Generals Holmes and Hindman in regard to the Indian troops and country has produced the results which long ago I predicted. In my opinion the Indian country is lost."

The Missourians, Pike informed Davis, "who had been sent to arrest me by their own confessions had plundered the houses of the Choctaws along the way."

Pike intended to go to Richmond when he was no longer in custody to "show how the Indian country, worth more to the Confederacy than the state of Virginia, has been wantonly thrown away."[18]

Pike did not stop with the letter to Davis; he also notified George W. Randolph, secretary of war. "I reassumed the command with the utmost reluctance and only in obedience to the President's wishes, as sent to me through Captain Mackey."[19] It is curious Pike failed to remind Davis about this.

As to the hostile Indians he had referred to, they were associated with the massacre of Agent Leeper and other white men of the agency. But they were not "hostile," they were the Reserve Indians at the agency. For some time they had been dissatisfied with Leeper and while he was in Texas, they told a man named Jones, acting in Leeper's absence, that they did not want the agent back. Jones either did not believe the threats, or was dilatory in notifying Leeper. When he returned on the night of October 23, the agency was invaded by the Reserve Indians who killed him and all other whites. The disaffected Indians placed the bodies in the agency building and set it afire.[20]

The Confederacy had no intention of abandoning Indian Territory regardless of Pike's commentary. As ordered by Davis, S.S. Scott, commissioner of the Indian Bureau, had visited the region. In a December 1862 address to the Five Civilized Tribes and other nations friendly to the Confederate States, Scott described his sojourn there. It was an auspicious opportunity to remind the nations of their ties to the South.

"You are, in every sense of the word, southern. The South was the home of your fathers. It was within the shadow of her deep forests and by the side of her sparkling streams, that they sported in their infancy and hunted the deer and the bear in their manhood, and it is in the bosom of her green valleys that their bones now lie buried."

He cautioned, as Pike had, of the dire consequences should the Union win the war. But, of course, that would never be as Gen. Lee and his army had just defeated "the grand army of the North" at Fredericksburg in Virginia. All future battles would be Confederate victories. "The southern Indian is the fighting Indian; the southern white man is the fighting white man and they can never be subdued by northern arms."

And there was the matter of "the fulfilment of certain promises made to you by the confederate government." The "great and terrible war" was the culprit, not the South. In the event future delays might occur they were to "bear in mind" that "the confederate government will comply strictly with all of its engagements to you." Under the care of the Confederacy "it will be easy for you in a few years to become powerful and prosperous nations."[21]

Small comfort these words must have been for the Rebel Indians who were without adequate arms to protect themselves and without clothing, shoes, and food. Indeed, the Rebel Indians were suffering the same vicissitudes as their fellow tribal members in Kansas. Even though the two factions were bitter toward each other, they were still Native People and therefore shared the common dupe of the white man.

Coffin's assurance to Dole that the whiskey traffic among the refugees, safely ensconced on the Sac and Fox Reservations, would be stopped had not tested true. Whiskey barrels had been found near the reserve and were destroyed. Cutler and the other agents had arrested a few white persons involved in the "nefarious business." Tried in U.S. courts, they were heavily fined to the point Cutler felt they would never recover. Yet, as soon as their fines and bonds were paid, and they were free, they returned to their operations. Obviously, these white men were subsidized by unknown parties. Obviously, they had threatened the refugees because Cutler could not "make an Indian testify" against them. When had an Indian making accusations against an American, in or out of court, ever been believed? Whiskey was plentiful, yet, in 1863, many of the refugees were naked and their condition "far from pleasant."[22]

In December, while Scott was addressing the Rebel Indians, there was a battle between Blunt and Hindman in northwestern Arkansas near Fayetteville. Hindman's forces were positioned in a semicircular line near a timbered area called Prairie Grove, their rear protected by the trees. Blunt's men, greatly outnumbered, were on the open plain. The battle lasted from early afternoon until dark. Blunt's batteries had kept up a deadly fire at close range while his men advanced steadily toward the timber. With nightfall, the fighting had stopped and Blunt, unaware of the damage that had been done to Hindman, planned to regroup and resume the battle at daylight.

Hindman sent a message to Blunt under a flag of truce. He wanted to meet Blunt at dawn in order to come to terms about removing his wounded. Blunt agreed, and later found out it had been a ruse. Hindman's army, with artillery wheels muffled by blankets, had hastily retreated over the Boston Mountains to safety during the dark, leaving some of the wounded on the field. The fierceness of Blunt's Army of the Frontier had proved too much for the southern gentlemen. And the way to St. Louis had been blocked for the Confederacy once more.

Among the Union soldiers penetrating the woods was the First and Second Indian Regiments. Little Captain, Billy Bowlegs and Haleck Tustunuggee of the First Regiment had distinguished themselves in the Union victory, and Lt. Col. Stephen H. Wattles reported they were "deserving of the highest praise." Lt. John T. Cox, Second Indian Regiment, mapped the campaigns of the country involved. His map of the Prairie Grove battlefield was published in *Harper's Weekly*.[23]

Chapter 27

We Are the Color
of the Earth

Coffin dictated this impromptu eulogy to his clerk and secretary, Henry Smith, on March 22, 1863, at the Sac and Fox Agency: "On arriving here I found the great king (O-poth-le-yo-ho-la) on his death bed; and though evidently struggling with the grim monster, yet possesses all the wonderful powers of mind that have characterized him through life, and forced the conviction upon all who have come in contact with him that he was no ordinary man. He manifests in an extraordinary degree that attachment for his people that has been the ruling passion of his life."[1]

In reporting Opothleyaholo's death, Cutler saw the leader as "probably the greatest Indian that has ever lived."[2] Fellow Creeks brought Opothleyaholo's body back to Woodson County. On a hill studded with oaks near Fort Belmont, he was buried beside the body of his beloved daughter.[3]

William W. Averell, bearer of the secret message to Emory, served with distinction in the Civil War and resigned in 1865 as brevet major general. He died February 3, 1900, at the age of 67 in Bath, New York.[4]

James G. Blunt was to engage in a bloody battle near Baxter Springs in October 1863. On October 4, the general, his staff and regimental band left Fort Scott to return to his command at Fort Smith. Near Camp Baxter on the 6th, they saw what they believed to be part of the troops from the small camp approaching them. As they were dressed in blue uniforms and carried the U.S. flag, Blunt's men believed them to be friendly. Yet, Blunt, apprehensive, approached them and was immediately fired upon. It was Quantrill and his men who had been on the move to Indian Territory when they stopped at Camp Baxter to harry the troops there. Of the 103 men with Blunt that day, 87 were killed including the band members and the little drummer boy. This chance encounter would be called the Baxter Springs Massacre. Blunt died

July 25, 1881, at Washington, D.C., a patient in the St. Elizabeth's government hospital for the insane.[5]

Billy Bowlegs, king of the Seminoles and captain of Company F, First Indian Home Guards, wrote several letters to Dole while serving in the army. Uppermost in Bowlegs' mind was to see his people returned to their country. In one of the letters he described his encounter with a "secesh" near Rhea Mills in Arkansas. During a tussle, the rebel took his two revolvers, saddle, bridle and horse. Bowlegs knew "that our Father will give me another gun."[6] In March 1864, Billy Bowlegs died of smallpox at Fort Gibson. He was never fated to see his people back in their own lands. Bowlegs is buried in the National Cemetery at Fort Gibson.[7]

Edwin H. Carruth died in the fall of 1863 and Milo Gookins was appointed as agent of the Wichita Agency.[8] William G. Coffin resigned his position as superintendent of the Southern Superintendency in the spring of 1865. Coffin was able to withstand the charge of malfeasance and other accusations associated with his tenure as superintendent. Opening a claims office in Washington, he practiced law and represented Indians until 1902.[9] He was 93 when he died in 1904 at Fort Scott.[10]

George W. Collamore was elected mayor of Lawrence, Kansas. He was there in August 1863 when Quantrill attacked the town. Family and friends, fearful that Quantrill would kill him, persuaded Collamore to hide in the well in a shed adjacent to his home. After it was safe for him to quit his hiding place, it was discovered that Collamore had died, a victim of the noxious fumes in the well.[11]

John T. Cox, who had supplied *Harper's Weekly* with a map of the Battle of Prairie Grove, was appointed Special Indian Agent in September 1863, and served until 1864. It was Cox, in February 1864, while in the Creek Nation, who found the regimental papers of Chilly McIntosh and private papers and correspondence of Gen. Cooper in a building near the Little River.[12] Cox drew a map of the retreat of the Loyal Indian Refugees to Kansas in 1861–62. This map is on file at the National Archives in Washington. He represented the government in the appraisal of the Cherokee Neutral Lands. As late as 1887 Cox was living in Fredonia, Kansas, where he had a real estate and insurance business. He served two terms as county surveyor.[13] Cox's mother, Mrs. Lydia Sexton, was the first woman chaplain at the Kansas Penitentiary in Lansing.[14]

Dr. George Cutler resigned as agent for the Creeks in the summer following Lincoln's assassination. He moved to Sherman, Texas, in the Red River country and established a newspaper, the *Patriot*. Robert S. Stevens, who had survived the bond scandal and the fleecing of the Indians, was involved in the building of the Missouri–Kansas–Texas (Katy) Railroad. The rail lines followed the old Texas Road in Indian Territory to Texas. Stevens persuaded Cutler to move to another area along the Red River where the railroad intended to build a town. Cutler complied, named his paper the *Red River Journal*, the headlines of its first issue in red ink. He, also, named the new town Red River City which became Denison. The former Indian agent was also vice-president of the Texas Press and Editorial Association in 1873. Cutler did return to Kansas and in 1883 was the postmaster at Geuda Springs in Sumner County, and maintained a drugstore and practiced medicine.[15]

Delaware Springs in Wilson County, where refugees camped and died, became a resort at the turn of the century. The spring water, thought to be beneficial for kidney trouble, was in demand throughout the United States. A sample of the water, a history of the springs, and a picture were sent to St. Louis for the Louisiana Exposition (World's Fair) in 1904 where it won a first prize, silver medal.[16]

William H. Emory, who led the Union Army out of Indian Territory, served in the Union Army during the Civil War. He was retired from active service on July 1, 1876, with rank of brig. general. Emory died December 1, 1887, at the age of 76, in Washington,[17]

James H. Lane was in Lawrence at the time of the massacre. Lane, on hearing that Quantrill was looking for him, escaped his home clad only in his underwear and took refuge in a cornfield. In this condition he rallied some men, hoping to prevent Quantrill's escape, but the effort proved unsuccessful. In 1866, Lane, in ill health and mentally unstable due to his political star descending, shot himself in the head, and died ten days later.[18]

Little Bear, Little Osage chief, died in 1868 at his village located at the confluence of the Verdigris and Fall rivers in Wilson County. Little Bear had remained loyal to the Union, disregarding Pike's oratory. However, Black Dog, the 7'6" Osage chief had journeyed to Tahlequah in September 1861 and joined the Confederacy. Little Bear's loyalty paid off in May 1863 when Confederate officers and men, on their way to enlist Rebels in the Colorado and New Mexico area, made the mistake of crossing Osage land. When they were discovered, they told the Osages they were scouts from Humboldt. But the Osages knew those scouts and in disputing their word, the Rebels took off across country heading northwest. A pursuit was launched and eventually coming around to the Verdigris near present Independence, Kansas, the Osages were victorious, killing all but two: Warner Lewis and John Rafferty. They had secreted themselves in brush along the river's bank. Lewis had been wounded in the shoulder by an arrow, and had lost his boots. He and Rafferty, sharing the latter's shoes, eventually made their way back to Jasper County, Missouri, where they had started.

The Osages scalped the Confederates and took all of their papers to show Capt. Willoughby Doudna, commander of Troop G, Ninth Kansas Cavalry, at Humboldt. One man was bald but had a heavy, long beard. The Osages not to be cheated of a coup merely removed the beard. All were decapitated, conforming to the Osages' belief that when the head was severed from the body, the person was dead.

In 1870, when the Osages left on their hunting trip, they did not return to southern Kansas. With the ceding of their remaining lands, they were moved into the hills of northern Indian Territory. Later, oil would be discovered on their lands and today, the Osages are described as the wealthiest Indian Nation in this country.[19]

Micco Hutki, one of Opothleyaholo's most trusted men, became the second chief of the Creek Nation in 1866.[20]

Albert Pike returned to law and journalism after the war. He remained active in Washington and Memphis. Some historians have linked his name with the organizing of the Ku Klux Klan. Pike died April 2, 1891, in Washington.[21]

John Ross, who had waited for federal help in defying the Confederacy, journeyed back east with his family to live. Ross died in Washington in 1866 at the age of 76. At the time of his death, he was negotiating a new treaty for the Cherokees.[22]

The Sac and Fox tribes presented a claim against the Loyal Indian Refugees for the "rent of 204 buildings" for the sum of $14,688 in 1864.[23] According to H.W. Martin, agent for the Sac and Fox, some of the refugees vandalized the houses. Martin's statement does not ring true, for at least 150 of the houses had suffered damage by the Sac and Fox. It does not seem logical that after enduring their horrendous living conditions along the Fall River, Verdigris and Neosho rivers that they would deliberately abuse any improved living quarters.[24]

It was the government expending money who had tried to civilize the Sac and Fox according to the *Emporia News*. As usual there was no information concerning the fact the Sac and Fox had paid for the frauds by the government. The Sac and Fox had shown their appreciation for the "comfortable stone houses" by tearing out the doors and partitions and using them for fuel while the remaining structure stabled their ponies. "The earth belongs to the workers. These human weeds have no right to withhold from tillage and improvement the magnificent domain they now occupy." The editor, in 1867, was happy to report their removal from Kansas to Indian Territory was imminent.[25]

Out of the "human weeds" would come Jim Thorpe, the world's greatest athlete. Thorpe had been born on the reservation in Indian Territory. In 1912, he won the pentathlon and decathlon in the Olympic Games and was stripped of his medals when it was discovered he had played semi-pro baseball. In 1920–21, Thorpe was the first president of the American Professional Football Association, now the NFL. After his death in 1953, the Olympic medals were returned to his family.

Opothleyaholo's family obtained rations at Fort Gibson in May 1865. There were listed, by number only, three children and four women which had been computed at five and one-half persons. The rations were issued for a ten day period. They received bacon, flour, hard bread in lieu of cornmeal, beans, hominy, tea, sugar, adamantine candles, soap and salt.[26]

Opothleyaholo's remains were never returned to Indian Territory.[27] It was believed that great leader, this great member of the Native People, was buried on the hill near old Fort Belmont. An Indian burial ground was discovered by some local people and was disinterred.[28] Perhaps one of the skeletons belonged to Opothleyaholo, who had met with two presidents—Adams and Jackson—and had fought at the Battle of Horseshoe Bend. He had defied the Confederacy to remain true to the Union, only to suffer starvation with his followers in Kansas.

In Kansas, he had supposedly died of old age. True, he was in his late sixties or seventies but he had dealt with the federal government since the 1820s and had endured nothing but lies by them. He had not been promised safe haven in Kansas, he had been promised the Union army's help to stay in his own land. And when the Confederacy realized he was a threat to their power in Indian Territory, the order was given that Opothleyaholo must concede or be driven from the territory. He did not yield to the pressure, nor did his followers. And, once again, he had been duped. Surely, this great leader had carried that onus with him during the years he had to stay in Kansas, and surely it had broken, at long last, his spirit.

In 1902 a history of Wilson County was compiled by the editor of the *Wilson County Citizen* in Fredonia. Contained within the county's history is an article about the Loyal Indian Refugees and their travail. John Gilmore wrote of how years later "bones of the ponies were widely strewn and skeletons of Indians whitened hillsides and lay scattered in forest glades." Due to the snow and sleet packed ground, the Indians were buried "in shallow graves." Many skeletons were discovered in "prostrate hollow trees." Often more than one skeleton was found "in a single trunk or log" with a stump of wood as a plug for the opening.

Gilmore's record of this horrible event is admirable, yet his consensus of the Native People is not, and exemplified the feeling of the Americans at that time. "These were the impressive and mournful evidences of the gloomy sojourn in Wilson County of a buffeted and inferior race who had demonstrated the possession of the qualities of fidelity, fortitude and self-sacrifice in a degree which deserved the unstinted praise and grateful approbation of the more civilized people whose wards they were."[29]

Just as Opothleyaholo has been denied his rightful place in the history of the United States, in death he was denied his correct name in the history of Kansas. In 1939 the WPA Writers Project of Kansas made an error that has

Wilburn Gouge (L), current speaker of the Muskogee nation; Thomas Yahola (R), member of the National Council, Tuckabatchee District, Muskogee Nation; lineal descendants of Opothleyaholo. *Courtesy Thomas Yahola.*

confused local historians for years. Citing the small town of Buffalo in northern Wilson County, it informed the general public traversing the area about the location of Fort Belmont. According to the writers, Hapo, an Osage chief, and his daughter were interred near the fort. The terse biography of misinformation was unfortunately about Opothleyaholo's heroic efforts during the Civil War. It also has created the belief that Chief Little Bear was buried there.[30]

In 1907, the Five Civilized Tribes saw their lands, which had been guaranteed by the federal government to be theirs as long as the grass grows and the waters flow, become the state of Oklahoma. Oklahoma is a Choctaw word meaning "Red Man" or "Red People."

In 1986 the site of Fort Row was commemorated. This event was not funded by any state or county money. Rather, more than 100 students of the Lincoln Elementary School in Fredonia participated in activities to raise the money needed to make a sign which recalled to passersby the grim occurrences in the winter of 1861–62.[31]

On August 22, 1993, fellow Muskogeeans gathered under a traditional arbor to induct Opothleyaholo into the National Hall of Fame for Famous American Indians at Anadarko, Oklahoma. The dedication speech was delivered by Thomas Yahola. Betty Butts, a Californian, presented the Muskogees with the unveiling of a bronze bust of Opothleyaholo.

In Yahola's speech, he talked about the earth and what it meant to them. He disclosed the Native People's affinity for the earth and how Opothleyaholo had tried to explain to the commissioners, almost 170 years ago, why they could not sell their mother, the earth. "We come from the earth; we go back to the earth; we are the color of the earth."

Notes

Chapter 1

1. Abel, *The American Indian As Participant in the Civil War*, p. 79–80.
2. *Annual Report of the Commissioner of Indian Affairs, Southern Superintendency, 1862*, p. 137; *Indian Office General Titles*, C-1526, February 13, 1862.
3. *Ibid.*, p. 138.

Chapter 2

1. Benton, *Thirty Years' View*, p. 64.
2. *Niles Weekly Register*, June 10, 1826, p. 257.
3. Interview with Thomas Yahola, Wetumka, Oklahoma.
4. *National Geographic*, V. 180, No. 4, October, 1991.
5. *American State Papers, Military Affairs*, V. 6, p. 643.
6. *American State Papers, Indian Affairs*, V. 2, p. 569.
7. Little Rock (Ark) *Daily State Journal*, January 10, 1862, p. 2, col. 3.
8. Thomas Yahola interview.
9. Hitchcock, *A Traveler in Indian Territory*, p. 112.
10. Thomas Yahola interview.
11. *Ibid.*
12. *Ibid.*
13. *American State Papers, Indian Affairs*, V. 2, p. 790.
14. *Ibid.*, p. 788.
15. *Ibid.*, p. 786, 788, 790.
16. *Ibid.*, p. 790.
17. Richardson, *Messages and Papers of the Presidents*, V. 1., p. 62, 68.
18. *Ibid.*
19. *American State Papers, Indian Affairs* II, p. 791.
20. *Ibid.*
21. Richardson, *Messages and Papers of the President*, V. 1., p. 70–72.
22. *Ibid.*, p. 118, 174.
23. *American State Papers, Indian Affairs*, V. 2, p. 792.

24. Hawkins, *Letters, Journals and Writings of Benjamin Hawkins*, V. 1, p. 352–354.

25. Hitchcock, *A Traveler in Indian Territory*, p. 129; *Bureau of American Ethnology of American Indians*, p. 364.

26. Thomas Yahola interview.

Chapter 3

1. Greeley, *The American Conflict*, 1866, V. I, p. 27, 30.

2. *American State Papers, Indian Affairs* II, p. 114.

3. Richardson, *Messages and Papers of the Presidents*, V. 1, p. 340.

4. Abel, *The History of Events Resulting in Indian Consolidation West of the Mississippi*, p. 249.

5. Richardson, *Messages and Papers of the Presidents*, V. 1, p. 340–342.

6. *Ibid.*, p. 396.

7. *Ibid.*, p. 386–387.

8. *Ibid.*, p. 388, 393.

9. *Ibid.*, p. 393.

10. Debo, *The Road to Disappearance*, p. 86–87; McKenney and Hall, *The Indian Tribes of America*, V. I, p. 263.

11. Eggleston, *Red Eagle and the Wars With the Creek Indians of Alabama*, p. 51, 54.

12. *Ibid.*, p. 63.

13. *Ibid.*

14. *Ibid.*, p. 63–64, 69.

15. *Ibid.*, p. 61–62.

16. *Ibid.*, p. 101, 104, 111–112.

17. Hawkins, *Letters, Journals and Writings of Benjamin Hawkins*, p. 665.

Chapter 4

1. Eggleston, *Red Eagle and the Wars with the Creek Indians of Alabama*, p. 310.

2. *Ibid.*, p. 321, 327.

3. Kappler, *Indian Affairs: Laws and Treaties*, V. II, p. 107–110.

4. McKenney and Hall, *Indian Tribes of America*, V. II, p. 178–193.

5. Halbert, *The Creek Wars of 1813–1814*, p. 276–277.

6. Hawkins, *Letters, Journals and Writings*, V. II, p. 696.

7. Richardson, *Messages and Papers of the Presidents*, V. I, p. 533.

8. *American State Papers, Military Affairs*, V. II, p. 119.

9. *Ibid.*, *Indian Affairs* II, p. 249–250.

10. *Ibid.*, p. 250.

11. *Ibid.*, p. 251.

12. *Ibid.*

13. *Ibid.*, p. 257.

14. *Ibid.*, p. 256.

15. *Ibid.*, p. 252.

16. *Ibid.*, p. 253.

17. *Ibid.*, p. 252.

18. *Ibid.*, p. 252–253.

19. *Ibid.*, p. 253.

20. *Ibid.*
21. *Ibid.*, p. 254.
22. Kappler, *Indian Affairs, Laws and Treaties*, V. II, p. 195–198.
23. *American State Papers, Indian Affairs* II, p. 254.
24. *Ibid.*, p. 259.
25. *Ibid.*, p. 748.
26. *Ibid.*, p. 260.

Chapter 5

1. *American State Papers, Indian Affairs* II, p. 746.
2. Richardson, *Messages and Papers of the Presidents*, V. II, p. 804.
3. *American State Papers, Indian Affairs* II, p. 736.
4. *Ibid.*, p. 570.
5. *Ibid.*, p. 565.
6. *Ibid.*, p. 255, 782.
7. *Ibid.*, p. 565.
8. *Ibid.*, p. 566.
9. *Ibid.*, p. 568.
10. *Ibid.*
11. *Ibid.*, p. 569.
12. *Ibid.*
13. *Ibid.*
14. *Ibid.*, p. 570.
15. *Ibid.*, p. 571.
16. Thomas Yahola interview.
17. *American State Papers, Indian Affairs* II, p. 571.
18. *Ibid.*
19. *Ibid.*, p. 572.
20. *Ibid.*, p. 573.
21. *Ibid.*
22. *Ibid.*, p. 572.
23. *Ibid.*, p. 573.

Chapter 6

1. *American State Papers, Indian Affairs* II, p. 574.
2. *Ibid.*
3. *Ibid.*
4. *Niles Weekly Register* V. XXVII, p. 222–224.
5. *American State Papers, Indian Affairs* II, p. 574.
6. *Ibid.*
7. *Ibid.*, p. 574–575.
8. *Ibid.*, p. 576.
9. *Ibid.*
10. *Ibid.*, p. 578.
11. *Ibid.*, p. 579.

12. *Ibid.*, p. 578–580.
13. *Ibid.*, p. 581.
14. Indian Springs State Park, Flovilla, GA.
15. *American State Papers, Indian Affairs* II, p. 581–582.
16. *Ibid.*, p. 582.
17. *Ibid.*, p. 583.
18. *Ibid.*
19. McKenney and Hall, *Indian Tribes*, V. II, p. 20.
20. *American State Papers, Indian Affairs* II, p. 583.
21. Kappler, *Indian Affairs, Laws and Treaties*, p. 214.
22. Indian Office Manuscript Records, 1825; Abel, *Indian Consolidation*, p. 346.
23. *American State Papers, Indian Affairs* II, p. 756.
24. *Ibid.*, p. 584.
25. Adams, *The Memoirs of John Quincy Adams*, V. VII, p. 12.
26. *American State Papers, Indian Affairs* II, p. 761.
27. *Ibid.*, p. 762.
28. *Ibid.*
29. *Ibid.*
30. *Ibid.*
31. *Ibid.*
32. *Ibid.*, p. 763.
33. *Ibid.*
34. *Ibid.*, p. 762.
35. *Ibid.*
36. *Ibid.*, p. 763.
37. *Ibid.*
38. *Ibid.*, p. 764.
39. *Ibid.*, p. 765.
40. *Ibid.*, p. 773.
41. *Ibid.*, p. 765.

Chapter 7

1. *American State Papers, Indian Affairs* II, p. 764.
2. *Ibid.*
3. *Ibid.*, p. 758.
4. *Ibid.*, p. 759.
5. *Ibid.*, p. 761.
6. *Ibid.*, p. 759.
7. *Ibid.*, p. 757–758.
8. *Ibid.*, p. 767.
9. *Ibid.*, p. 768.
10. *Ibid.*
11. *Ibid.*
12. *Ibid.*, p. 770–771.
13. *Ibid.*, p. 768.
14. *Ibid.*
15. *Ibid.*, p. 768–769.
16. *Ibid.*, p. 767.

17. *Ibid.*, p. 768.
18. *Ibid.*, p. 769.
19. Adams, *Memoirs*, V. VII, p. 3.
20. *Ibid.*
21. *Ibid.*
22. *Ibid.*, p. 5.
23. *Ibid.*
24. *Ibid.*, p. 8.
25. *Ibid.*, p. 11.

Chapter 8

1. *Niles Register*, V. XXIX, 9/3/1825, p. 17–18.
2. *Ibid.*, p. 5.
3. *American State Papers, Indian Affairs* II, p. 795.
4. *Ibid.*, p. 798.
5. *Ibid.*, p. 796.
6. *Ibid.*
7. *Ibid.*, p. 797.
8. *Ibid.*, p. 808.
9. *Ibid.*, p. 809.
10. *Ibid.*, p. 852.
11. *Ibid.*, p. 807.
12. *Ibid.*, p. 806.
13. *Ibid.*, p. 817.
14. *Ibid.*, p. 818.
15. *Ibid.*, p. 831.
16. *Ibid.*
17. *Ibid.*, p. 832–833.
18. *Ibid.*, p. 833.
19. *Ibid.*, p. 800.
20. *Ibid.*, p. 800–801.
21. *Ibid.*, p. 801.
22. *Ibid.*, p. 801–803.
23. *Ibid.*, p. 809.
24. *Ibid.*, p. 810.
25. *Ibid.*
26. *Ibid.*, p. 811.
27. *Ibid.*, p. 815.
28. *Ibid.*, p. 816.
29. *Ibid.*, p. 852.
30. *Ibid.*, p. 855–858.

Chapter 9

1. Abel, *Indian Consolidation*, p. 245.
2. Tindle, *Wilson County, Kansas: People of the South Wind*, p. 2.

3. Kappler, *Indian Treaties*, V. II, p. 167.
4. *Ibid.*, p. 217–221.
5. *Ibid.*, p. 246–248.
6. *Niles Register*, V. XXIX, 11/26/1825, p. 194.
7. Wilson, *Washington, the Capital City*, p. 203–205.
8. Adams, *Memoirs*, V. VII, 11/26/1825 p. 61–62.
9. *Ibid.*, p. 62.
10. *Ibid.*
11. "Talk of Poethleyoholo," 11/30/1825, *Indian Office Letter Book*, Ser. II. No. 2, p. 272.

Chapter 10

1. Adams, *Memoirs*, V. VII, p. 76.
2. *American State Papers, Indian Affairs* II, p. 741.
3. Richardson, *Messages and Papers of the Presidents*, V II, 1/31/1826, p. 872.
4. McKenney and Hall, *Indian Tribes*, V. II, p. 24–25.
5. National Archives RG75, T–494, Roll 1, frames 0777–81.
6. *Niles Register*, V. XXX, 6/10/1826, p. 257.
7. National Archives, RG75, T–494, Roll 1, frames 0798–99.
8. Adams, *Memoirs*, V. VII, p. 78–79.
9. *Ibid.*, p. 90.
10. *Ibid.*, p. 89.
11. *Ibid.*, p. 90.
12. *Ibid.*, p. 106.
13. *Niles Register*, V. XXX, 6/10/1826, p. 257.
14. Kappler, *Indian Treaties*, V. II, p. 264, 268.
15. Adams, *Memoirs*, V. VII, p. 108.
16. *Niles Register*, V. XXX, 6/10/1826, p. 257–258.
17. *Ibid.*, p. 258.
18. *Ibid.*, p. 257.
19. *Ibid.*
20. *Ibid.*, p. 258.
21. *American State Papers, Indian Affairs*, II, p. 665.
22. Kappler, *American State Papers, Indian Affairs, Laws and Treaties,* V. II, p. 284–286.
23. *Chronicles of Oklahoma, Choctaw Academy*, V. VI, p. 453–480.
24. *Niles Register*, V. XXX, 6/10/1826, p. 277–279.
25. *Ibid.*, p. 279–280.
26. *American State Papers, Indian Affairs* II, p. 644–646.
27. Abel, *Indian Consolidation*, p. 356.
28. *American State Papers, Indian Affairs* II, p. 737.
29. *Ibid.*, p. 749.
30. National Archives, RG75, Letters sent to Office of Indian Affairs, Letter Book III, p. 78–80.
31. *Ibid.*, Creek Agency 1825–26, M–234, Roll 220, frames 0274–77, 9/30/1826.
32. *American State Papers, Indian Affairs* II, p. 744.
33. *Ibid.*
34. *Ibid.*

35. *Ibid.*, p. 749.
36. *Ibid.*, p. 864.
37. *Ibid.*, p. 866.
38. *Ibid.*, p. 865–866.
39. Abel, *Indian Consolidation*, p. 354.
40. *American State Papers, Indian Affairs* II, p. 864.
41. *Ibid.*, p. 865.
42. Richardson, *Messages and Papers of the Presidents* II, p. 370–373.
43. McKenney and Hall, *Indian Tribes* II, p. 22–29.
44. Richardson, *Messages and Papers of the Presidents* II, p. 960.
45. *Niles Register*, V. XXVII, 10/18/1828, p. 123.
46. *The Bicentennial Almanac*, 1975, p. 96.
47. Richardson, *Messages and Papers of the Presidents* II, p. 1020.
48. *Ibid.*, p. 982.
49. *World Book Encyclopedia*, 1965, V. IV, p. 504.
50. *Niles Register*, V. XXXV, 9/20/1828, p. 58.
51. *Ibid.*
52. Foreman, *Indians and Pioneers*, p. 250–251.
53. Bureau of American Ethnology, Bulletin 30, p. 385, 387
54. *Ibid.*
55. *Ibid.*
56. *The Bicentennial Almanac*, p. 44.
57. *World Book Encyclopedia*, V. XIV, p. 22.
58. Richardson, *Messages and Papers of the Presidents*, V. II, p. 1001.
59. *Ibid.*, p. 1099–1104, 1020–1021.

Chapter 11

1. Richardson, *Messages and Papers of the Presidents*, V. II, p. 1001.
2. *Ibid.*, p. 1020.
3. *Ibid.*, p. 1021.
4. *Ibid.*
5. *Military Affairs*, V. IV, p. 129–133.
6. Richardson, *Messages and Papers of the Presidents*, V. II, p. 1082.
7. *Ibid.*
8. *Ibid.*, p. 1084–1085.
9. Greeley, *The American Conflict*, V. I, p. 105–106.
10. Eneah Micco and others to secretary of war, 4/8/1831, Office of Indian Affairs, Creek Emigration.
11. *Niles Register*, V. XL, 7/16/1831, p. 344.
12. *Ibid.*
13. James, *The Raven*, p. 162.
14. *Niles Register*, V. LI, 9/17/1836, p. 37.
15. *American State Papers, Indian Affairs*, V. II, p. 247.
16. Foreman, *Indian Removal*, p. 116.
17. Richardson, *Messages and Papers of the Presidents* II, p. 1252.
18. *American State Papers, Military Affairs*, V. VI, p. 723–724.
19. Yoakum, *History of Texas*, 1855, p. 328.
20. *Ibid.*

21. *American State Papers, Military Affairs*, V. VI, p. 752.
22. *Ibid.*
23. *Ibid.*, p. 723.
24. *Ibid.*
25. *Ibid.*
26. *Ibid.*
27. *Ibid.*, p. 723–724.
28. *Ibid.*, p. 752.
29. *Ibid.*, p. 724.
30. *Ibid.*, p. 725–726.
31. *Ibid.*, p. 776.
32. *Ibid.*, p. 727.
33. *Ibid.*, p. 728.
34. *Ibid.*
35. *Ibid.*, p. 729.
36. *Ibid.*
37. *Ibid.*, p. 733.
38. Hitchcock, *Traveler in Indian Territory*, p. 145.
39. Abel, *Indian Consolidation*, p. 387; Greeley, *American Conflict*, V. I, p. 106.
40. Thomas Yahola interview.
41. *Ibid.*
42. *American State Papers, Military Affairs*, V. VI, p. 776–777.
43. *Ibid.*
44. *Ibid.*, p. 642–643.
45. *Ibid.*
46. *Ibid.*
47. *Ibid.*, p. 744.
48. *Ibid.*
49. *Ibid.*
50. *Ibid.*
51. *Ibid.*
52. *Ibid.*, p. 757.
53. *Ibid.*, p. 758.
54. *Ibid.*, p. 773.
55. Foreman, *Indian Removal*, p. 144.

Chapter 12

1. *American State Papers, Military Affairs*, V. VI, p. 150.
2. *Ibid.*, p. 152.
3. *Ibid.*, p. 13.
4. *Ibid.*, p. 532.
5. *Ibid.*, p. 730.
6. *Ibid.*, p. 747–748.
7. *Ibid.*, p. 748.
8. *Ibid.*, p. 749.
9. *Ibid.*, p. 750.
10. *Ibid.*, p. 759–760.
11. Crockett, *Life of David Crockett*, p. 75.

12. *American State Papers, Military Affairs*, V. VI, p. 751–753.
13. *Ibid.*, p. 762.
14. *Ibid.*, p. 763.
15. *Ibid.*, p. 769.
16. *Ibid.*, p. 769–770.
17. *Ibid.*, p. 771.
18. *Ibid.*
19. *Ibid.*
20. *Ibid.*
21. *Ibid.*, p. 763.
22. *Ibid.*
23. *Ibid.*
24. *Ibid.*, p. 761.
25. *Ibid.*, V. VII, p. 953.
26. *Niles Register*, V. LI, 1836, p. 37–38.
27. *Ibid.*
28. *Ibid.*
29. *Ibid.*
30. *Ibid.*
31. *Ibid.*
32. *Ibid.*
33. *Ibid.*
34. Richardson, *Messages and Papers of the Presidents*, V. III, p. 1538.
35. Greeley, *American Conflict*, V. I, p. 143.
36. *American State Papers, Military Affairs*, V. VII, p. 347–348.
37. *Niles Register*, V. LI, 2/25/1837, p. 416.
38. Hitchcock, Ethan, Notes, February 3, 1842, Manuscripts Div., Library of Congress.
39. *Ibid.*
40. *American State Papers, Military Affairs*, V. VII, p. 954.
41. *Ibid.*, p. 952.
42. Gatschet, *A Migration Legend of the Creek Indians*, p. 147.
43. Thomas Yahola interview.
44. Hitchcock Notes, 2/3/1842.
45. McKenney and Hall, *Indian Tribes*, V. II, p. 190–191.
46. Hitchcock Notes, 2/3/1842.
47. Thomas Yahola interview.
48. *Ibid.*
49. *Arkansas Gazette*, 11/5/1836.
50. Thomas Yahola interview.
51. *American State Papers, Military Affairs*, V. VII, p. 952; Thomas Yahola.

Chapter 13

1. Hitchcock Notes, 2/3/1842.
2. Kappler, *Indian Affairs, Laws and Treaties*, V. II, p. 524–525.
3. Hitchcock Notes, 2/3/1842.
4. *Ibid.*
5. *Ibid.*

6. *Ibid.*

7. Tindle, *Wilson County*, Kansas, p. 4.

8. Hitchcock Notes, 2/3/1842.

9. *Ibid.*

10. Abel, *Indian as Slaveholder and Secessionist*, p. 193; *Little Rock Daily State Journal*, 1/10/1862, p. 2, col. 3.

11. Foreman, *The Five Civilized Tribes*, 1934, p. 191.

12. Thomas Yahola interview

13. Richards, *Headquarters House and the Forts of Fort Scott*, 1954, p. 2.

14. Fischer, *The Civil War Era in Indian Territory*, p. 20.

15. *Ibid.*, p. 19.

16. Greeley, *American Conflict*, V. I, p. 163.

17. *Ibid.*, p. 164.

18. *Ibid.*, p. 165.

19. *Ibid.*, p. 169.

20. *Ibid.*, p. 158.

21. *Ibid.*, p. 157.

22. *Ibid.*, p. 159.

23. *Ibid.*, p. 158.

24. *Ibid.*, p. 162

25. *Ibid.*, p. 163.

26. *Ibid.*, p. 186–187.

27. Silver, *Edmund Pendleton Gaines, Frontier General*, p. 260.

28. Greeley, *American Conflict*, V. I, p. 187.

29. *Ibid.*

30. Silver, *Edmund P. Gaines*, p. 260, 270.

31. Singletary, Otis A., "The Mexican War," *Reader's Digest Family Encyclopedia of American History*, p. 718.

32. *Ibid.*

33. Stephenson, *The Political Career of General James H. Lane*, V. III, p. 27.

34. Richardson, *Messages and Papers of the Presidents*, V. IV, p. 2334.

Chapter 14

1. Greeley, *American Conflict*, I, p. 204.

2. Connelley, *Kansas and Kansans*, V. I, p. 298–299.

3. Richardson, *Messages and Papers of the Presidents*, V. IV, p. 2754.

4. Dept. of the Army, US Military Academy, Special collections, West Point, NY.

5. Barry, *The Beginning of the West*, p. 1191.

6. Connelley, *Kansas and Kansans*, V. I, p. 320.

7. *Ibid.*, p. 338, 361.

8. *Ibid.*, p. 546.

9. *Ibid.*, p. 478

10. Barry, *Beginning of the West*, p. 1178, 1197, 1202.

11. Cutler, *History of Kansas*, p. 559.

12. *Kansas Historical Collections*, V. IV, p. 354.

13. Connelley, *Kansas and Kansans*, V. II, p. 636.

14. Tindle, *Wilson County, Kansas*, p. 15.

15. Connelley, *Kansas and Kansans*, V. I, p. 479–481.

16. Cutler, *History of Kansas*, p. 914.
17. *Ibid.*, p. 559.
18. *Ibid.*

Chapter 15

1. *Annual Report of the Commissioner of Indian Affairs*, 1859, p. 417.
2. *Ibid.*, p. 163–164.
3. *Ibid.*, p. 190.
4. *Ibid.*, p. 172.
5. Richardson, *Messages and Papers of the Presidents*, V. V, p. 3010–3011.
6. *Ibid.*, p. 3012.
7. Connelley, *Kansas and Kansans*, V. I, p. 267–268; Cutler, *History of Kansas*, p. 1530.
8. Cutler *History of Kansas*, p. 1530.
9. *Ibid.*
10. *Ibid.*
11. *Ibid.*
12. *Annual Report, Commissioner of Indian Affairs*, 1859, p. 219.
13. *Ibid.*
14. *Ibid.*, p. 215.
15. *Ibid.*, p. 217–218.
16. *Ibid.*, p. 218.
17. *Ibid.*
18. *Ibid.*
19. *Ibid.*, p. 215.
20. *Ibid.*, p. 218.
21. *Ibid.*, p. 167.
22. *Ibid.*
23. Abel, *Indian as Slaveholder and Secessionist*, p. 75–76.
24. Prentis, *History of Kansas*, p. 91–92.
25. Greeley, *American Conflict*, V. I, p. 410–411.
26. Connelley, *Kansas and Kansans*, V. I., p. 177.
27. *Ibid.*, p. 165–167.
28. *Ibid.*
29. *Ibid.*, p. 177.
30. *Ibid.*
31. *Ibid.*
32. Greeley, *American Conflict*, V. I, p. 410.
33. *Ibid.*, p. 410–411.
34. *Ibid.*
35. *Ibid.*
36. *Ibid.; Dictionary of American Biography*, p. 252.
37. Greeley, *American Conflict*, V. I, p. 346.
38. *Ibid.*, p. 342.
39. *Ibid.*, p. 344.
40. *Ibid.*
41. *Ibid.*
42. *Ibid.*, p. 347.
43. *Ibid.*, p. 348.

44. *Ibid.*, p. 349.
45. Isley and Richards, *Four Centuries in Kansas*, p. 87–88.
46. Connelley, *Kansas and Kansans*, V. II, p. 708; Isley and Richards, *Four Centuries in Kansas*, p. 161.

Chapter 16

1. Greeley, *American Conflict*, V. I, p. 414.
2. *Ibid.*, p. 442.
3. *Ibid.*, p. 409.
4. *Ibid.*, p. 408.
5. *Ibid.*, p. 410.
6. *Ibid.*, p. 411.
7. *Ibid.*, p. 411–413.
8. *Ibid.*, p. 412.
9. *Official Records of the War of the Rebellion*, Ser. I, V. LIII, p. 630. (Hereafter, *Official Records*)
10. *Ibid.*, p. 624.
11. *Ibid.*
12. *Ibid.*, p. 630.
13. *Ibid.*, p. 626.
14. *Ibid.*, p. 629.
15. *Official Records*, Ser. IV, V. I, p. 322–325.

Chapter 17

1. *Official Records*, Ser. I, V. LIII, p. 493–494.
2. US Military Academy Archives, West Point, NY, 31st Annual Reunion, 6/12/1900, p. 119–122.
3. Greeley, *American Conflict*, V. I, p. 449.
4. *Official Records*, Ser. I, V. LIII, p. 488.
5. *Ibid.*, p. 493.
6. *Ibid.*, Ser. I, V. I, p. 656.
7. US Military Academy Archives, 19th Reunion, 6/11/1888, p. 51–54.
8. *Official Records*, Ser. I, V. I, p. 656, 659–660.
9. *Ibid.*, p. 656.
10. *Ibid.*, p. 660.
11. *Ibid.*, p. 662.
12. *Ibid.*, p. 660.
13. *Ibid.*, p. 662.
14. *Annual Report, Commissioner of Indian Affairs*, 1862, p. 4–5.
15. *Official Records*, Ser. I, V. I, p. 661.
16. *Ibid.*, p. 665, 656.
17. *Ibid.*, p. 662, 668.
18. *Ibid.*, Ser. I, V. LIII, p. 494–496.
19. *Ibid.*, Ser. I, V. I, p. 665.
20. *Ibid.*, Ser. I, V. LIII, p. 496.
21. *Ibid.*, Ser. I, V. I, p. 648.

22. *Ibid.*, p. 652, Report #11.
23. *Ibid.*, p. 648.
24. *Annual Report, Commissioner of Indian Affairs*, 1860, p. 156.
25. Rainey, *The Cherokee Strip*, p. 53.
26. *Officials Records*, Ser. I, V. I, 665.
27. US Military Academy Archives, 19th Reunion, p. 53–54.
28. *Official Records*, Ser. I, V. LIII, 494–496.
29. *Annual Report, Commissioner of Indian Affairs*, 1861, p. 35.
30. *Official Records*, Ser. I., V. LIII, p. 679.
31. *Ibid.*, p. 682.
32. *Ibid.*, Ser. I, V. I, p. 648.
33. *Ibid.*, Ser. I, V. LIII, p. 682.
34. *Ibid.*, Ser. I, V. I, p. 653.
35. *Ibid.*, Ser. I, V. III, p. 575–576.
36. *Ibid.*, p. 583
37. *Ibid.*, Ser. I, V. I, p. 575.
38 *Ibid.*, p. 649.

Chapter 18

1. *Official Records*, Ser. IV, V. I, p. 785.
2. Abel, *Indian as Slaveholder and Secessionist*, p. 128.
3. Allsopp, *Albert Pike*, p. 91; Duncan, *Reluctant General*, p. 153, 157.
4. Duncan, *Reluctant General*, p. 151.
5. *Official Records*, Ser. I, V. III, p. 573.
6. *Ibid.*, p. 574.
7. *Ibid.*, p. 590.
8. *Ibid.*, p. 587; Ser. IV, V. I, p. 323.
9. Cutler, *History of Kansas*, p. 74, 247.
10. *Annual Report of the Commissioner of Indian Affairs*, 1859, p. 163.
11. Richards, *Headquarters House and Forts of Fort Scott*, p. 27.
12. *Official Records*, Ser. I, V. III, p. 572.
13. *Ibid.*, Ser. IV, V. I, p. 359–360.
14. *Ibid.*, p. 359.
15. *Ibid.*, Ser. I, V. III, p. 591–592, 596–597.
16. *Ibid.*, p. 594–595.
17. *Ibid.*, p. 595.
18. *Ibid.*, p. 578–579.
19. National Archives, Indian Office Special Files #201; Abel, *Indian as Participant in the Civil War,* p. 46–47.
20. *Ibid.*, Southern Superintendency, B567, 1861.
21. *Official Records*, Ser. I, V. III, p. 599.
22. *Ibid.*, p. 591, 600.
23. Barry, *Beginning of the West*, p. 1067–1068.
24. *Official Records*, Ser. IV, V. I, p. 443.
25. *Ibid.*, Ser. I, V. III, p. 614.
26. *Ibid.*, p. 589.
27. *Ibid.*, Ser. IV, V. I, p. 426–443.
28. *Ibid.*, p. 443.

29. Greeley, *American Conflict*, V. II, p. 34.

30. Pike to Commissioner of Indian Affairs, 2/17/1866; Thoburn, Joseph B., "The Cherokee Question." *Chronicles of Oklahoma* II, 1924, p. 174–175; Duncan, *Reluctant General*, p. 175–176.

31. *Official Records*, Ser. I, V. III, p. 623–624.

32. *Ibid.*, p. 597.

33. *Ibid.*, p. 624.

34. *Annual Report of the Commissioner of Indian Affairs*, 1865, p. 328.

35. *Ibid.*

36. *Ibid.*, 1859, p. 179.

37. *Ibid.*, p. 159.

38. *Ibid.*

39. *Ibid.*, p. 160.

40. *Ibid.*, 1860, p. 124.

41. *Ibid.*

42. *Ibid.*, 1859, p. 168.

43. *Ibid.*, p. 161.

Chapter 19

1. *Oskaloosa Independent*, June 19, 1861.

2. *Ibid.*, August 3, 1861.

3. *Ibid.*

4. *Ibid.*

5. *Leavenworth Daily Conservative*, January 16, 1862.

6. Pollard, *Southern History of the War*, p. 142.

7. *Official Records*, Ser. I, V. III, p. 692.

8. *Ibid.*, Ser. I., V. I, 683–684; V. XIII, 490–491.

9. Allsopp, *Albert Pike*, p. 188.

10. *Official Records*, Ser. I, V. III, p. 673, 691.

11. *Ibid.*, Ser. I, V. III, p. 692.

12. *Ibid.*

13. *Annual Report of the Commissioner of Indian Affairs*, 1861, p. 34.

14. *Ibid.*, p. 3–4.

15. *Ibid.*, p. 34–35.

16. *Official Records*, Ser. I, V. III, p. 454–455.

17. Indian Affairs, General Files, Kansas, 1855–1862, B774.

18. *Ibid.*

19. *Annual Report of the Commissioner of Indian Affairs*, 1861, p. 11.

20. Indian Office Letter Book #66, p. 485.

21. *Annual Report of the Commissioner of Indian Affairs*, 1862, p. 138.

Chapter 20

1. Abel, *Indian as Slaveholder and Secessionist*, p. 245; Indian Office Letter Book #67, p. 78–79.

2. *Annual Report of the Commissioner of Indian Affairs*, 1865, p. 330.

3. *Official Records*, Ser. I, V. VIII, p. 25.
4. *Ibid.*, p. 26.
5. *Ibid.*
6. *Annual Report of the Commissioner of Indian Affairs*, 1861, p. 41–43.
7. *Ibid.*
8. *Ibid.*
9. *Official Records*, Ser. I, V. III, p. 490.
10. *Ibid.*, p. 446.
11. *Eureka* (Kansas) *Herald*, 2/12/1869.
12. *Ibid.*
13. *Official Records*, Ser. I, V. III, p. 490.
14. Blunt, "Civil War Experiences," *Kansas Historical Quarterly*, V. 1, No. 3, p. 214.
15. Indian Office, Special Files #201, Central Superintendency W474, 1861.
16. *Official Records*, Ser. I, V. III, p. 490.
17. Cutler, *History of Kansas*, p. 1199.
18. *Neosho–Wilson County History*, p. 822–823.
19. Kansas Historical Collections, V. XVII, p. 701–702.
20. *Ibid.*, V. I, p. 233.
21. Tindle, *Wilson County, Kansas*, p. 15.
22. Bureau of American Ethnology of American Indians, Bulletin 30, p. 1004.
23. *Ibid.*, p. 321.
24. Cutler, *History of Kansas*, p. 900.
25. Tindle, *Wilson County, Kansas*, p. 99.
26. Irving, Washington, *A Tour on the Prairies*, p. 12.
27. *Wilson County Citizen*, 9/16/1941.
28. *Ibid.*

Chapter 21

1. *Annual Report of the Commissioner of Indian Affairs*, 1861, p. 38.
2. Cutler, *History of Kansas*, p. 669.
3. *Official Records*, Ser. I, V. III, p. 490.
4. *Ibid.*, p. 500; *Leavenworth Daily Conservative*, 9/26/1861.
5. *Official Records*, Ser. I, V. III, p. 196, 506.
6. Coffin to Dole, 12/17/1861, Letters Received, Southern Superintendency, 1851–1871.
7. *Leavenworth Daily Conservative*, 2/18/1862.
8. *Oskaloosa Independent*, 11/2/1861.
9. *Official Records*, Ser. I, V. XIII, p. 857–858.
10. *Ibid.*, Ser. I, V. XXII, Pt. I, Reports, p. 329.
11. *Kansas Historical Quarterly*, 1973, V. XXXIX, p. 496.
12. Indian Office Special Files #201, Southern Superintendency C1400, 1861.
13. *Annual Report of the Commissioner of Indian Affairs*, 1861, p. 43–44.
14. *Ibid.*
15. *Ibid.*, p. 44.
16. *Ibid.*, p. 46.
17. *Ibid.*, p. 49.
18. *Ibid.*, p. 46–49.
19. *Ibid.*, p. 49.

20. *Leavenworth Daily Conservative*, 12/14/1861, from *Burlington Register*.
21. *Annual Report of the Commissioner of Indian Affairs*, Central Superintendency, 1863, p. 255.

Chapter 22

1. *Tulsa Tribune*, 11/19/1939.
2. *Van Buren* (Ark) *Press*, 10/16/1861, p. 1, col. 7.
3. *Tulsa Tribune*, 11/19/1939.
4. *Ibid.*
5. *Ibid.*
6. *Official Records*, Ser. I, V. VIII, p. 5.
7. *Ibid.*
8. *Ibid.*
9. *Ibid.*, p. 6.
10. *Ibid.*, p. 14–15.
11. *Tulsa Tribune*, 11/19/1939.
12. *Official Records*, Ser. I, V. VIII, p. 7.
13. *Chronicles of Oklahoma*, V. XXIX, No. 4, *Ekvn-hv'lwuce*, p. 404–406.
14. *Leavenworth Daily Conservative*, 1/28/1862.
15. Richardson, *Messages and Papers of the Presidents*, V. 5, 1910, p. 3253.
16. *Leavenworth Daily Conservative*, 1/28/1862.
17. *Ekvn'hv'lwuce*, p. 406.
18. *Official Records*, Ser. I, V. VIII, p. 7.
19. *Ibid.*
20. *Ibid.*, p. 7–8.
21. *Ibid.*, p. 8.
22. *Ibid.*, p. 17.
23. *Ibid.*, p. 8.
24. *Ibid.*
25. *Ibid.*, p. 9.
26. *Ibid.*, p. 10.
27. *Ibid.*, p. 16.
28. *Ibid.*, p. 10.
29. *Leavenworth Daily Conservative*, 1/28/1862.
30. Abel, *Indian as Slaveholder and Secessionist*, p. 268–269; Indian Office Letter Book No. 67, p. 271–272.
31. *Leavenworth Daily Conservative*, 1/28/1862.
32. *Official Records*, Ser. I, V. VIII, p. 11.
33. *Ibid.*
34. *Ibid.*, p. 22.
35. *Ibid.*, p. 12.
36. *Ibid.*, p. 22.
37. *Ibid.*, p. 13.
38. *Ibid.*, p. 23.
39. *Ibid.*
40. *Ibid.*, p. 23, 29.
41. *Ibid.*, p. 24.
42. *Ibid.*, p. 32.

43. *Ibid.*
44. *Ibid.*, p. 12.
45. *Ibid.*, p. 13.
46. *Ibid.*
47. *Ibid.*
48. *Ibid.*, p. 713–714.
49. *Ibid.*, p. 715.
50. *Ibid.*, p. 31.

Chapter 23

1. *Leavenworth Daily Conservative*, 12/28/1861.
2. *Official Records*, Ser. I, V. VIII, p. 482; *Kansas Historical Quarterly* XXXIX, p. 499.
3. Indian Office, General Files, Southern Superintendency, 1859–1862, Coffin to Dole, 12/28/1861.
4. Indian Office Special Files No. 201, Southern Superintendency, C1443, 1862.
5. *Annual Report of the Commissioner of Indian Affairs*, 1862, p. 138.
6. *Ibid.*, p. 136, 138, 148, 152.
7. *Neosho–Wilson County History*, p. 823.
8. *Annual Report of the Commissioner of Indian Affairs*, 1861, p. 151–152.
9. *Leavenworth Daily Conservative*, 1/28/1862.
10. *Annual Report of the Commissioner of Indian Affairs*, 1862, p. 156.
11. *Leavenworth Daily Conservative*, 1/28/1862.
12. *Ibid.*
13. *Ibid.*, 1/17/1862.
14. *Ibid.*, 1/28/1862.
15. *Official Records*, Ser. I, V. VIII, p. 534.
16. *Annual Report of the Commissioner of Indian Affairs*, 1862, p. 152–154.
17. *Ibid.*, p. 154–155.
18. *Ibid.*, p. 148.
19. *Ibid.*, p. 136.
20. *Ibid.*, p. 171.
21. Barry, *Beginning of the West*, p. 250–251.
22. *Ibid.*, p. 1137.
23. *Ibid.*, p. 1218.
24. Cutler, *History of Kansas*, p. 881.
25. *Annual Report of the Commissioner of Indian Affairs*, Central Superintendency, 1859, p. 158.
26. *Ibid.*, Southern Superintendency, 1862, p. 171–172.
27. *Ibid.*, p. 145–147.
28. Indian Office Letter Book #67, p. 448.
29. *Leavenworth Daily Conservative*, 2/14/1862.
30. *Annual Report of the Commissioner of Indian Affairs*, 1862, p. 146.
31. *Ibid.*, p. 138.

Chapter 24

1. Indian Office,General Files, Southern Superintendency, 1859–1862, C1544, Coffin to Dole.

2. *Ibid.*, C1541, Coffin to Dole, 2/28/1862.

3. Abel, *American Indian as Participant in the Civil War*, p. 105.

4. Indian Office,General Files, Southern Superintendency, 1859–1862, C1544, 3/3/1862.

5. *Official Records*, Ser. I, V. VIII, p. 831.

6. Abel, *American Indian as Participant in the Civil War*, p. 97.

7. Indian Office Land Files, 1855–1870, 043, 1862.

8. Indian Office, General Files, Southern Superintendency, 1859–1862, C1544.

9. Hamilton, Sr., "Indian Refugees in Coffey County," *LeRoy* (Kansas) *Reporter*, 8/14 and 8/21/1931.

10. Abel, *Indian as Slaveholder and Secessionist*, p. 275.

11. *Ibid.*

12. *Battles and Leaders of the Civil War*, V. I, p. 314–337.

13. *Official Records*, Ser. I, V. VIII, p. 624–625.

14. Indian Office Land Files, 1855–1870, 043, 1862.

15. *Ibid.*

16. *Leavenworth Daily Conservative*, 3/5/1862.

17. *Annual Report of the Commissioner of Indian Affairs*, 1862, p. 155–158.

18. *Ibid.*, p. 173–175.

19. Indian Office General Files, Southern Superintendency, C1571, 1862.

20. *Annual Report of the Commissioner of Indian Affairs*, 1862, p. 148.

21. Indian Office General Files, Southern Superintendency, C1578, 1862.

Chapter 25

1. *Leavenworth Daily Conservative*, 4/16/1862.

2. *LeRoy Reporter*, 8/21/1931.

3. Thomas Yahola interview.

4. *Official Records*, Ser. I, V. VIII, p. 418.

5. Blunt, *Civil War Experiences*, p. 222–223.

6. *Leavenworth Daily Conservative*, 5/8/1862.

7. *Ibid.*

8. *Annual Report of the Commissioner of Indian Affairs*, 1862, p. 149.

9. *Leavenworth Daily Conservative*, 5/8/1862.

10. *Ibid.*, 5/10/1862.

11. *Ibid.*, 6/17/1862.

12. Indian Office General Files Southern Superintendency, 1859–1862, Coffin to Dole, 6/25/1862.

13. Abel, *Indian as Participant in the Civil War*, p. 108.

14. *Official Records*, Ser. I, V. XIII, p. 450.

15. Indian Office General Files Southern Superintendency, 1859–1862, C1684.

16. *Official Records*, Ser. I, V. XIII, p. 839–840.

17. *Ibid.*, p. 850.

18. *Ibid.*, p. 954–962.

19. *Ibid.*

20. *Ibid.*

21. *Ibid.*

22. *Kansas Historical Collections*, V. XIV, p. 239.

23. *Annual Report of the Commissioner of Indian Affairs*, 1862, p. 162–164.

24. *Ibid.*
25. *Official Records*, Ser. I, V. XIII, p. 963–965.
26. *Annual Report of the Commissioner Indian Affairs*, 1862, p. 162.
27. *Official Records*, Ser. I, V. XIII, p. 857–858.
28. *Ibid.*, p. 859–860.
29. *Annual Report of the Commissioner of Indian Affairs*, 1862, p. 158–160.
30. *Ibid.*, p. 163.
31. Blunt, *Civil War Experiences*, p. 223.
32. *Official Reports*, Ser. I, V. XIII, p. 475–476.
33. *Ibid.*, p. 489.
34. *Ibid.*, p. 484–485; *Annual Report of the Commissioner of Indian Affairs*, 1862, p. 163.
35. *Official Reports*, Ser. I, V. XIII, p. 482–483.
36. Blunt, *Civil War Experiences*, p. 223.
37. *Ibid.*, p. 224.
38. *Ibid.*
39. *Ibid.*
40. *Official Reports*, Ser. I, V. XIII, p. 478.
41. *Ibid.*, p. 481, 511–512.
42. *Annual Report of the Commissioner of Indian Affairs*, 1862, p. 160–161.
43. *Ibid.*, 1862, p. 162.
44. *Official Records*, Ser. I, V. XIII, p. 860–869.
45. *Ibid.*, p. 531.

Chapter 26

1. *Annual Report of the Commissioner of Indian Affairs*, 1862, p. 138–140.
2. Indian Office Special Files #201, Southern Superintendency, C1565, 3/28/1862, Coffin to Dole.
3. *Annual Report of the Commissioner of Indian Affairs*, Southern Superintendency, 1863, p. 184–185.
4. *Ibid.*, p. 190.
5. *Ibid.*, p. 195.
6. *Ibid.*, p. 197.
7. *Annual Report of the Commissioner of Indian Affairs*, Southern Superintendency, 1865, appendix p. 437; *Leavenworth Daily Conservative*, 6/19/1862 from Fort Scott Bulletin.
8. Indian Office Consolidated Files, Neosho, C1904, Coffin to Dole, 11/16/1862; Abel, *Indian as Participant in the Civil War*, p. 207.
9. Indian Office Special Files #201, Southern Superintendency C1565, 3/28/1862.
10. *Ibid.*
11. *Ibid.*
12. *Annual Report of the Commissioner of Indian Affairs*, Southern Superintendency 1862, p. 138, 140.
13. *Ibid.*, p. 170.
14. *Ibid.*, p. 167–169.
15. *Official Records*, Ser. I. V. XIII, p. 923.
16. *Ibid.*, p. 869–871.
17. *Ibid.*, p. 860; 918.
18. *Ibid.*, p. 921–922.
19. *Ibid.*, p. 925–926.

20. *Ibid.*, p. 919–920.

21. *Annual Report of the Commissioner of Indian Affairs*, Southern Superintendency, 1863, p. 225–227.

22. *Ibid.*, p. 181–183.

23. Blunt, *Civil War Experiences*, p. 232–234; *Official Records*, Ser. I, V. XXII, Pt. I, Reports, p. 93–94; Cutler, *History of Kansas*, p. 903.

Chapter 27

1. *Annual Report of the Commissioner of Indian Affairs*, 1863, Southern Superintendency, p. 198.

2. *Ibid.*, p. 182.

3. Morrison, *Progress in Kansas*, V. I, No. 8, July/1935.

4. USMA, West Point, 31st Reunion, 1900, 119–122.

5. *Baxter Springs Citizen*, 10/7/1963; *Oswego Independent*, 9/7/1951.

6. Indian Office General Files, Seminole, 1858–1869, B317, 5/13/1863.

7. *Ibid.* S291; "Billy Bowlegs (Holata Micco) in the Civil War" Pt. II, Porter; *Florida Historical Quarterly*, V. XLV, No. 4, April, 1967.

8. *Annual Report of the Commissioner of Indian Affairs*, Southern Superintendency, 1864, p. 319.

9. William G. Coffin, Lincoln's Superintendent of Indian Affairs for the Southern Superintendency, Holman; *Kansas Historical Quarterly*, 1973, V. XXXIX, p. 514.

10. *Fort Scott Daily Tribune*, 2/1/1904.

11. Cutler, *History of Kansas*, p. 322; Connelley, *Quantrill and the Border Wars*, p. 352.

12. *Annual Report of the Commissioner of Indian Affairs*, Southern Superintendency, 1864, p. 321.

13. Cutler, *History of Kansas*, p. 903.

14. *Kansas Historical Collections*, V. XIV, 1915–1918, p. 391.

15. Cutler, *History of Kansas*, p. 559; *Golden Jubilee History of the Texas Press Association*, 1929, p. 110.

16. Tindle, *Wilson County Kansas*, p. 33.

17. USMA, West Point, 19th Reunion, 1888, p. 51–54.

18. Stephenson, *Political Career of James H. Lane*, p. 115, 159.

19. Tindle, *Wilson County Kansas*, p. 9–10, 7–8; Connelley, *Kansas and Kansans*, V. I, p. 228–229.

20. Debo, *Road to Disappearance*, p. 183.

21. Raschke, *Painted Black*, p. 37.

22. *Family Encyclopedia of American History*, p. 972.

23. Indian Office Land Files, Southern Superintendency, 1855–1870, 5/14/1864.

24. *Annual Report of the Commissioner of Indian Affairs*, Central Superintendency, 1863, p. 256.

25. *Emporia News*, 1/26/1867.

26. Indian Office, Southern Superintendency, I.D. Files, Bundle No. 54.

27. Thomas Yahola interview.

28. Newman, *Early Day History of Fort Belmont*, p. 2.

29. *Neosho and Wilson County History*, p. 890–893.

30. *Kansas: A Guide to the Sunflower State*, p. 474.

31. Tindle, *Wilson County, Kansas*, p. 23–24.

Bibliography

Books

Abel, Anna Heloise, *The Indian as Slaveholder and Secessionist*, V. I. Cleveland: Arthur H. Clark, 1915; reprint, Lincoln: University of Nebraska Press, 1992.

_____. *The Indian as Participant in the Civil War*, V. II. Cleveland: Arthur H. Clark, 1919.

Adams, John Quincy. *The Memoirs of John Quincy Adams, 1795–1848*. 12 volumes, Charles Francis Adams, ed. Philadelphia: J.P. Lippincott, 1874–1877.

Allsopp, Fred W. *Albert Pike: A Biography*. Little Rock, AR: Parke-Harper, 1928.

Barry, Louise. *The Beginning of the West*. Topeka: Kansas State Historical Society, 1972.

Battles and Leaders of the Civil War, four volumes. New York: Castle Books, 1956.

Benton, Thomas H. *Thirty Years View or a History of the Working of the American Government for Thirty Years*. New York: Greenwood Press, 1968.

Bureau of American Ethnology of American Indians, Bulletin 30, Pt. I. *Handbook of American Indians of North America*. Fredrick Webb Hodge, ed., two parts. Washington, D.C.: Govt. Printing Office, 1912.

Connelley, William. *Kansas and Kansans*, five volumes. Chicago: Lewis, 1918.

_____. *Quantrill and the Border Wars*. Cedar Rapids, IA: The Torch Press, 1910.

Crockett, David. *Life of David Crockett*. Bedford, MA: Applewood; reprint 1993.

Cutler, William G. *History of the State of Kansas*. Chicago: A.T. Andreas, 1883.

Debo, Angie. *The Road to Disappearance*. Norman: University of Oklahoma Press, 1941.

Dictionary of American Biography. New York: Charles Scribner's Sons, 1935.

Duncan, L. Wallace and John Gilmore. *Neosho–Wilson County History*. Ft. Scott, Kansas: Monitor, 1902.

Duncan, Robert Lipscomb, *Reluctant General, The Life and Times of Albert Pike*, New York: E.P. Dutton, 1961.

Eggleston, George Cary. *Red Eagle and the Wars with the Creek Indians of Alabama*. New York: Dodd, Mead, 1878; reprint AMS, Los Angeles.

Federal Writers Project of the Work Projects Administration for the State of Kansas. *Kansas: A Guide to the Sunflower State*. New York: Viking, 1939.

Field Enterprises Educational Corp. *World Book Encyclopedia*, 20 volumes. International Copyright, 1965.

Fischer, LeRoy. *The Civil War Era in Indian Territory*. Los Angeles: L.L. Morrison, 1974.

Foreman, Grant. *Five Civilized Tribes*. Norman: University of Oklahoma Press, 1971.
_____. *Indians and Pioneers*. Norman: University of Oklahoma Press, 1936.
_____. *Indian Removal*. Norman: University of Oklahoma Press, 1986.
Gatschet, Albert S. *A Migration Legend of the Creek Indians*, two volumes. Philadelphia: 1884. New York: Knaus, 1969.
Greeley, Horace. *The American Conflict*, two volumes. Chicago: O.D. Case, 1866.
Halbert, H.S. and T.H. Ball. *The Creek War of 1813–1814*. Chicago: 1895; reprint, Frank L. Owsley, Jr., ed. University of Alabama Press, 1969, 1995.
Hawkins, Benjamin. *Letters, Journals and Writing of Benjamin Hawkins*, V. I. 1796–1801; V. II. 1802–1816. C.L. Grant, ed. Savannah, Georgia: Beehive, 1980.
Hitchcock, Maj. Ethan A. *A Traveler in Indian Territory*. Foreman, Grant, ed. Cedar Rapids, Iowa: The Torch Press, 1930; reprint, Norman: University of Oklahoma Press, 1996.
Irving, Washington. *A Tour on the Prairies*. McDermott, John Francis, ed. Norman: University of Oklahoma Press, 1985.
Isley, Bliss and W.M.Richards. *Four Centuries in Kansas*. Topeka: State Printer, 1944.
James Marquis. *The Raven*. Indianapolis: Bobbs–Merrill, 1929; reprint, Marietta, GA: Cherokee, 1991.
Kappler, Charles J. *Indian Affairs, Laws and Treaties*. V. II, Washington: Government Printing Office, 1904; reprint, Buffalo: W.S. Hein, 1995.
Linton, Calvin D., ed. *The Bicentennial Almanac, 1776–1976*. Nashville & New York: Thomas Nelson, 1975.
McKenney, Thomas L. and James Hall. *The Indian Tribes of America with Biographical Sketches and Anecdotes of the Principal Chiefs*. Edinburgh, Scotland: J. Grant, 1933–1934.
Pollard, E.A. *Southern History of the War*, 2 volumes. New York: Charles B. Richardson, 1866.
Prentis, Noble L. *A History of Kansas*. Topeka: Carolyn Prentis, 1904; 1909.
Rainey, George. *The Cherokee Strip*. Guthrie, Oklahoma: Co-operative Publishing, 1933.
Raschke, Carl A. *Painted Black*. New York: Harper Collins, 1992.
Reader's Digest. *Family Encyclopedia of American History*. New York: Pleasantville, 1975.
Richards, Ralph. *Headquarters House and the Forts of Fort Scott*. Fort Scott, Kansas: *Fort Scott Tribune*, 1954.
Richardson, James. *Messages and Papers of the Presidents*, 10 volumes. New York: Bureau of National Literature and Art, 1907.
Silver, James W. *Edmund Pendleton Gaines: Frontier General*. Baton Rouge: Louisiana State University Press, 1949.
Stephenson, Wendell Holmes. *The Political Career of General James H. Lane*, V. III. Topeka: Kansas State Historical Society, 1930.
Tindle, Lela J. *Wilson County, Kansas: People of the South Wind*. Dallas: Curtis Media, 1988.
Wilson, Rufus Rockwell. *Washington the Capital City*, two volumes. Philadelphia and London: J.B. Lippincott, 1902.
Yoakum, H., Esq. *History of Texas, 1855*. Temecula, California: Reprint Services, 1993.

Historical Papers

Early Day History of Old Fort Belmont, Jo Newman.
Golden Jubilee History of the Texas Press Association, Austin.

Interview

Thomas Yahola, Muskogee Nation, Wetumka, Oklahoma.

Library of Congress

Hitchcock, Ethan A., Maj., Notes, 2/3/1842, Manuscripts Div.

National Archives

Indian Office: Consolidated Files, General Files, I.D. Files, Land Files, Letter Book, Letters Received, Manuscript Records, Special Files.
Office of Indian Affairs: Creek Emigration, 1831.
Microfilm: Letters rec'd, Creek Agency, Records of the Bureau of Indian Affairs, Record Group 75, T–494, Roll I: Letters Rec'd, Indian Affairs, Letter Book III, Record Group 75, M–234, Roll 220.

Newspapers

Arkansas Gazette, Little Rock, AR.
Baxter Springs Citizen, Baxter Springs, KS.
Emporia News, Emporia, KS.
Eureka Herald, Eureka, KS.
Fort Scott Daily Tribune, Fort Scott, KS.
Leavenworth Daily Conservative, Leavenworth, KS.
LeRoy Reporter, LeRoy, KS.
Little Rock Daily State Journal, Little Rock, AR.
Niles Weekly Register, Baltimore, MD.
Oskaloosa Independent, Oskaloosa, KS.
Oswego Independent, Oswego, KS.
Tulsa Tribune, Tulsa, OK.
Van Buren Press, Van Buren, AR.
Wilson County Citizen, Fredonia, KS.

Pamphlets and Periodicals

Indian Springs State Park, Flovilla, GA.
National Geographic
Progress in Kansas

Report

Abel, Anna Heloise. *The History of Events Resulting in Indian Consolidation West of the Mississippi River*. American Historical Assoc., 1906.

State Historical Collections

Chronicles of Oklahoma, Oklahoma Historical Society, Oklahoma City, OK.
Florida Historical Quarterly, The Florida Historical Society, Tampa, FL.
Kansas Historical Collections, Kansas State Historical Society, Topeka, KS.
Kansas Historical Quarterly, Kansas State Historical Society, Topeka, KS.

U.S. Government Documents

The American State Papers, Documents, Legislative and Executive of the Congress of the United States. Ed. by Walter Lowrie et al. 39 vols. Washington, D.C.: Government Printing Office, 1832–1861.
Documents from this source that were used in researching the present work are as follows (listed under volume title and number):

INDIAN AFFAIRS, V. II

"Claim of Alabama to Certain Lands."
"Claims Against the Creeks."
"Conditions of the Indians."
"Extinguishment of Indian Title to Lands."
"Intrusion on Creek Lands by Georgia."
"Proceedings in Relation to a Creek Treaty."
"Provision for Carrying into Effect a Treaty."
"Treaties with Several Tribes."
"Treaty with Indian Tribes at Chicago."
"Treaty with the Creeks."

MILITARY AFFAIRS, V. II

"Troops Raised Without Consent of Congress."

MILITARY AFFAIRS, V. IV

"Militia of the United States."

MILITARY AFFAIRS, V. V

"Condition of the Military Establishment, Etc."

MILITARY AFFAIRS, V. VI

"Defence of the Western Frontier."
"Indian Hostilities in Florida."
"Military Road."

MILITARY AFFAIRS, V. VII

"Creek Warriors Engaged in Hostilities, Etc."
"Military Courts of Inquiry."
"Protection of the Western Frontier."
"Report of the Secretary of War."

Annual Report of the Commissioner of Indian Affairs. Washington, D.C.: Government Printing Office, 1859–1866.
War of the Rebellion: Official Records of the Civil War. 128 vols. Washington, D.C.: Government Printing Office, 1880–1904.

INDEX